the new
architecture
of europe

AN ILLUSTRATED GUIDEBOOK AND APPRAISAL

the new architecture of europe

G. E. KIDDER SMITH

Meridian Books

THE WORLD PUBLISHING COMPANY
Cleveland and New York

G. E. KIDDER SMITH

G. E. Kidder Smith, a Fellow of the American Institute of Architects, graduated from Princeton in 1935 and received his M.F.A., also from Princeton, in 1938. In addition to teaching at M.I.T. and at Yale, he has lectured at schools of architecture and at museums throughout the United States and much of Europe. His writings, which cover the contemporary architecture of twenty-three countries, include ITALY BUILDS *(1955) and* SWEDEN BUILDS *(1957), and he is now preparing a comprehensive book to be called* THE NEW CHURCHES OF EUROPE. *Among the fellowships awarded to Mr. Smith have been grants from the American Scandinavian Foundation and the John Simon Guggenheim Memorial Foundation, the President's Fellowship from Brown University, a Fulbright Award for Research in Italy, and the Arnold W. Brunner Scholarship from the New York Chapter of the American Institute of Architects which made* THE NEW ARCHITECTURE OF EUROPE *possible.*

AN ORIGINAL MERIDIAN BOOK

Published by The World Publishing Company
2231 West 110 Street, Cleveland 2, Ohio
Copyright © 1961 by The World Publishing Company
All rights reserved
Library of Congress Catalog Card Number: 61–11474

First printing May 1961
Manufactured in the United States of America
Typography and design by Elaine Lustig

CONTENTS

ACKNOWLEDGMENTS

This book was made possible by the generous Arnold W. Brunner Scholarship—and extension—awarded the author by the New York Chapter of the American Institute of Architects. Deep appreciation goes to the founder of this wonderful series of grants and to the chapter that administers them. Many projects in architectural research would not have been possible without such support.

In Europe several architects and editors were most helpful with ideas and guidance: the members of Arbeitsgruppe 4 in Vienna, Pierre Vago in Paris, and very particularly indeed, Jim Richards in London. John Engh in Oslo, Erik Christian Sørensen in Copenhagen, the office of Inter Nationes in Bonn, Alfred Roth in Zürich, and Ernesto Rogers in Milan also offered many useful suggestions.

In the United States Douglas Haskell of *Architectural Forum* and Thomas Creighton of *Progressive Architecture* were ever generous with facilities and ideas. Each meant a great deal in assembling this material, as did Frederick Gutheim of Washington, D.C. Per Guldbeck of Cooperstown, New York, aided in translations; Nancy Smith Druse of Richfield Springs, New York, beautifully typed the manuscript under pressure conditions; and Prof. Albert Bush-Brown of M.I.T. cast his knowing eye over much material, always to its betterment. Eunice Sudak's eagle eye and well-pointed blue pencil honed every page. Columbia University's Avery Library—an unequaled archive of architectural knowledge—was of constant use, and its director, Adolf Placzek, was a never-failing source of information. My wife's discerning touch and suggestions can be seen throughout. To all of the above and to the many architects in Europe who so kindly furnished information my deep gratitude.

Finally to Arthur Cohen, Vice President of The World Publishing Company, who undertook this guide, and to Elaine Lustig, who beautifully put it together, my thanks and admiration.

G.E.K.S.

INTRODUCTION

The introduction of rolled steel and reinforced concrete (both approximately 100 years ago), then plate glass, new forms of factory processed (i.e., laminated) wood, and most recently, plastics, has revolutionized man's building means. Moreover, when one demands totally fresh building types—skyscrapers, large hospitals, community halls, housing projects, expansive schools, industrial plants, and not forgetting that terror, the automobile, garages and suspension bridges—the result will inescapably and logically produce a new architecture. Furthermore, this has been and is being colored by a newly egalitarian society, one assailed by changes more profound and rapid than ever before in history.

Europe gave the world this new architecture. And Europe, with its manifold geographical, cultural, material, and national variations, has taken it to its most protean and significant heights.

This book has been written for those who, not satisfied with viewing aged masterpieces only, would like to examine personally the provocative postwar architectural achievements of Europe.

While it is unquestionably true that the United States can muster a greater number of significant postwar buildings—the word "postwar" must be underlined—than any single country elsewhere, there are few building types in the U.S. which are not surpassed in excellence by European examples. Indeed, excepting the contributions of our own pioneer genius, the late Frank Lloyd Wright (himself a powerful influence on European building), the present advanced state of U.S. architecture can be traced directly to the influx here of extraordinarily talented architects from the Continent, and to the influence of their pioneering, teaching, and achievement.

Strangely enough it is in large-scale thinking and large-scale construction techniques that the "small" countries of Europe almost invariably surpass us. The United States has, for instance, no housing authority that can touch the scope and quality of work being done in London or Stockholm, while American industrial planning is—in the factory-housing-community sense—embryonic

8

relative to that embodied in the new Finnish industrial towns. Our use of large prefabricated concrete components and panels (an inevitable constructional development) stands in knee pants compared to similar work in Italy, England, France, and Scandinavia—as, indeed, does our ordinary concrete construction. Wall-sized factory-fabricated panels are regularly employed in much of Europe (especially for housing), while the small-unit prefabricated work of Nervi in Italy is world renowned. As for imaginative work in metal, it is of interest that the famous $25,000 annual R. S. Reynolds Memorial Award for creative work in aluminum (of which the U.S. produces by far the world's largest output) has gone to Europe three out of five times—once it went to Australia and not until this year did it, for the first time, go to the United States. Moreover, the standardization of building materials and techniques and the constant necessity of using only stock items make much American architectural practice somewhat like assembling a gigantic Meccano set. Expensive U.S. labor and relatively inexpensive U.S. materials contrast with inexpensive—and prideful and imaginative—Continental labor and high European material costs and limitations, adding another element of difference between architecture here and abroad.

Two hundred and twenty-five buildings in sixteen countries are analyzed here. Obviously there are not two hundred and twenty-five works of contemporary architectural genius in Europe—or anywhere else. However, Europe certainly counts two hundred and twenty-five—and more—stimulating and significant recent buildings. This group has been sought out. The buildings have been selected and arranged to present not only an over-all picture of architectural achievement but also a cultural barometer of each nation's postwar abilities in shelter. There is at times an obvious lack of equality in similar building types in different places. For example, housing in, say, Greece does not equal housing in Sweden—and is, indeed, surpassed by Stockholm examples not even mentioned. However, one of the functions of this book is to set forth the outstanding work in each country. Thus the traveler even in the less developed nations can readily find what new buildings of merit are about. It is further hoped that pointing out progressive structures in a country where few others exist might be a spur to future developments.

There are many ways of evaluating a building aside from the "pure design" standpoint. Final design is, of course, the final arbiter—and design criteria have determined the backbone of selections made for this guide. However, determinants on sociological, philosophical, constructional, and even national bases are responsible for a few choices, examples of architecture that are pregnant in thought in spite of certain shortcomings in appearance. Merit alone is not sufficient for the inclusion of a building: it must have ideas and stimulation as well. In some cases a building that demonstrates fresh and constructive thinking, or explores a new facet of space, but suffers design weaknesses, has been chosen over a similar example of routine thought but superior execution.

Some buildings that I personally do not particularly admire are included here. However, they are so important as indexes to trends or as outstanding examples of certain schools of architectural thought that it would be negligent to omit them. Obviously each reader will find incomprehensible the inclusion of some buildings—and the omission of others. (Several prominent lacunae are the result of architects' requests; in a few instances technical difficulties prevented a building's inclusion.) It is pertinent to remember that two of the greatest architects of our time, men whose influence has transformed U.S. architecture and architectural education, see virtually nothing of merit in Ronchamp. The rest of us hold this chapel to be one of the truly significant creations of the ages! *De gustibus non disputandum est.*

The buildings described here represent what are considered the finest postwar works in sixteen countries. This is the cream: do not expect to find the general level anywhere near this high.

As this book is primarily a guide, buildings are grouped by location—always starting with the nation's most important city—and not by architect or building type; these are indexed in the back of the book for the convenience of the reader seeking to follow the work of a particular architect or architects, or to probe new thoughts in housing, schools, churches, etc.

No private houses are listed, nor are exhibitions (sprightly though many be) or buildings, such as shops, apt to vanish or change markedly overnight. As regards the first, it would be an intrusion for owners of distinguished homes to have hordes of curious visitors descending upon them. Exhibitions are here today and gone tomorrow. Shops can be virtually ruined over the weekend.

This guide does not—cannot—probe deeply into the myriad aspects involved in every structure. With one photograph and limited text—and no plans or sections—this is obviously impossible. The book essays to set the general scene, then to bring out each building's salient contributions, tell precisely where it is and who did it, and in the index, when it was done. It concentrates largely on work of the past few years, but for fuller understanding and depth it goes back to the outbreak of World War II and winnows the telling work from that sad era. The book seeks to function as an introduction to the wonderful richness of architectural thought evident in Europe today: it most definitely does not constitute a history of modern architecture, nor should it be read at one sitting—or rashly considered a substitute for personal visits to the buildings described.

A selection such as must be made here is a thankless job. No two people would agree on the two hundred and twenty-five most stimulating buildings of postwar Europe. However, on personal examination of most and thorough study of all of the buildings mentioned—plus hundreds eliminated—those that follow seem in broad perspective to be those of the greatest interest. The author would appreciate suggestions or corrections.

G. E. Kidder Smith

163 East 81st Street
New York 28, N. Y.

March 1961

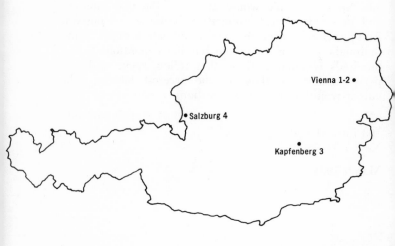

Vienna 1-2 •

• Salzburg 4

•
Kapfenberg 3

AUSTRIA

10 20 30 40 50 M

20 40 60 80 KM

AUSTRIA

Austria, smallish (about the size of Maine) and relatively poor, is struggling to get back on its feet after the onslaughts of war—and postwar—upheavals. Its architectural situation naturally reflects the crises the country has experienced, and until recently emergency and utilitarian building dominated construction. Now a certain security and affluence have appeared, and architecture is beginning to blossom.

Austria's future contributions should be substantial, for the seeds of modern architecture were planted early here, and they flourished. In the first part of this century Otto Wagner, Adolf Loos, and Joseph Hoffmann—their Viennese *Sezession* was an early revolt against the *Art Nouveau* so prevalent throughout the Continent—produced works that were among the significant pioneering designs of our time. The Steiner home in Vienna, built by Loos in 1910, is generally held to be the first "modern" house. Although Loos never built extensively at any time, and although he suffered an architectural aberration with his Doric-column skyscraper proposal for the 1923 *Chicago Tribune* competition, this "Viennese Socrates"—as his distinguished pupil Richard Neutra calls him —was, from 1910 until his death in 1933, one of the great architectural catalysts in Austria. Le Corbusier has proclaimed him: "one of the first to have realized the splendor of industry and its close connections with esthetics."

The United States is fortunate that Richard Neutra (born in Vienna in 1892), himself one of the most brilliant of Austrian architects, has practiced in this country since 1923. It can well be said that Neutra advanced America's architectural thinking by a decade. Victor Gruen (born in Vienna in 1903) has also contributed very significantly to planning and building in the United States. Bernard Rudofsky, too, has been a most stimulating import to the United States after a brief but brilliant sojourn in Brazil. A little-known Austrian who remained at home but who has had a world effect on building is Ludwig Hatschek (1856–1914): he invented asbestos cement.

In spite of the fact that Austria was one of the early

13

Continental protagonists of large-scale housing (the 1930 Karl Marx Hof in Vienna and the famous Werkbundsiedlung of 1932 being particularly well known) postwar building in this line has been distinctly disappointing. The recent work of Roland Rainer and Carl Auböck for the Fertighaussiedlung in Vienna (Vietingergasse)—next to the Werkbundsiedlung—is of merit, particularly in its use of prefabricated materials, but far too much new Austrian housing is poor in design, poor in site plan, and poor in internal arrangement.

Vienna is the natural center for postwar work; its new sports and communal arena is its most interesting building. Other promising work is beginning—the new Böhler Building (Elisabethstrasse 14) by Roland Rainer is a fine small office-block and St. Florian, Wiedner Hauptstrasse, by Rudolf Schwarz, the German architect, should be seen—but no great volume of significant work can be expected for several years.

1 City Auditorium and Sports Hall (Stadthalle)

Märzpark, Vienna
Roland Rainer, architect

The closed competition (held in 1952) for this municipal hall and covered stadium was the most significant architectural event in postwar Austria. A number of Europe's distinguished architects, including Alvar Aalto and Pier Luigi Nervi, participated. Although Aalto and Roland Rainer split first prize honors, Rainer, being Viennese, received the commission. Rainer's design is very handsome, though not as daring and expressive as Aalto's cable-suspended roof, nor as dramatic as Nervi's pure, precise statement—which somewhat resembled his Palazzo dello Sport in Rome (and which received honorable mention). The project is primarily a gigantic *Sportpalast* of great flexibility, with a huge multipurpose main room and separate smaller pavilions for gymnastics, roller skating, ice skating, and basketball. The great hall can be used for varied activities—cycle racing, ice skating, boxing, circus performances, conventions—and even as a theater. Capacity varies from 4,000 for films to 7,409 for theater and 15,400 for boxing (with half the audience seated, half standing). In section, two great banks of seats rise on either side of a flat floor. As needs determine, this floor can be filled with chairs or provided with a ramp for cycle racing, or it can be taken up altogether. A 340-foot-wide, hip-truss roof spans the auditorium. The ancillary halls beyond the main room contain specialized sports facilities, but even these can be converted to lecture halls and smaller assemblies if necessary. The exterior of the *Stadthalle* is vigorously stated with a fitting and businesslike angularity, but the interior of the main hall is somewhat a victim of its own flexibility—particularly in the helter-skelter ceiling treament of lights and utilities. Altogether this is a pivotal unit in Austria's rebuilding, one that should do much to encourage modern architecture throughout the country.

2 Gänsehäufel Lido

Gänsehäufel Island (in "Old" Danube outside Vienna)
Eugen Wörle and Max Fellerer, architects

The 80-acre island of Gänsehäufel, some five miles from downtown Vienna, has been a favorite recreation spot for Viennese since the early part of the century. The first bathing facilities there were destroyed during the war, and in 1946 Vienna's city council decided to expand the entire concept of this as a riverside resort. Professor Wörle's and the late Max Fellerer's main job was to preserve as many as possible of the island's thick natural trees and as much as possible of its vegetation, concentrating their "changing" facilities in an or-

15

dered central area and leaving the rest of the island untouched. In addition to 14,000 bathers, for whom lockers and cubicles were necessary, an equal number of nonbathers visits the resort; separate circulation was necessary for each group. For the nonbathers the northwest end of the island has been provided with tennis courts, a café, and a series of rentable cottages. The "changing" cubicles are mostly in 2-story blocks, with some single-story private cabins. All such facilities are grouped—a touch rigidly—in pavilions separated from one another by small open courts. Material is primarily reinforced concrete, for durability and ease of upkeep. A simplicity and straightforward directness characterize Gänsehäufel; this and its sympathetic scale make the result a success although it lacks the sophisticated felicity of similar baths in Switzerland.

3 Community Center (Volksheim)

Kapfenberg, Steiermark (90 miles SW of Vienna)
Arbeitsgruupe 4 (Holzbauer, Kurrent, and Spalt), architects

This binuclear building consists of a community hall on a slightly raised and terraced platform joined by a glass link to a 2-story-and-basement office-block. The hall, which can seat a maximum of 300, contains a stage at the far end, with rear exit to a small café and a kitchen, which double as dressing rooms on demand. Lounges and coatracks occupy a foyer

along one side of the hall; the opposite wall, all of glass, looks onto a garden strip and terrace. The 40-foot-wide terrace finds extensive use in summer. The basement of the office block contains hobby rooms for both young and old, including a photographic darkroom and television room. The city library occupies one end of the main floor, which has various municipal offices and clubrooms along its double-loaded corridor. The top floor contains trade-union offices and a conference room. The trim, even stark, quality of the architecture is emphasized by the dark reinforced-concrete frame against the light panel infilling.

4 Parish Church of the Holy Blood

Gaissmairstrasse 6, Salzburg-Parsch
Arbeitsgruppe 4 (Holzbauer, Kurrent, and Spalt), architects

Using an ancient barn as a base, three imaginative young Viennese architects have put together an impressive church in an east Salzburg suburb. The old portion consists of three low bays of three vaults each (nine vaults altogether), producing a somewhat medieval nave. The architects put a pent roof at 45° above and pointing away from the last line of barn vaults, producing a spacious and brilliantly illuminated chancel with dropped roof behind. The altar thus stands bathed and free in the flood of light about it. This contrast of the low somber with the bright lofty is highly effective, a polarity of means too little seen in church design.

17

Beyond the chancel proper, at the far end of the rectangle of the church, are five more ranks of pews, giving a total seating capacity of 450. Oskar Kokoschka painted in line two strangely amateurish door panels. The exterior of the new (east) end is a bit overscaled in its great angled-roof and window, but all in all—not forgetting its origins as an aged barn—this church achieves very commendable results.

Amsterdam 1-2
Aerdenhout 3
Hilversum 4
Amersfoort 5
Rotterdam 6
Geleen 7
Brussels 1-2
Liége 3

BENELUX

BENELUX

The contemporary architectural situation in Belgium, the Netherlands, and Luxembourg, the three small but densely settled and wealthy countries of Benelux, is puzzling. (The Netherlands and Belgium are the first and second most densely populated nations on earth; if the United States were so thickly settled, it would contain more than three *billion* people, well over the world's total population. As to wealth, Luxembourg and Belgium have—or had until July 1960—the second and third highest per capita income in Europe, Switzerland having the greatest.) Just as England and Spain might be said to offer the most surprising postwar architectural contributions in Europe, so Benelux must be said to have the most disappointing.

Luxembourg, a charming political anomaly, possesses a latent liveliness but nothing as yet of contemporary architectural significance. The recent competition for a national theater, won by Alain Bourbonnais of Paris, has intriguing possibilities, and the Kirchberg plateau extension of the capital by Henri Luja seems promising. However, since the time when the Romans roamed through, few buildings of distinction have materialized.

BELGIUM

Belgium has produced little of merit, architecturally speaking, since the first World War. With turn-of-the-century pioneers like Baron Horta and Henri van de Velde behind Belgian architectural efforts, this is doubly disturbing. Of all European countries, Belgium is least to be excused for not contributing more to contemporary architecture. Having a thoroughly literate and capable population of nine million and an extremely high living-standard, the mediocrity of its architecture can be explained only by the indifference of its officials, the inadequacy of its educational system, and a flabby materialism.

Belgians won the R. S. Reynolds Award in 1958 for the temporary Transportation Pavilion at the Brussels Fair, but this is the only bright mark on a dismal report. Housing aspires to the monumental, in the Ecole des Beaux-Arts manner of a generation ago. "Du reste, la Belgique n'occupe pas une position enviable en ce qui concerne la production de nouveaux logements" (*Logement Social et Santé*, Brussels, September 1960). The proposed Heysel development near the site of the Brussels exposition appears absolutely frightening—a gigantic fortress of apartments. The dwellings—and technical buildings—at the new nuclear-energy center at Mol, by Wybauw and Thiran, are good, and the Liége housing shown below expresses imaginative construction technique, though it is poorly laid out. Little else of housing merit can be seen. Several other buildings are of general interest and worth a small look, but the total situation is lamentable.

1 Foncolin Building

rue Montoyer 3, Brussels
André Jacqmain, architect

A handsomely detailed two-part office-block (connected on the third floor by a glazed passage) for an insurance firm. Bands of concrete horizontals (the floor slabs) play against the nervous tension of metal frames and thin wood rails that project out in front of the window wall. These extended slabs give protection from the sun and lend plastic interest to the façade. The main wall itself is well detailed in pre-fabricated vibrated-concrete units of slender dimensions. Thermopane windows fill the wall panels from floor to ceiling. With a façade so full of interest and movement, it is unfortunate that a projecting fire stair has been so prominently attended to, and that the top floors of each block have assumed unnecessary self-importance. The basic module, though, is both clever and fresh.

2 Apartment Hotel

avenue Louise, Brussels
René Stapels, architect

An agreeable, urbane residence-hotel mildly reflecting Le Corbusier's Clarté Flats in Geneva. Above a ground floor containing the usual reception area, bar, and restaurant (which can also send meals directly to the apartments), are imposed six floors of 20-foot-high duplexes, with eight apartments on each floor except the top. Each apartment consists of a lofty 2-story living-room with completely equipped kitchenette and services on back wall, plus bedroom "half-floor" with bath and closets above. This can be closed off by curtains if desired. All interior decoration and furniture are by Knoll International. The haphazard top floor does nothing to help an exterior otherwise simple and expressive.

3 Champ des Manoeuvres Housing

avenue Georges Truffaut at avenue Reine Astrid, Liége
C. Carlier, H. Lhoest and J. Mozin, architects

Containing 1,800 apartments for some 7,000 people (154 per acre), these flats directly on the River Meuse represent one of the largest housing developments in Benelux. Crèches, schools, church, library, shops, and community hall are integrated with the 16 housing units. The development's faults lie in its uniform 12-story buildings, which breathe a formidable air, its rigid site-planning, its interior traffic which makes mincemeat of the area (yet all buildings face on exterior streets), and in a principal avenue that (through no fault of the housing architects) separates the inhabitants from the river. Its merit resides mainly in its construction technique: each apartment block rests on V-shaped supports, all of which were prefabricated and craned into place; further, the double window-bays were made of prefabricated vibrated-concrete, finely detailed and of such size (approximately 12 feet wide by 9 high) that construction was greatly speeded.

THE NETHERLANDS

The Netherlands, in contrast to Belgium, has been a country of architectural pioneering. In the 1920's and 30's, exhorted by Oud and Rietveld—early leaders of the famous *De Stijl* movement—and augmented by Duiker, Dudok, and others (with Berlage before them) the Dutch bequeathed us many buildings important in the evolution of a contemporary architectural approach. Hilversum abounds in excellent examples of this period: Dudok's grand, though Wrightish, town hall; Duiker's Zoonnestraal Sanatorium, and Gooiland Hotel; and the radio station by Merkelbach and Karsten. Housing and planning were also particularly fine in this era.

Since World War II, however, a pronounced falling off in quality has become evident. Although some excellent things have been realized—the Lijnbaan shopping center in Rotterdam is one of the finest urban rehabilitations to be found anywhere, and a children's home in Amsterdam bursts with ideas—having been led to expect so much from prewar achievement, we must feel disenchanted by most postwar work. In addition, there has been an architectural apostasy on the part of the Delft School and of certain men, such as Oud, who have on occasion turned too heavily to romantic cul-de-sacs (e.g., the Shell Building) or seemingly conscious confusions of forms (Secondary School in The Hague). The book *Na-oorlogse bouwkunst in Nederland* ("Postwar Architecture in Holland") is a painful volume, while buildings such as the Groote Schouburg (Large Theater) in Rotterdam, the new railroad stations in Flushing and 's Hertogenbosch, and the provincial center at Arnhem would garner many votes as outstanding recent Continental horrors.

However, as mentioned, a few, very few, excellent buildings are being erected, plus a modicum of others (the best of which are shown below): one's quarrel is that we—and the Dutch—deserve more. Among the buildings not illustrated later are several churches and schools: the Church of the Good Shepherd, Oosterbeek-hoog (near Arnhem), by F. A. Eschauzier (simple and pleasant interior); the neoromantic Cross Church, Charlotte de Montpensierlaan, Amstelveen (near Amsterdam's Schiphol Airport), by Marius Duintjer; Maranatha Church, Kuinderstraat 12, Amsterdam, by Groenewegen and Mieras (fair interior); and the Reformed Church at Burgemeester Honnerlage-Gretelaan, Schiedam, by van den Broek and Bakema, which many find spiritually vacant (its chancel wall is one third clear-glass and overlooks the rear end of a housing development). Among the schools of some interest—but not in a class with English or Swiss examples—are Oud's school, mentioned above, in The Hague on Goudsbleemlaan (good on some interiors); and van den Broek and Bakema's Montessori Secondary School, Schimmelpenninckstraat, Rotterdam (well organized though somewhat brutal).

A word on planning in the Netherlands. Having almost 900 people per square mile, the entire country is rapidly becoming one enormous city—or concatenation of cities. Much of the land on which these cities are built is being snatched from the sea itself: such man-made real estate thus assumes a monumental value. Planning under these conditions is no academic matter, but takes on a significance considerably more urgent than in the Western Hemisphere, where unused acreage is ubiquitous. It has been said that the Dutch countryside is so precisely, indeed rigidly, arranged and organized that it is little wonder Mondrian painted as he did!

Rotterdam—the world's second busiest port—having been the victim of an exercise in extermination bombing (25,000 houses, 2,300 stores, 62 schools, and 13 hospitals destroyed or damaged in one hour), should be the luminous example of the finest in European replanning. However, although much was accomplished, the light somehow failed. Central Rotterdam was indeed liberated in rebuilding, as reference to plans of 1940 and 1960 will attest, reducing the area covered by building from 55% of the total to a reported 31%, and unbinding a medieval accumulation so that the city could breathe easily. However, far too much was rebuilt as was; the city center is still amorphous, coreless; and traffic is rather less than brilliantly handled. To paraphrase Paul Valéry, it does not sing as a city.

Housing in the Netherlands is not in a class with that in Sweden, Finland, or England, but one partly nonarchitectural aspect merits interest: the Dutch are probing more deeply than any other country into the mental factors involved in housing—factors too often overlooked thus far. Having achieved physical health statistics that are usually the best in the world, plus a very high material prosperity, the Netherlands has experienced a rapid rise in mental problems (as has the rest of the world) that gives pause to think. Small apartments with all the family crowded together, lack of privacy, intra-apartment noise even in well-planned developments, lack of sufficient contact with nature, and the inability (particularly in the crowded Netherlands) to enjoy nature alone, all of these are coming in for scrutiny. Their architectural manifestations will not be without interest.

1 Children's Home

Amstelveenscheweg at Ysbaanpad, Amsterdam
Aldo van Eyck, architect

This temporary home for 125 children on the western edge of Amsterdam (just south of the Olympic Stadium) is among the most provocative new buildings of Europe. Built by a semiprivate institution to take care of children (babies to 20-year-olds) who are not being taken care of properly—or at all—at home, this "transit station"—children stay from several weeks to almost a year—seeks to provide a friendly, com-

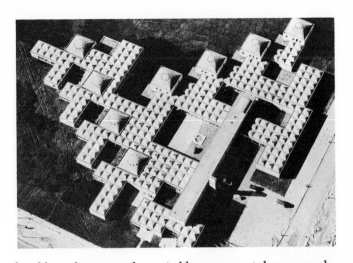

fortable welcome until a suitable permanent home can be found. It is manned by a staff of 30 (social-welfare people, doctors, nurses, teachers), 12 of whom live in. Both the architectural means and the architectural philosophy of the building are impressive. A staggering number (336) of prefabricated lightweight concrete cupolas 11 feet square, plus 8 larger cupolas, 33 feet square, are grouped around a series of small and large inner courts (for sheltered games and play) of geometric shape, but with a totally irregular over-all periphery. The entire building is built on an 11 foot module. Altogether there are 8 contiguous divisions, each formed and equipped for a particular age group. Gymnasiums and play halls are convenient to each. Living quarters for the resident staff occupy the long elevated block above the entrance, with administration, central kitchen, and services grouped about it. The children eat and sleep in their own unit. A small hospital is also included. Two large playing fields adjoin the home. The building's pungent architectural philosophy begins with its relation to the site and street and continues even in details. The meeting of side wall and roof was, for instance, the object of closest scrutiny and reflection, and a special glazed beam was evolved as an intermedium in order to avoid vitiating the inner space (which glass against ceiling would do) and to preserve a feeling of enclosure while not presenting a shut-in sensation. Doors, moreover, are rarely flush sections of a wall but serve as occasions for transition from one space to another, and are thus usually set in depth. Hard and sometimes arbitrary, this is a highly exciting building.

2 Opstanding Church

Bos en Lommer Plein at van Artevelde Straat, Amsterdam-West

M. F. Duintjer, architect

In spite of an overly zealous and curiously scaled tower, plus a somewhat abrupt entry, the interior of this Reformed church merits a look. Its U-shaped nave is uniformly surrounded by a series of vertical ceiling-high baffles, and these louvers are so set that the congregation sees no direct source of light (except when leaving and facing the entrance). A flood of sunshine slices through these louvers, focusing on and playing over the chancel with an alive intensity. Beneath the church proper, which is elevated almost a full floor above grade because of soil conditions, are placed a series of community rooms, youth rooms, and related services.

3 Reformed Church

Leeuweriken Laan, Aerdenhout (just SW of Haarlem)

Karel L. Sijmons, architect

A strong, positive church (13 miles west of Amsterdam), clearly divided into its main elements of worship, entry, and classrooms. The nave, which seats 400, embodies a space of restrained tension. Its higher, central section plays against low sides, one the approach, the other with raised platform for the Communion table. (In Dutch Reformed churches the congregation in turn moves to and actually sits at the table with the minister for the bread and wine.) These ancillary spaces about the nave also provide visual depth and spatiality. The window wall to the left, though obviously influenced by

Le Corbusier, possesses a strength and personality of its own. Its deep reveal and several glass colors are well done. The entrance, somewhat too self-effacing outside, gives onto a generous hall within, with nave to the left and Sunday school, community rooms, and administrative offices to the right. Well worth the drive from Amsterdam.

4 World Broadcasting Center

Lage Naarderweg, hoek Nieuwe Crailooseweg, Hilversum
 (15 miles SE of Amsterdam)
van den Broek and Bakema, architects

This impressive new group now going up just outside of Hilversum will augment the comely town's first broadcasting studio of architectural consequence, the famous one by Merkelbach and Karsten on 's Gravenlandsche Weg, the early stages of which were completed in 1936. In basic plan the new building consists of an elevated T-shaped administrative block, the long leg of which surmounts two (eventually three) lozenge-shaped clusters of small studios; the top of the T rests on a smaller lozenge containing a large studio.

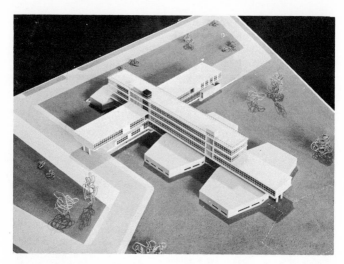

The studio groups "float" under the office block above and are structurally independent, double-walled, and totally sound insulated. The architectural expression of the two components—the concrete "platform" of the elevated offices against the low block studios sweeping underneath—is the most striking feature of a design otherwise marked by a certain hardness and a staccato fenestration of the offices.

5 Zonnehof Exhibition Hall and Museum

Arnhemseweg, Amersfoort (30 miles SE of Amsterdam)
Gerrit T. Rietveld, architect

A small (one display room and a mezzanine) museum—the most recent work of the talented Rietveld, and a permanent sequel to his elegant but unfortunately temporary Sculpture Pavilion in Arnhem. Its architecture is etched precisely in a dark steel frame, white, black, and blue brick panels, and glass. A module of 3 meters was used both horizontally and vertically. Two window-wall sections give a fine inpouring of natural light, and a central skylight provides supplementary illumination for sculpture. The balcony, reached by a nicely detailed open stair, serves for small pictures. The entire interior presents a quiet, relaxed, and spacious background for its works of art. Office, toilets, storage room, and heating plant (note the firm exterior expression of chimney) complete the building.

6 Lijnbaan Shopping Center

Lijnbaan (just off Coolsingel), Rotterdam
van den Broek and Bakema, architects

The Lijnbaan in downtown Rotterdam is probably the finest mid-city redevelopment of limited size yet made in either Europe or America. It comprises only some 65 shops, but it stands for excellence in almost all particulars. Gaiety, pleasure, scale, extraordinary flowers and planting, sculpture, birds singing, weather protection, reasonable signs, agreeable street furniture, and most important of all, liberation of the pedestrian from most traffic cares all induce one to spend. The overly high neighboring housing breathes down one's neck and the parking is not fully resolved, but the shopping area itself exudes ideas. Downtown Rotterdam was practically erased in one day of war (May 14, 1940), and the problem of its rebuilding was one of the most difficult the Netherlanders had to face. One unusual principle was adopted when it was decided to put a number of apartments in the central core of the city to create a full life there, not one that simply lasted during business hours. The Lijnbaan itself was to be a traffic-free group of shops no more than two stories high laid out in an L-shape, largely surrounded by apartments, and only a block from Coolsingel, Rotterdam's main avenue. Through this happy L one can stroll, not rush; one can pause in an outdoor café (glass-shielded against brisk weather); or one can—as one generally does—buy from one or several tempting shops of friendly 2-story size. A continuous marquee provides weather protection and lends to the pleasant intimacy of the scale. The Ter Meulen, Wassen, and Van Vorst combined stores, together with Martin's

restaurant (all van den Broek and Bakema) mark the entrance to Lijnbaan on Binnenweg, and Marcel Breuer's famous De Bijenkorf department store (with the extravagantly scaled Gabo sculpture in front) stands just around the corner on Coolsingel. The replanning of downtown Rotterdam itself disappoints (insufficient traffic and parking provisions, too little urban joy), but the Lijnbaan proper, in spite of a certain rigidity and lack of focus—plus intruding 13-story apartments along the side—is one of the fascinating shopping complexes in Europe. Absolutely tops.

7 Reformed Church
Parklaan at Op de Vey, Geleen (12 miles N of Maastricht)
Bart van Kasteel, architect

An unusual church on a tight triangular lot in southernmost Holland. The sanctuary floor is elevated physically (and spiritually) above the nondescript neighborhood. On the ground floor are placed the meeting hall and offices, and alongside, a detached residence for the minister. One reaches the nave via a gently curved exterior ramp or by an internal stair on the opposite side. The nave proper, which with the balcony, seats a maximum of 350, is a starkly simple room. The presbytery is handsomely bathed in indirect natural light from a single continuous roof window; four ceiling lightwells supplement this. Karel Appel, one of the foremost contemporary artists in the Netherlands (he won the 1960 Guggenheim prize), designed the colored-glass window at left.

Thornton 23

Richmond 22

Wigan 21

Dublin 1

West Bromwich 20

Hunstanton 1

Coventry 19

Brynmawr 18

Harlow 13

Swindon 17

London 1-9

Mitcham 10

Northflee

Hinkley Point 16

Gatwick 11

Marchwood 15

ENGLAND AND IRELAND

50   100   150 M

50   100   150   200   250 KM

ENGLAND AND IRELAND

ENGLAND

Intellectually the contemporary architectural situation in Great Britain is on one of the highest planes in Europe. Much of the excellence of English architectural development can be traced to the Industrial Revolution, which England sired, and to its incalculable effect on spans and structures: first the bridges of Telford, Paine, and Stephenson, and then, in 1851, Paxton's remarkable Crystal Palace—one of the most prophetic buildings in the history of architecture. Following these startling achievements a ferment of architectural ideas, with a concern for moralistic, stylistic, and other architectural values, erupted with Ruskin and William Morris, and was kept in motion by Voysey and Macintosh. As Jürgen Joedicke wrote in *A History of Modern Architecture:* "The seeds of modern architecture were first sown in England."

Unfortunately, these nineteenth-century beginnings, which stirred all the Continent and significantly influenced the German founders of the modern movement, withered in England itself. For almost the entire first half of the twentieth century Great Britain saw little of architectural significance. The 1930's counted brave pioneers like Wells Coates, Joseph Emberton, Raymond McGrath, Owen Williams, Maxwell Fry, F. R. S. Yorke, and Frederick Gibberd (from England and the Empire), Serge Chermayeff and Berthold Lubetkin (from Russia), and temporarily at least, Eric Mendelsohn, Walter Gropius, and Marcel Breuer (from Germany). However, in spite of the excellence of their work, these men blazed lonely trails. (Remember the Penguin Pool in Regent's Park Zoo and the Highpoint Flats, North Hill Road, in London?) As far as the general public was concerned, architectural progress was more talked about than acted upon.

Then came World War II. Afterward, instead of returning to a norm of complacency—as the French and Dutch did largely—the British (and the Italians) determined to create a new architectural environment. This

35

"revolution" was, of course, intensified by Britain's social upheaval (i.e., the welfare state) and by the need for replacing an awesome number of buildings. Early post-war work, of necessity in an austerity mold, was basically concerned with housing the homeless and providing schools for the young. And as these housing and educa-tion matters were affairs of state, the rebuilding of Britain was initially almost exclusively "officially" in-spired. Government architecture in most of the world (including the U.S.) slides with a common norm of little distinction; in England, however, its achievements have often been superb. Indeed the London County Council's architectural staff has produced some of the finest housing and some of the finest schools in all Europe, and much famous provincial work (the Hertfordshire and Middlesex schools, for example) can also be at-tributed to government architects.

The London County Council, started late in the last century, attained its postwar excellence largely through the brilliant early leadership of Robert Matthew and Leslie Martin and a young corps of inquiring, eager architects. (After all, no private work of size could be done.) Its program was enormous, for, as regards schools alone, of the 1,200 in use in London in 1939, only 50 escaped damage or destruction during the war! (Figures from *Architectural Design,* June 1959.) And other pub-lic building needs of London County's three and a third million people also had to be met—including (at present) some 7,000 or more dwelling units a year.

Government architects (at the L.C.C. and elsewhere) early realized that traditional methods of building—to say nothing of traditional designs—were not sufficient for the staggering job that faced them, a job that was not made any easier by shortages of skilled labor and materials. All agencies, especially the British Building Research Station, hence undertook searching studies into every phase of building—from the early postwar prefabs of merit (untold thousands of "Churchill Villas" were built) to the high-density high-rise apartments now dominant in all cities, although previously rare in Britain. Standardization and prefabrication became routine procedure to a degree that makes similar U.S. practice (especially in housing) seem almost nineteenth-century.

Since the war no country anywhere has concentrated architectural and related talents upon the manifold problems of building as completely as has Great Britain. These efforts have paid off handsomely, first in housing and schools, and most recently, in hospitals. Furthermore, the "new" architecture that thus arose has had a powerful effect in introducing contemporary architectural concepts to a very broad range of the British public. Modern architecture has arrived.

The English achievement in building schools is recognized everywhere. Walter Gropius—no stranger to education—has said that Britain has the most advanced new schools in the world (*Architectural Forum*, May 1952). Unfortunately, only a few of these can be examined in a survey such as this.* However, three critical points should be kept in mind: most English primary and secondary schools crowd too many pupils to a classroom (40 is frequent); many of them are far too large (with over 2,000 students); and, in common with most of the world's schools (except those in Switzerland), too few of them boast enough art. On most other counts, however, English schools (and those in Switzerland) are the finest to be seen in Europe.

---

* English schools of distinction not covered later: Architects' Co-Partnership's Secondary School, Nottingham Road, Chaddesden, Derbyshire, Girls' School, City Road, Sheffield, Yorkshire, and Secondary School, Great North Road, Hatfield, Hertfordshire; the day nursery, St. Alban's Road, Garston, the junior school in Croxley Green, and Summerswood Junior School, Boreham Wood, by C. H. Aslin (Hertfordshire County Architect); Denis Clarke Hall's Woodfield County Secondary, Woodfield Road, Cranford, Middlesex; Drake and Lasdun's Hallfield Primary, Bishop's Bridge Road, Paddington, London W 2; London County Council's Catford Secondary, Bromley Road, Lewisham, SE 13, Garratt Green School, Aboyne Road, Wandsworth, SW 17, and Spencer Park School for Boys, Trinity Road, Wandsworth, SW 18; Peter Moro's Fairlawn Primary School, Honor Oak Road, London SE 23; Powell and Moya's Mayfield Girls' School, West Hill, Putney, London SW 15; the T. P. Riley Comprehensive School, Bloxwich, Walsall (Birmingham), by Richard Sheppard, Robson and Partners; the Bridgnorth Secondary Boys' and Girls' Schools, by Paul Yarker and A. H. Colquhoun; and Yorke, Rosenberg and Mardall's Secondary School, Stevenage New Town, and Susan Lawrence School, Poplar, London E 14. On the university level the following are notable: Sheffield University's library, by Gollins, Melvin, Ward and Partners; the physics building at Liverpool University, by Basil Spence; and the addition to St. John's College, Oxford, by the Architects' Co-Partnership.

Housing is the main field in which the British have done intense research. As a consequence, few countries can match the achievements of this branch of English architecture. From the urban rehabilitation standpoint, not even the Swedes can touch the British housing. The London County Council, abetted by buzz bombs, has done splendid work in creating economical new neighborhoods throughout the city. Quantity not quality marked its results until the mid-fifties, but quality appears frequently today. Roehampton (q.v.), for instance, is probably the finest low-cost housing in the world. Other outstanding L.C.C. developments: Loughborough Estate, Brixton, SW 9 (formidable in the over-all but good in its high-slab design); Ackroydan Estate, Wimbledon Parkside, SW 19 (fine in its high flats); and Brandon Estate, Kennington Park, Hillingdon Road, SE 17. Private architects, too, have produced first-rate public-housing. In addition to those described and illustrated later, the following are of merit: Hallfield Estate, Bishop's Bridge Road, London W 2, by Tecton, Drake and Lasdun; Tile Hill, Coventry (very fine in parts; note shopping center) by Gibson and Ling; the flats at Ham Common, Richmond, by Stirling and Gowan (imaginative small apartments); and nearby, off Upper Ham Road, Parkley's Estate (good in parts), by Eric Lyons. It should be emphasized that such housing represents the best only. British speculative housing, now that financial controls are off, is universally ghastly: among Europe's worst.

By far the largest statements of housing and planning in England can be seen in the New Towns. These—along with several large-scale Swedish experiments—are the most important architectural and urban developments in Europe. Although they suffered severe growing pains (which were to be expected), and although their density often is ridiculously low, chewing up the landscape and militating against a "town" as opposed to a "garden city" atmosphere, they nonetheless abound in lessons. In many cases as much—or more—can be learned from their failures as from their successes. Paramount among their positive features are their scale and their inhabitants' sense of belonging. The English have the faculty of being able to make a whole city seem like a private club, and every on-looker a member. In far too many coun-

38

tries (including the United States) "identity" of the citizen has disappeared from urbanism or been pasteurized to a mockery.

The New Towns, although they were originated in an effort to get people out of the clutch of the great cities, primarily greater London, are not dormitory satellites, but self-contained cities, complete with their own offices and industries, and their own recreational facilities. Eight of the fifteen New Towns are grouped around London itself (at distances of up to 30 miles), as this megalopolis is in direst need of relief; but there are four others in England proper, and three in Scotland (notably, that at Cumbernauld, 15 miles northeast of Glasgow). The New Towns have been placed relatively close to their "mother" cities so that the people whom these developments wish to attract will still be able to run up to London, etc., with comparative ease for special cultural and entertainment events, or for personal reasons—and hence will feel freer to move from city to New Town than they otherwise would. Physical and psychological linkage with large cities is especially important in the formative years of New Towns; as their maximum foreseen populations (up to 80,000) are approached, the New Towns become more completely self-contained.

The finest of the New Towns is probably Harlow, which is shown below. Although neither it nor any of the other New Towns is spectacularly planned—none of the New Towns is, for example, comparable to Stockholm's Vällingby—all are of considerable importance. The very fact of their existence is imposing. What other country in the world can claim so much large-scale creativity in housing? Sweden, perhaps, but no other; certainly not the United States.

Although planning in the New Towns has ranged from fair to good, as mentioned, replanning in the old cities has been sickeningly disappointing. None of the English cities will have again—we trust—the planning opportunities that war cruelly thrust upon them, yet none of them can point with pride to over-all outstanding achievement —in spite of the hopes inherent in the wartime Uthwatt Report and the Town Planning Act of 1947. London, for which such bright planning expectations were held, is obviously going rapidly ahead—an impressive 14 acres of rebuilding a week is the figure sometimes quoted—and building within the framework of the London Development Plan. But because so much more could have been done had the issue been firmly seized at war's termination, one weeps for lost chances. Traffic in London has been no more than touched. Total paralysis—of minds and motors. Coventry made a brave replanning effort, but though the results are agreeable in spots, they are spatially formalistic; progress has been generally thwarted by the merchants who insisted that cars drive up to their front doors; traffic, of course, is chaos. Little people, little results.

In summarizing postwar British architectural achievements one is struck by a puzzling paradox: in some respects they are superb; in a few others, antediluvian. This may be explained in part by that elusive and intriguing British temperament. When the totally new is a challenge, the English (and Scotch) can't be beat. Radar and penicillin, first commercial jet planes, the world's fastest car, fastest boat, first turbine car, first industrial use of atomic power—all were developed by the British. Yet with the familiar, only the tried and true will do. Another and more tangible factor in this architectural plus and minus reflects the client: where the government, or at any rate, a select agency like the L.C.C., has been in charge, the building level has been very high; where big business, private wealth, and commerce—and above all speculative builders—are concerned the picture degenerates into the second-rate or worse. None of the new office blocks and corporate headquarters in London and the Midland cities can, for example, touch Italian or German counterparts; many are on a dubious par with the Dutch: self-important, egregious. Theaters and the architecture of pleasure, though only beginning to appear following austerity, are chrome-bedecked and "moderne" in spite of the spritely example of the 1951 Festival of Britain (which did much, incidentally, to awaken the British public to modern architecture). Churches with few exceptions—generally in the "free" churches—are the most architecturally reactionary in Europe. Except the Coventry Cathedral (now being built), the Church of England has commissioned nothing, absolutely nothing, of real merit. Yet hundreds of new

40

churches have gone up. Is it any wonder that church attendance in Great Britain is slipping? There are more fine new churches around Basel or Cologne than in the whole of the United Kingdom. To flip through *Sixty Post-War Churches* (Incorporated Church Building Society, London, 1957) will make even the most devout an agnostic.

One technical detail, of domestic utilities, is bewildering—and perhaps revealing. Central heating and hot water, particularly in houses, is, one gathers, still suspiciously regarded. However, there's hope: a recent London newspaper headlined "We're Becoming Central Heating Minded"! Moreover, kitchens, even in luxury flats, consist of a sink and perhaps a stove. No effort is made to integrate all fixtures, to build in suitable cupboards, to organize the housewife's most important workshop into an efficient and delightful whole. And in the bathrooms one almost always finds the hot water tap in its little corner and the cold in its. Never the twain shall meet. Flagellating.

However, the future holds promise. Clients are catching up with architects. Several of the schools of architecture are excellent. The two chief professional magazines are particularly fine—the *Architectural Review* being the most highly regarded architectural journal in the world. Their self-criticism and their perceptive crusading for a finer environment, to say nothing of their deep concern for architectural appreciation, make them models. (Unfortunately, the lay press in England is not as alert.) Books, too, cover every phase of architectural achievement; they are excellent, numerous, and find a ready audience. The Council of Industrial Design (with headquarters at 28 Haymarket, London) assiduously champions a finer ambience. Unlike France with Le Corbusier, Italy with Nervi, or the Scandinavian countries with Aalto, Markelius, and Jacobsen, England has no towering architectural genius. But a surprisingly potent contribution is being made, one about to blossom mightily. When the accomplishments of British architects overseas, particularly the work of Maxwell Fry and Jane Drew in Ghana and Chandigarh, of Raglan Squire in Rangoon, and of James Cubitt from Burma eastward, are considered, the picture looks even brighter.

Within a decade the contemporary architecture of Great Britain might well be the best in Europe.

1 Roehampton Estate

Roehampton Lane at Portsmouth Road, London SW 15
London County Council, architects (Hubert Bennett, in succession to J. L. Martin and Robert H. Matthew)

Roehampton is probably the finest low-cost housing development in the world, and as it accommodates some 9,500 people, it is also one of the largest. A gloriously unspoiled 128 acres (formerly the grounds of five Victorian houses), adjacent to Richmond Park, provided an ideal site with superb trees and uneven topography. Every tree, every natural feature was used wherever possible. The buildings consist of a variety of high and low types, with large 10- and 11-story "point" (freestanding, high) houses and slab blocks accommodating more than half the population, and 4-story walkup buildings containing maisonettes (duplex apartments), roughly one third. The other units are 2- and 3-story terraced blocks and unusual buildings with single-story one-room apartments for old people. There are altogether some 2,611 dwellings, with a population density of 110 people to a built-up acre. The 11- and 12-story blocks, which visually dominate the entire development, are found on the high ground at both east and west ends. The twenty-five "point" houses, (each is a chubby rectangle in plan) have (in the newer west groups) two two-bedroom and two one-bedroom flats per floor. These tall, assertive blocks, well separated and beautifully landscaped, form three impressive groups as one walks or drives about on ever-curving roads. They are well planned inside and handsome outside. Nicely scaled reinforced-concrete panels, approximately 20 inches wide, cover them on four sides. The five large slab buildings (in the north corner of the development) decidedly recall Le Corbusier's

unités with their mass raised on *pilotis*, their 2-story apartments with loggias, their bold scale and rough concrete. All the apartments in these buildings are of the balcony-access, two-bedroom, duplex type and are 12 feet wide and 38 feet deep including loggia. (The first *unité*'s apartments are 12 feet wide and 80 feet deep.) They cost approximately £2,350 ($6,580) apiece. Raising them on stilts created wet-weather play areas for the children and absorbed the marked unevenness of the ground. Furthermore, the open, see-through quality achieved by use of the stilts gives the buildings a lightness in the landscape. Like the tall "point" houses, the slab blocks are sheathed with prefabricated concrete units and use precast floor-slabs and staircases. The 4-story walkups, the other major building type, also contain duplex, balcony-access apartments, but these are wider (16 feet) than the apartments in the slabs and contain three bedrooms and outside bath. The wonderful visual variety generated by these three major building types, and to a lesser degree,

43

the others, is one of the strong points in the pleasures of Roehampton. The freedom of the road net and the variety of vistas it provides is also excellent. Weaknesses lie in the pronouncedly stiff layouts of all the low housing, in a certain institutional atmosphere in the slab region, in a lack of garaging (which will soon be acute), and in the lack of more "local" shopping and communal facilities. A new and elaborate shopping center is being built on the central periphery; this, however, should be supplemented by more neighborhood stores—and by more neighborhood atmosphere. But in its use of the land, in advanced construction technique, in visual satisfaction, in apartment planning, and in its high blocks, especially the "point" houses, Roehampton rates very, very high.

2 Churchill Gardens Development
Pimlico, Grosvenor Road, London SW 1
Powell and Moya, architects

An extensive development, stretched along the Thames and adjacent to the Chelsea section of southwest London—one of the pivotal building groups in immediately postwar England. Its success prompted other large-scale thinking. Winning a competition for its design in 1946, the architects spent the next nine years evolving a four-stage series of flats and maisonettes which now houses some 6,500 people in 1,650 apartments. In addition, there are some 30 shops, nurseries and nursery schools, a community center, pubs, etc. As the group is largely low-cost, and as construction subsidies were provided by the Ministry of Housing, economy of building and a high density (200 people per acre—this is a very thickly settled section of town) were both necessary. The tree-bordered river was the take-off point in over-all layout; virtually all high units (10 to 11 stories) are perpendicular to the river, and from upper floors especially, enjoy a fine view. Another conscious feature of the layout is the juxtaposition of high elevator and low walk-up housing, and the creation of composed spaces with these varying heights. A series of intimate "neighborhoods" has been created, with no endless vistas or rigidly parallel or stiffly geometric relations. Architecturally the buildings range from good to very good, although a too restless vocabulary of types rankles in such tight and sparsely planted areas. As nice accents, several small old buildings on the site have been left intact. Color, too, has been well handled, Block 7 on Lupus Street being particularly fine. The famous 126-foot-high glass-encased

heat-accumulator, which gets waste hot water from the Battersea power station directly across the river, provides a handsome accent. With more planting and more space—and perhaps more communal buildings—Churchill Gardens would attain great distinction. Even as it is, nothing in New York can touch it.

3 Golden Lane Housing

Golden Lane, Fann Street, Goswell Road, London EC 1
Chamberlin, Powell and Bon, architects

On a dull mid-city lot with no natural features whatever, an attractive solution to the problem of urban living has been realized for 1,400 people. Winning a competition for its design in 1952, the architects have molded seven acres, which had been completely cleared by bombings, and whose interior streets were subsequently eliminated, into a tight (200 to the acre) but agreeable *mise en scène.* Located only a short distance (5 8 of a mile) north of St. Paul's, it provides particularly convenient accommodations for working couples. The chief virtue of Golden Lane lies in its imaginative use of the site: by means of a periphery of 4- and 6-story buildings (containing maisonettes) and a 16-story block of flats in the center, a series of four delightful, varied, and gracious courts and gardens has been created. Furthermore, the courts are each different in character, and each serves a particular need: the court for pedestrians (built over the garage) opens onto Fann Street; the community-center court has a hall for 200, a youth club, etc.; the inner court serves for quiet activities; and the physical-recreation court provides several levels for outdoor bowls, as well as space for ball games and badminton. All traffic has been confined to the periphery and to underground access. A London County Council school will be built in the northeast corner. A series of shops, a restaurant, and other facilities are placed at ground-floor level in the peripheral buildings. The high-rise unit, which is well related in scale and a handsome contrast to the low buildings, contains 120 bedroom-and-living room flats; these two rooms can be thrown together for half their depth by a large sliding wall-panel. Clever. Estate offices, hobby rooms, and laundry facilities occupy the ground floor of the tall building, which has an elaborate roof terrace on top, dominated by a dubiously exuberant swooping canopy that folds over the roof utilities. The planning of the maisonettes is tight as a drum; i.e., in many one must traverse the whole apartment, including the living room, to reach the stairs to bedroom level. This, however, carps a detail in a highly provocative downtown redevelopment.

4 Holford Square Estate

Holford Square off Percy Circus, London WC 1
Skinner, Bailey and Lubetkin, architects

Beginning with the still highly impressive Highpoint Flats
of 1935, the famous firm of Tecton did much to improve the
housing of London. Though Tecton dissolved some years ago,
the original participants, among them Skinner, Bailey, and
Lubetkin, have sometimes associated since the war. In addition to the development shown here, their ambitious low-
cost housing projects include, among others, Hallfield Estate,
Bishop's Bridge Road, W 2 (Tecton, Drake and Lasdun),
and Priory Green Estate, Wynford Road, Calshot Street, N 1
(Skinner, Bailey and Lubetkin). The Holford Square development, though smaller than either of these, is more unusual
because of its broadly stated three-arm plan. This Y-shaped
8-story building contains 118 one- and two-bedroom low-in-
come apartments. The east and west wings are of the balcony-
access type and are arranged so that all bedrooms and living
rooms face southerly, with kitchen and bath only on the
north (access) side. The south arm of the plan provides three-
bedroom duplex apartments, to which there is alternate floor
access. Though the apartments in all three arms are compactly planned, each, particularly each duplex, suffers from
a grievous lack of closets—the municipality's, not the architects', shortsightedness. Apartments are served by two elevators at the nodal point, plus a very clever stair, which is
worth a look. The façades vary from the prosaic on the sunny
sides to the lively on balcony-access sides. A small, detached
4-story block for twelve families occupies part of the scheme.
Over-all density is 129 per acre.

5 Bethnal Green Housing

Claredale Street (off Hackney Road), Bethnal Green, London E 2

Denys Lasdun and Partners, architects

Imaginative, ingenious, even off-beat, low-cost housing. As such it contrasts pointedly with the standard parade of blocks that characterizes urban development throughout most of the world, including, incidentally, the world at the foot of this quadrifurcated tower. This is no frivolous revolt, but an inquiring experiment, and a valuable—and probably successful—one at that. The 14-story cluster-block to be discussed here is joined by two long and rather boorish 6-story maisonnettes to make up this development in a poorer London quarter. The total population is 576. The cluster high-rise is composed of four identical, angled "wings" which are attached by narrow "bridges" to a central but freestanding vertical circulation-and-utility tower. These wings contain

two apartments per entry floor; except for those on the fifth floor, which has bed-living-room flats, all are duplexes. Balcony access leads to all, and no rooms except interior stair-halls, bathrooms, and w.c.'s have windows onto this public balcony. On the other side, facing easterly, southerly, and westerly, are private balconies extending much of the width of each apartment. Boiler and oil storage rooms, utilities, and tenants' bulk storage occupy the ground floor. The elaborate means used to fractionalize this housing into five units instead of one not only provide each tenant with greater privacy, visual and aural, but also make each apartment more of an aerie—with its accompanying sense of freedom—than could any slab or even "point" house. From the surrounding streets, this cluster block proclaims itself more a member of a small-scale neighborhood than would a perfunctory arrangement of large-unit buildings. It belongs. The inner core area is tight; an inexplicable exterior "panel" mars each end wall; bedroom windows should run full, not partial, room width; storage is insufficient; and unnecessary compartmentation (between living room and dining-kitchen, etc.) chops up the plan. Still, this housing represents a searching approach to new and appropriate forms and is highly provocative. "For this reason, Denys Lasdun's cluster-blocks in Bethnal Green . . . are works of architectural and historical importance, insofar as they embody one of the prime concepts of the anti-diagrammatic programme and give it successful visual form" (*Architectural Review*, May 1960).

6 Luxury Flats

26 St. James Place, London SW 1
Denys Lasdun and Partners, architects

Down from the Ritz, up from Pall Mall, and overlooking Green Park—no finer spot could be chosen for an upper-bracket London apartment. Hidebound for generations in garlanded and corniced whispers of the past, luxury housing has been England's most reactionary building type. Until the last few years few units had been built since 1939. This 8-story apartment has finally achieved a break-through, and a handsome one it is. The new flats had to run a frightening gantlet of critics, being, for one thing, located next to Spencer House, an eighteenth-century building of distinction. Approval had to be obtained from the Minister of Housing and Local Government, the Minister of Works, the Royal Fine Art Commission, the London County Council, and the Crown Estates Commissioners. As the architect states: "The archi-

tectural relationship, in terms of harmony between the new building and Spencer House, is achieved not by means of formal correspondence, one building with the other, but by each building having a common concern with what is authentic in architecture of any time." The new block, though tightly bounded on its site, finds escape in ingeniously planned interlocking levels. Its four large apartments have 40-foot-long duplex living-rooms and 6-foot-wide terraces on the park. Even the smaller flats advertise living rooms that face the park. Almost every foot of outside wall is glazed, perhaps overly so in the northeast bedrooms. Although un-necessarily—and formalistically—choppy at the "cutout" corners without, and inexcusably deficient in closet and storage space (and in kitchen equipment) within, this is sophisti-cated building.

7 Royal Festival Hall

South Bank of Thames at Waterloo Bridge Road, London SE 1

Robert H. Matthew and J. L. Martin (of London County Council), architects

A cocoon wrapped in concrete inside a shell states the structural essence of this concert hall for 3,000. Elaborate insulation was necessary because the hall is tightly sandwiched between the Hungerford Railroad Bridge and Waterloo Bridge, both heavy with traffic, and is directly on the banks of the Thames with its river noises. A subway runs underneath. Built as the one permanent building of the 1951 Festival of Britain, it forms an important element of postwar architecture in England. Its rectangular auditorium rises a story and a half above ground level and is encased in two 10-inch-thick walls with a 12-inch air-space between them. The roof is of similar double-thickness construction. Two features distinguish the auditorium: the steeply and continuously canted floor, and the famous "staggered" box-stalls, twelve on one side, eighteen on the other, looking like so many regal toboggans. (Both floor slant and projecting boxes have had a marked influence on concert-hall design on the Continent, particularly in Germany.) The auditorium further boasts finer acoustics than any other concert hall of our time. In this regard it is interesting to realize that the side walls are parallel and the floor and ceiling raked—the reverse of "standard" practice. As inner *pilotis* support the auditorium, the restaurant and public areas could be placed beneath it and circulation could be simplified. Actually, the generous circulation areas surrounding the auditorium proper—a series of promenades, bars and restaurants, overlooking a garden and the river—and the wonderful flow of space between them on numerous levels, are the greatest architectural delights of the whole building. This part is brilliant. However, "well enough" was obviously not left sufficiently alone in detailing, for there is too little visual repose and there are too many busy-busy contesting elements within, while on the outside too many cooks stirred the various façades. But in basic thinking—and basic results —we could ask no more of an auditorium and its inner approaches.

8 Bousfield Primary School
Old Brompton Road at The Boltons, London SW 10
Chamberlin, Powell and Bon, architects

An absolutely charming school; among the finest primary schools yet designed. Note the sensitive spaces—open and enclosed—that distinguish it. The use of a water garden along the sidewalk to control pedestrian circulation is inspired. Other gardens, and changes in level, are wrapped around the school proper and nestle the building easily into its residential neighborhood. Belying its inconspicuous appearance the

school accommodates 560 pupils (at 40 pupils to a room!); it is divided into a junior school, to the north, and a primary, to the south. To take care of so many students, yet fit the whole school into a discreet residential neighborhood—the school occupies the site of several bombed houses—was no mean architectural achievement. However, by subtle changes of levels and a considerate scale, the architects were able to pacify the initial qualms of the district. The school was built on a strict module (40 inches) and largely of prefabricated materials. In plan, the school splits into well-defined zones: two large assembly halls, each flanked by services, are back to back in the center and are separated by enclosed courts from the two classroom banks. Structure is boldly expressed —permission was obtained to leave the steel exposed on an experimental basis—and a fine use of color is seen throughout. In many respects this is one of the best schools in Europe.

9 Secondary School for Girls

Gray's Inn Road at Sidmouth Street, St. Pancras, London WC 1

London County Council, architects (P. Nicoll and R. J. Herron, job leaders)

Although less than a half mile south of the King's Cross and St. Pancras stations, and not far from the British Museum, this mid-city school for 480 girls enjoys a pleasant park and a sizable nearby playing field. The school will eventually be

enlarged and changed into a local college, and this long-term requirement was anticipated in the present stage. The school's most striking features include its imaginative use of several outdoor levels, its interesting detached assembly-hall, and its classroom block on stilts. By excavating and clearing the basements of the houses previously on the site, a sunken playground, which flows right under the east end of the elevated teaching-block, was created so that outdoor recreation could be enjoyed even in bad weather. The gymnasium, a separate unit to the east, with dressing rooms beneath, is reached by a "bridge" over the playground. The main block of the school is composed of three classroom stories on stilts, with entry and services taking up part of the ground floor. Most of the general classrooms face southerly. The assembly hall in the backyard resembles a slightly angled glass-sided box, delightfully transparent and unobtrusive in the neighborhood. A stage across the far end of the hall enables it to be used for theatricals. Construction throughout is of reinforced concrete.

10 Methodist Church

Cricket Green, Mitcham, Surrey
Edward D. Mills, architect

With a sensitive design and disposition of its main elements, this is one of the most pleasant of the new English churches. Replacing a blitzed church that had stood nearby, the new one overlooks a cricket field in a south London suburb, just

off the main London Road. Its two main units, arranged in an L-shape, are the church proper, seating 300, and the parrish hall, which accommodates 200. Vestries, classrooms, clubrooms, dressing rooms, and services are grouped behind these two. The whole is set back behind a picket fence in a garden containing several fine trees, a well-placed free-standing cross, and a small parking area. The nave proper is roofed with folded planes of concrete (designed by Ove Arup and Partners) which project on the west side to provide a fine covered passage both to the church and to the hall. The sharp folds of this roof are fully expressed within, where they are covered with narrow tongue-and-groove boards in a natural finish. A somewhat questionable feature of the interior is the use of the York-stone panel that fills the chancel wall; the over-all design of the interior is so clean and direct that this seems an unnecessary intrusion. An unusual—and successful—feature is the sunken organ at the front of the pews, with the choir placed at right angles to the other pews directly across the aisle from it. The architect designed the furniture (except the altar which came from the old church): pulpit, pews, and altar rail are especially good.

11 Gatwick Airport

Gatwick (near Crawley), Sussex (25 miles S of London)
Yorke, Rosenberg and Mardall, architects

The cleverest feature of this south of London airport—an alternative to the main London field in dirty weather—is the coalescing of three forms of transportation—air, rail, and highway—under one roof. Rarely has this been accomplished so effectively. One steps off the plane and whisks into Victoria Station via the Southern Railway in far better time than highway transportation can provide. Or if leaving by car or bus, one steps directly from the concourse into the vehicle. Another admirable feature is its quality of "airport-ness": as soon as one arrives one feels that this is an airport and no other transportation service. One is architecturally, indeed physically, projected into the field and made a part of its excitement, for no solid wall ever rises between the passenger and his aerial transportation. On arrival (by train, bus, or car) passengers are processed—on one level—through the upper (main) floor of the building; they then proceed to the long (900-foot) finger, where stairs lead to the planes. The design of the main building itself is crisp and businesslike, though structurally it is somewhat puzzling in that the internal supports are of concrete, while the building's exterior

strongly proclaims steel (with, strangely enough, wood mullions). The long, long finger has a clever structural detail, for the tubular handrails are the top chords of the "bridges" spanning the 40-foot widths between supports. The buildings thus far constructed represent the first stage of development. When completed the present terminal will be doubled in size and will have a 5-story administration block on top. Two additional access fingers will also be built.

12 Bowater Paper Mill

Crete Hall Road, Northfleet (near mouth of Thames)
Farmer and Dark, architects

A large industrial group 25 miles down the Thames from London, on the south bank opposite Tilbury (whence leave the Scandinavian passengers ships). Strategically situated to receive pulp from abroad and to export finished paper by freighter, and with good highway connections on the opposite side, this is just one of a series of large industries that have proliferated along the Thames in recent years. Located on the site of an old chalk pit, and tightly packed between river and township, it could not partake of the continuous production flow and relaxed layout in the landscape that characterize much new industry on the Continent and in the United States. Nonetheless a capable group of buildings has been—and is being—erected, the most distinguished individual structure being the engineering division, a single-story unit directly opposite the employees' entrance. An

enormous 200,000-gallon water-tower, 143 feet high, dominates the group. Interestingly enough it was found cheaper
to build a series of full floors under this than to use regular
bracing. These floors have been enclosed and are utilized on
lower levels. The wall enclosing the plant is the most sophisti-
cated touch apt to be seen by the visitor; of white concrete
frame, with large flint-pebble panels, it is very handsome.
The same architects have also done an imposing power station a bit up the river at Belvedere.

13 Harlow New Town

Harlow (23 miles N of London), Essex
Frederick Gibberd, chief architect-planner

Harlow is probably the finest New Town to date, and though
it will not be finished for several years, it now boasts a population of approximately 50,000 (at a density of approximately
60 persons per acre), and its basic pattern is well established.
It anticipates a population of 80,000. Harlow focuses on its
own center—"The High"—with its market square, shops, offices, bus station, and communal pleasures. To the north, well

separated by topography and trees and a major sports area,
lie the industrial belt and the railroad station. Three major
housing sections are grouped about the centrum, divided
from each other but tied by main roads to the core. These
basic housing groups, each with secondary shopping facilities, a pub, a community hall, primary school, etc., are subdivided into a series of neighborhoods composed of from
150 to 400 dwellings—all graciously deployed over the countryside. A separate group of architects designed each of these
neighborhoods; this not only speeded initial development
but also, and far more importantly, created agreeable changes
in character and treatment. As approximately four out of five
families in Harlow prefer 2-story attached houses with gardens to accommodations in flats, enlivening variations of the
basic building types became necessary. It should be pointed
out, however, that there is a great variety of types, enough
to fit all tastes. Unusually, houses are cheaper to build than
flats in England. As regards design, do not look for shining
brilliance in Harlow's individual buildings: it rarely appears.
Housing runs a broad gamut from the dowdy to the good
(Gibberd's "The Lawn") to the very good ("Tanys Dell" and
"The Chantry" by Fry, Drew and Partners). The central

shopping area is probably the weakest section, being tight, fidgety in scale, and without that neglected but essential element that makes one spend: joy. In addition, an important road inexcusably bisects the market square. The shopping center at Stevenage New Town (L. G. Vincent, chief architect) is far finer, being full of atmosphere and empty of cars. Harlow for all its faults is, however, an impressive achievement, one that all can study with profit. Its impact and lesson lie in its vast scope, its land usage, and indeed, in the very fact of its existence.

14 Secondary School

King's Lynn Road at Downs Road, Hunstanton, Norfolk
Alison and Peter Smithson, architects

This, one of the first of the great new schools in England (it was finished in 1954), exerted a strong influence on subsequent work. Winning a competition, its young architects

were determined to produce a formal, compact, rather pristine 2-story main block with all noisy (or odoriferous) related activities in 1-story adjuncts. The main block, 103 by 240 feet, is strictly symmetrical, with a large 2-story assembly hall in the center (not walled in as a separate room), and two interior courts, 52 by 72 feet each, on either side. All administrative and group activities take place on the ground-floor level; all classrooms (for 510 pupils) are on the second floor. Connected to the north (and entrance) side in separate 1-story pavilions are the kitchen-pantry wing, the adult housecraft room, boiler house, and two back-to-back workshops. A large, detached gymnasium with dressing rooms is placed near the southwest corner. One of the most interesting features of the philosophy of the school's design is the location of the classrooms: by having them all on the second floor, grouped in pairs, and reached by a series of small stairs—not by long corridors—each room could be completely glazed from floor to ceiling on both its north and its south side. This provides a maximum of controllable natural light. Indeed the lively transparency that runs throughout the building is its strongest feature. Technically, the school is beautifully put together, with exposed steel frame and brick wall-panels of an obvious Miesian background. Although hard almost to the point of brittleness, and with inner-looking design (enclosed courts) when views over all the flatlands of Norfolk are about, this distinguished school has many provocative elements. Philip Johnson calls it "an extraordinary group of buildings" (*Architectural Review*, September 1954).

15 Marchwood Power Station

Marchwood, Hampshire (6 miles SW of Southampton)
Farmer and Dark, architects

The design of power stations, a building type that through gargantuan size and ordered complexity impresses no matter how treated, is fortunately evolving from the monument neurosis that in the past draped its units with a heavy masonry disguise. We are now getting instead a precise statement of envelope, the envelope closely reflecting contents, set off by a lean and virile play of ancillary units— ramps, stacks, smaller buildings. We have found architectural truth stronger than fiction. This power station along the shipping lanes to Southampton is among the most impressive in Europe. Not only is it impressive at a distance—as almost any power station is—it readily bears close inspection. The major unit is an enormous turbine house—600 feet long, 109

feet wide, and 97 feet high. This is parallel to and connected
with a similarly large boiler-house, which rises even higher.
Directly behind are two 425-foot chimneys. The plant can
use either oil or solid fuel, and being on the water's edge,
needs no cooling tower. The turbine house is particularly
handsome for the manner in which its steel structural frame
is clad: a curtain wall of ridged aluminum, is set in seven
continuous bands, which are splayed out to make a vertical
saw-tooth. Each splay is glazed on top. Thus natural, glareproof light floods the interior by day, while at night the
interior's artificial illumination shines up on the canted surfaces
without. The lower levels are encased in reinforced-concrete
blocks as blast protection. The only unfortunate ·element
from the design standpoint is the abrupt manner in which a
graceless switch-annex punctures the turbine hall along almost the entire length of its base.

16 Nuclear Power Station

Hinkley Point (Bristol Channel, 8 miles N of Bridgwater)
Frederick Gibberd, architect

England was the first country in the world to produce commercial power by nuclear energy, opening its famous Calder
Hall in 1956. Since then several other units have been put
in operation, or will be shortly. The newest is this 500-
megawatt station now being finished on the south shore of
the Bristol Channel. Thus far only photographs of the model
and an accompanying description of Hinkley Point have been

released, but they are sufficient to show that this will be one of the impressive industrial complexes of our day. Besides the usual administrative building (located at the left corner of the illustration), the main units are an enormous turbine house (foreground) and two reactor buildings directly behind. The turbine building is long, low, and sheathed with aluminum; a constant clerestory runs its length on each side. The reactor buildings, which are more interesting visually, are

cages, 180 feet high, almost totally glazed on four sides; thus one can see the forms of the reactors and heat exchangers from any angle. This transparency also lessens the effect of enormous mass in the scenic area in which the station is set. As the architect writes: "The buildings have been considered as being in scale with the estuary and have been related to them in natural color and texture. It is (further) proposed to use large areas of aluminum sheeting which will weather a soft, powdery grey colour, which is almost identical with the stones of the foreshore." What a wonderful regard for nature!

17 Princess Margaret Hospital

Okus Road, Swindon, Wiltshire (30 miles SW of Oxford)
Powell and Moya, architects

The first building stage of this new hospital is enough by itself to put this among the architecturally significant hospitals in Europe today. Virulently opposed to the monumental-block approach, it presents instead a friendly, welcoming group of connected units; each of these has a private garden-court or a view of the Wiltshire downs. One thus enjoys constant contact with nature. As the architects write: "The Departments are planned as a series of 'islands,' connected one with another by covered and glazed links. As a result, when walking from one part of the hospital to another, it is easy to grasp the planning of the whole and of its

various parts and to find one's way around, instead of being lost in a seemingly limitless mass of building." When stages two and three are eventually completed, giving a capacity of 600 beds, this delightful intimacy will still be maintained. Walking distances will not be too great either. It should be noted that this hospital's intimacy results from scale and from relation to nature, not from a "cosy-cosy" architecture: indeed the individual buildings are sometimes hard to the point of flintiness. The entrance marquee in particular is so ponderous and uncompromising that one half expects Lazarus himself to appear pushing it up. Glass, concrete, stone, and mahogany are the prime materials throughout. As the 22-acre site slopes pronouncedly down to the south, two "ground-floor" levels are possible: an upper for outpatients and visitors, a lower for staff. An auspicious look at hospital design.

18 Rubber Factory

Waen Pond, Brynmawr, Brecknockshire (SE Wales)

Architects' Co-Partnership, architects; Ove Arup and Partners, consulting engineers

The first postwar building in England to command world attention (it was finished in 1951), this extremely handsome factory was perhaps even more important on the national scene than it was internationally, for it showed British industrialists the advantages of working with architects as well as with engineers. Both contributed significantly to the design of

the plant, which is located directly south of a previously depressed town (population 7,000) and beside an old reservoir, from which it draws water for cooling at the rate of
1,000 gallons a minute. Making small-unit, flexible products,
the factory could be more compactly laid out than is possible
in many industries; the main building is thus one deep rectangle, approximately 325 feet wide by 450 long. If expansion should be needed in the future, a separate building
will be constructed: no addition will be made. The great imagination of the plant lies in its compact layout and in the

ingenious roofing that makes this practicable. To provide for
wide uninterrupted floor areas on the main production (top)
floor, and to light these areas with daylight whenever possible,
a series of nine bays of reinforced concrete was used to cover
the factory. The low domes (3 inches thick) that fill these
bays have arc-shaped clerestories on four sides; in addition,
each has eight overhead skylights. Supplementary fluorescent strips are also provided. Spacious and flexible within,
these domed bays are also handsome without. Other areas of
the factory are likewise thoughtfully laid out and designed.
A superior industrial building.

19 St. Michael's Cathedral

Cathedral Square, Coventry

Basil Spence and Partners, architects

Although this great cathedral for 2,000 will not be completed until 1962, progress thus far is very tangible. While Europe as a whole is peppered with fine new churches—very, very few, incidentally, in England—this will be the first contemporary cathedral. Strangely enough, as Banister Fletcher points out, "the only complete English Gothic cathedral designed for the Protestant faith [before Coventry] is Liverpool." This labored Gothic affair was begun in 1903. To have a Protestant cathedral with contemporary convictions and a handsome appearance is thus doubly welcome. Such a building credits both Basil Spence—who won a competition for its design in 1951—and the battered people of Coventry, whose previous cathedral was razed in one of the infamous "Baedeker Raids." One of the acute problems in evolving the new was what to do with the ruins of the old, only the tower and part of the walls of which were left. Spence has brilliantly utilized these remains by making them the most impressive forecourt in Christendom; a tragically bombed old church with sightless windows and grass-filled floor evoking an overwhelming poignancy. Furthermore he has carried the "module" used in the vaulting of the old church into that of the new (which is set at right angles to it). The new building—to judge from progress to date and the architects' drawings—will be very handsome indeed, in spite of a marked inconsistency in structure and an overly attenuated plan. The structural dichotomy lies in the fact that the ten great floor-to-ceiling splayed wall-panels are of heavy local masonry, while the inner structure rests on slender prestressed-concrete columns; no intimation of the inner is suggested by the outer. Unquestionably there should be a visible separation and statement here. The length of the plan is excessive—far more Gothic than current liturgy recommends. The art in the new Coventry Cathedral is and will be outstanding, and will grow with the church. Graham Sutherland has designed the largest tapestry ever made, which will dominate—let us hope not overdominate—the sanctuary wall; Jacob Epstein did an impressive (if somewhat wooden) St. Michael; and a brilliant series of windows is being produced by John Piper, Lawrence Lee, and others. Konrad Adenauer has made an appropriate gift of all the glass in the Chapel of Unity. Basil Spence has also designed small, economical, similar neighborhood churches for three of the new suburbs of Coventry; the best of these is St. Oswald's at Tile Hill, west of the city.

20 Churchfields School

Church Vale at Vale Street, West Bromwich (Birmingham)
Richard Sheppard and Partners, architects

Probing deeply into the problem of the gigantic school and
its impact on young minds, the Sheppard associates have come
up with a deeply understanding solution: a group of "houses"
gathered about a central core of libraries, workshops, and
assembly halls (a scheme not dissimilar to that at most English private schools). Thus, instead of cramming 1,600 to
2,000 students into one vast box, where the individuality of
each child must perforce suffer, 180 to 360 students are accommodated in each of a series of extremely attractive separate
"schools" grouped about a core of communal facilities. These
school units, providing all theoretic teaching and meals, but
differing in response to varying requirements, become the
children's bases, educationally and socially. Thus far, twelve
2-story buildings joined by low kitchen-dining wings—to make
six separate "houses"—have been built. Practical and specialized teaching (workshops, etc.) and general assembly—plus
over-all administration—are in units in the central area. The
idea of separate "houses" is beautifully perceptive in itself;
its architectural realization proves equally fine. The individual buildings combine concrete, steel, and wood well, and
each enjoys highly agreeable spatial relations with the
others. One can quarrel with an educational system that permits so many young students to attend a single school, but
one will not quarrel with this splendid solution.

21 H. J. Heinz Factory

Walthew House Lane, Kitt Green, Wigan, Lancashire
*J. Douglas Mathews and Partners, with Skidmore, Owings
and Merrill (New York), architects*

Situated in open country between Liverpool and Manchester, and designed between London and New York, this trimly turned factory represents much of the best of two worlds. The American influence can be seen particularly in the compact over-all disposition and in the artificially lighted warehouse half of the main building (general European practice uses skylights wherever possible). The complex is divided into three main units, all capable of expansion: a 2-level factory-warehouse block, an administration and personnel building, and a can plant. The main block (shown at left in photograph) receives raw materials and prepares and cooks them on its upper level; canning and labeling, storage of the finished products, and shipping are all handled on the lower level. All vegetables and ingredients are gravity fed. The west, or receiving, shipping, and warehousing end (raw materials above, finished goods below) is of solid-wall construction. In contrast, the east, or preparation, half of the main building is all glass. In front of the factory is the administration and personnel building (right in photo); following ground contours, it rises one story at its west end and two at its east, or canteen, end. This is a beautifully scaled structure with a white concrete frame and red brick infilling. Its breadth of scale contrasts sharply with the finicky fenestration of the glass-walled factory, to which it is attached by a covered "bridge." Except for this discrepancy—and the juncture of access ramp to main building—the group is a vigorous example of industrial architecture.

22 Secondary Modern School

off Richmond-Darlington Road, 3/4 mile NE of Richmond, Yorkshire

Clarke Hall and Scorer, architects

An ingenious and clever school, built on a pronounced slope and realized with a limited budget. With such a trying lot, the architects had a choice of leveling the site or breaking the school into a number of blocks and stepping them down the grade—either would have been expensive—or of projecting one unit perpendicular to the hillside. This last was done. The resulting building is a simple block 300 feet long by 70 feet wide, with two floors at the high (north) end and four at the lower. It contains all of the school's facilities except a small separate workshop, laboratory, and garden room. All twenty-three classrooms for the 600 pupils are on the top floor, along with the library, which has a pleasant, south-facing, balcony. At ground level at the upper end are administration and staff rooms; the kitchen and dining room are placed toward the building's midriff. A 2-story assembly hall, which has a stage, is stepped down the hillside and is adjacent to a double-height sound-insulated gymnasium. At lowest level (at south end), directly under the gym, and adjacent to the playing fields, are the boys' and girls' locker rooms. To emphasize the positive statement of this 4-level, stepped form, the architects expressed the top floor as an emphatic self-contained, continuously glazed box, cantilevered beyond the inferior floors along much of its length. To make this structurally feasible, a system of 10-foot-deep reinforced-concrete beam-walls was set up on columns spaced 25 feet (e.g., the classroom width) apart. Solid on the top (classroom) floor except for central corridor and two emergency doors, each beam-wall rests on two reinforced-concrete columns, set in 10 feet from its outer edge, and carried down as structural supports through the various heights of the lower floors. Clever structure and fine expression.

23 Rothes Colliery

Strathore Road, Thornton, Fifeshire, Scotland
Egon Riss, architect

Across the Firth of Forth from Edinburgh, inland and 3 miles north of Kirkcaldy, rises one of the most positive architectural organizations of coal mining yet seen. Sinewy directness characterizes all components, particularly the masterful dominating winding-towers. These two reinforced-concrete towers, 191 feet high and 500 feet apart, house the enormous wheels and machinery which wind the cables and bring the cars from seam depths of over 2,500 feet. Connecting the towers at ground level is the car-circulation hall, which gives onto the coal-preparation plant. This plant straddles the railroad tracks. Offices, canteen, pit-head baths, and shops are placed in separate buildings, well related to the shafts for optimum circulation of miners and staff.

Eire not only has almost no contemporary building of merit, the Irish apparently prefer life this way. The country is wrapped in an anachronistic past that virtually forces bright young people, of whatever profession, to emigrate—hardly a lovely stage of progress. As the Irish themselves put it: "Emigration is a legitimate adjustment to economic conditions provided it is limited and controlled by these conditions. The present wave of emigration has many signs of arising from much more emotional causes. Many of our trained and experienced people have been forced to emigrate to provide a livelihood for their dependents but many others are now going because they see no future in this country." (Luan P. Cuffe, *Architectural Survey*, The Parkside Press, Dublin, 1957.) This, if it continues—fortunately, there are indications of incipient improvement—will be ominous for Ireland and equally unhappy for the rest of the world. Talent in many forms is not unknown to the Emerald Isle; if given half a chance. . . . It is not insignificant that the chief of design in Eero Saarinen's distinguished office was born and educated in Dublin.

1 Bus Terminal and Office Block
Beresford Place, Dublin
Michael Scott, architect

Considering that this capable, impressive building was Ireland's first (1953) contemporary structure of significance, and bearing in mind its location directly opposite the historic 1781 Customs House, it is doubly rewarding to find such contemporary excellence. However, it is doubly puzzling that Eire has since built so little else of such merit. The building comprises two separate units: a bus station, which occupies the basement and the ground floor; and an L-shaped office-block above. Because of height restrictions, the office block was split into two low masses rather than constructed as one high mass. The offices, initially intended for the National Transport Services, were taken over by the Department of Social Welfare while they were in construction. The Minister's offices are marked on the exterior by the loggia bay in the center of the taller office-unit. The bus station fits easily under the office block, the busses entering under the low wing and leaving under the high in a straight-line operation. They back into their proper loading platforms—there are 17—and when loading is completed, depart via a ring road that avoids heavy traffic. As many of the busses are double-deckers, high clearance and a high protective canopy were needed. The sinusoidal profile of this canopy dominates the interesting architectural features. A large 2-story-and-mezzanine waiting-room, with the usual facilities, occupies all of the ground floor except for the entrance lobby to the offices. A small cinema, staff cycle park, and storage take up most of the basement level. If the junction of the two office wings had been more fully expressed and the topmost floor of the tall block more simple of profile, this building would have been even more successful. (Michael Scott and Associates has also done a handsome lecture hall extension for University College, Galway, and two capable factories: Messrs. Brown & Polson Ltd., Goldenbridge, Inchicore, Dublin, and The Kire Manufacturing Company Ltd., Barracks Hill, Kinsale, County Cork.)

Le Havre 16

Baccarat 8

Saint-Lô 17

Paris 1-6

Fontaines-les-Grès 7

Ronchamp 9

Audincourt 10

Nantes 18

Evian-les-Bains 11

Eveux-sur-l'Arbresle 12

Royan 19-20

Vence

Marseilles 13-14

Lacq 21

Lourdes 22

FRANCE

50   100   150 M

50   100   150   200   250 KM

FRANCE

France, which heretofore has been overly dominated in all professions by a veneration of the old, is now coming very much alive to the problems of mid-twentieth-century architecture and urbanism. Unprecedented new building needs, the architectural effulgence of the rest of Europe (and of the United States), and the impact of that towering genius, the Swiss-born Le Corbusier, are washing thin the desiccated academicism of the Ecole des Beaux-Arts. The climate for modern architecture in France, which throughout the century has been in puzzling contrast to that for modern art, is definitely improving. Under de Gaulle a wonderful wave of confidence, affluence, and achievement began to sweep over the "new" France.

The significant new structures of France are still few and widely scattered, but a half a dozen years ago there was virtually nothing of recent merit except the works of Le Corbusier. The authoritative *Architectural Review* has said: "France is the most conservative country in Western Europe, with about the same amount to contribute [architecturally] as Portugal" (March 1957). The present polarities between which France is torn can be illustrated by the extreme reaction of the French Right on one hand and the brilliant progressiveness of French transportation on the other. C. L. Sulzberger writes thus of France's still potent archconservatism: "The French Right refuses to admit that this is a changing world and aspires to the long-lost era of the Bourbons. . . . The French Right seeks its own destruction with the desperate illogic of those lemmings who seasonally drown themselves. Unlike the German, Italian and British Right, the French Right refuses to adjust to time. It never learns, never forgets, and prefers suicide to co-existence" (*The New York Times*, January 9, 1961). However, another element in France, epitomized by transportation, looks to the future: in rail and medium-range air-transport the French are supreme. *Le Mistral* is the fastest train in the world (80 m.p.h. between Paris and Lyon—318 miles); French locomotives hold the world's speed record (206 m.p.h.); while Sud-Aviation's twin-jet *Caravelle* is so outstandingly advanced that it has been licensed to Douglas and is now being built in the U.S.A.

The architectural withdrawal that made most French buildings until recently anachronistic palimpsests of former glories can be explained in part by the fact that France was invaded three times in seventy years, the last two times brutally so. As an almost inescapable corollary of the repeated destruction of French towns and cities—and the accompanying psychological implications—the French people were pushed toward an architectural womb, a retreat into the familiar expressed by rebuilding what they had had before.

Another, more intangible but nonetheless potent, reason for France's unfortunate architectural atavism has been the near-catastrophic influence of the older men, *les grands maîtres*, who seemingly control public taste and perpetuate it in all public buildings. Until recently, the younger man in France (outside the arts) has rarely had a chance to express himself. This was, apparently, as true in medicine, law, and banking as it was in architecture. In education, too, the old ruled; in architectural education, with a mighty hand.

France without question needs at least a half a dozen major and completely independent architectural schools deployed throughout the country—as all the other large (and many smaller) nations of Europe already have. It needs them in a hurry, and it needs them staffed with bright young men from a variety of backgrounds. French architectural training, in spite of recent improvements and some decentralization, is still not only rigid and stultifying but without real alternatives. The dissatisfaction of the students provides regular copy for the French journals. One goes to the Ecole Nationale des Beaux-Arts (1,700 students and some 200 graduates a year) or to the Ecole Spéciale d'Architecture (360 students and some 50 graduates a year), or one goes abroad. And, as a recent issue of *L'Architecture d'Aujourd'hui* stated, "if you aspire to municipal work, the Beaux-Arts diploma will get a better hearing than any other." In a country of 45,000,000 highly talented people this school system was and is preposterous; most of the work of the past forty years clearly shows this preposterousness.

Furthermore, the "taste makers," until recently, saw to it that what we rather vaguely term "modern architecture" was not particularly fashionable. As a result, its level of public acceptance, compared with that in Scandinavia or Italy, for instance, was low indeed. This, of course, has not been without its effect on clients—national, corporate, and private. The level of popular taste and the ready availability of well-designed furniture (with the exception of the sensitive work of Charlotte Perriand) have also suffered. The architectural magazines themselves (the leading journal appears only six times a year) have had until lately too little intellectual curiosity concerning the profession and the environment it shapes. This general apathy is further seen in the lack of books on the new architecture. In contrast with England, Switzerland, Italy, and Germany, France produces almost no current architectural literature of value.

As indicated, this dismal picture is, however, brightening perceptibly. It had to. France in the earlier part of this century—to say nothing of the last—gave so much to the modern movement that its demise there today would be unthinkable. The pioneering of men like Dutert and Cottancin with their Galerie des Machines of 1889 and of Gustave Eiffel with his famous tower of the same year opened a new world of spans and a new world of means in metal. And in recent years new applications of metal to lightweight, demountable, industrialized building-components have been notably advanced by the work of Jean Prouvé. Since 1925 Prouvé, a self-styled *constructeur*, but one deep in creative architectural problems, has been working with leading practitioners all over the country.

In reinforced concrete France has played an even more significant role. (The Romans, of course, knew and used concrete, but without the metal reinforcing that gives this material strength in tension to match its native strength in compression.) Ferroconcrete was largely invented by a Frenchman (Joseph Monnier is generally credited with it) a hundred years ago, and three Frenchmen, Coignet, Hennebique, and de Baudot, showed the world how to use it in the latter part of the nineteenth century. Then Auguste Perret (1874–1954), beginning almost sixty years ago, "transformed reinforced concrete

77

from a structural system like the steel frame into an organic element of a new architecture with its laws of monolithic continuity, different from any that came before" (Erno Goldfinger, *Architects' Year Book*, No. 7). It should, however, be pointed out, that Perret was at times a greater technician than he was an architectural creator (actually he was never *diplômé*); his later search for "a French style," especially as evidenced in his postwar work, was almost disastrous. Another brilliant contributor to reinforced concrete has been Eugène Freyssinet, born in 1879 and still active. His superb (now destroyed) dirigible hangar at Orly stunned the world in 1916 with its 320-foot span and 195-foot height. Freyssinet furthermore perfected (in 1923) the system of prestressing concrete which has since so revolutionized the medium. Bernard Laffaille, also, has been a great concrete engineer, building the first known hyperbolic paraboloid in 1933 in France.

As will be realized, the men and works mentioned above represented greater conquests in engineering and construction than in creating and modeling space. The engineering aspect of French architecture has always been among the country's strongest building contributions. Today this is apparent in the C.N.I.T. building in Paris (q.v.), the slender tower of the proposed Maine-Montparnasse project, Gillet's water tower and center at Caen, the roof of the Marignane hangar at Marseilles, and several impressive dams in the Alps. At Nancy-Beauregard, Jean Prouvé has applied his technology to mass producing wall-sized elements of concrete to encase an enormous (but architecturally disappointing) housing development.

The pillar of architectural strength in France was—and still is—the man whom many consider the greatest architect in half a millennium, Le Corbusier. Although his forebears some four hundred years ago had to flee southeast France because of their Calvinism, Le Corbusier since 1917 has made his home in Paris and not in his native Switzerland. His work from the 1920's to date has been incomparable. Would that he had also done UNESCO (his nomination was stupidly killed by Americans) and that his influence and public acceptance had been earlier manifest. Besides Le Corbusier and

Perret, other pioneer architects of note were Robert Mallet-Stevens, André Lurçat, Eugène Beaudouin, and Marcel Lods.

Contemporary planning, in the comprehensive and professional meaning of the word, arrived late in France. Several architects dabbled in *urbanisme*, but with the exception of Tony Garnier's prophetic "Cité Industrielle" project of the early 1900's—and, always, excepting the ideas of Le Corbusier—most planning has been regarded as an esthetic, primarily Beaux-Arts exercise. Thus, after World War II (as, indeed, after World War I), when France had to undertake enormous reconstruction (roughly 2,000,000 were homeless), competent talent was in short supply. When meagerness of abilities conspired with innate die-hard conservatism and the "architectural womb" complex mentioned earlier—and was compounded by early postwar *malaise politique* and financial crises—little could be expected. And as in Germany and England, which had similar opportunities, little of real urban merit was realized. Perret, for instance, rebuilt Le Havre with a desiccated monumentality; it is rigid, didactic, almost treeless, a town for pawns, symmetrical ones at that. Even trying to forget its esthetics and dummy windows, few of the urban problems sired by our age (traffic, parking, neighborhood identity, etc.) are properly solved in the new Le Havre. The Cité de la Benauge at Bordeaux, by Carlu, Joly, and Babin, is almost as monumental and self-important—as soul crushing—as the housing along the Stalin Allee in East Berlin. Amiens, Calais, and Lisieux are "magpie collections of motifs." Royan, Toulon, and Boulogne-sur-Mer—to name other large-scale rebuildings—are fortunately better but are not distinguished. Even the project for a new Paris, the "City of Today," by Marcel Lods (*L'Architecture d'Aujourd'hui*, No. 88), is an inhuman affair of terrifying scale in spite of its obvious cleverness. As the perceptive French architect and editor Paul Damaz (now in the U.S.) wrote: "Experience in France has proved that a very good architect might fail as a town planner." The problem of expansion for Paris now rages bitterly in the capital. The first Salon d'Architecture, which closed at the Grand Palais in January 1961, highlighted France's thinking in this regard. The "Paris

Parallèle" proposal for a detached second city separated from the capital by a green belt vied with the arch-conservative plan of the government to maintain and reorganize but not extend the city. Let us hope that the bolder—and altogether more sensible—plan triumphs and that its lesson is not lost on other cities—European and American.

It remains for completely new industrial towns to offer the brightest lessons in French urbanism. Several of these are very good—at least in parts: Mourenx, at Lacq, in the Pyrenees (q.v.); Bagnols-sur-Cèze (north of Avignon); and Fontenay-aux-Roses (near Paris). It is more than regrettable that the tragedies of war's destruction have not been seized upon as opportunities in France—or anywhere else in Europe, west of the Curtain, or east.

However, a handful of housing developments—the largest building element of urbanism—have shown startling improvement in France in the last three years, achieving a scope and design excellence of high rank. Around Paris, where restrictions on rents and on construction succeeded in throttling building for generations, many new and large neighborhoods have sprung up. The best of these are illustrated later. But as over-all construction of housing operated at such a slow pace before the war (and even then there was a desperate housing shortage), the present flood of it has too often produced only mediocrity (as in much of Europe) with an overassertiveness and a monument complex even in the best. With the exception of the work of Emile Aillaud, who has been conducting a sometimes interesting, sometimes alarming, one-man campaign of "serpentine" developments against the endless parallel blocks of apartments, most new housing in France is laid out in checkerboard fashion, with precise 90° angles throughout. Strange: housing designed as pattern on theoretically flat ground, with no concern for site unevenness! As a matter of fact, the theoretical is often dominant in such designing; instead of a welcoming atmosphere encouraging the dignity of man, as is found in housing throughout Scandinavia and England, a distinctly unpalatable stretch of gigantic barracks greets the unfortunate Frenchman. Look again at Lods's "City of Today," or at the already built Maisons-Alfort, Aubervilliers, Bondy, Epinay-sur-Seine, or La Meinau at Strasbourg. It is as though these were composed for their aerial graphic effect (on flat ground) rather than as means for the daily life of human beings. Intra-apartment planning varies from very good to poor, with—as in most Europe—never enough built-in closet or storage space.

But, as has been mentioned, there are several superior housing developments, the best of which are illustrated later. Two groups should be especially pointed out for their success in confining all automobiles to their peripheries, leaving central, and safe, garden areas for their tenants. These are Marly-les-Grandes-Terres, shown below, and "Les Buffets," the best part of the new industrial town of Fontenay-aux-Roses (Lagneau, Weill, Dimitrijevic and Perrottet, architects).

The brightest building in postwar France is found in the new churches. Contemporary religious architecture can indeed be said to have begun in France, first with de Baudot's hints in the 1890's, then concretely with Perret's Notre Dame at Le Raincy (avenue de la Résistance) of 1923. This small church, just east of Paris, is (on the interior) one of the most influential buildings of our time, and in spite of the revolution it occasioned all over Europe, it has rarely been surpassed. In post-World War II years French church building has again pioneered—or should one say revived a Middle Ages concept?—in bringing the finest contemporary artists into church work. The late Father M. A. Couturier, O.P., was largely responsible for getting "living artists" to work for the church. His first important commission was the embellishment of a new church at Assy, near Chamonix, in 1950. Though its architecture (by Maurice Novarina) is by no means advanced, being actually somewhat neo-Romanesque, the artists that Father Couturier brought in (Léger, Rouault, Richier, Lurçat, Lipchitz, etc.) were among the most progressive in France. In 1951 Novarina built the Church of the Sacred Heart in Audincourt (q.v.), an industrial town near the Swiss border; again, the architecture is of scant importance but the art magnificent—Léger designed a scintillating band of seventeen clerestory windows, and Jean Bazaine a lovely all-glass baptistery. Elsewhere, the windows of Alfred

81

Manessier (such as at Hem, near Lille) and of Leon Zack (Notre Dame des Pauvres, in Issy-les-Moulineaux, a southwest suburb of Paris) are likewise excellent. Gabriel Loire, at Chartres, has been one of the prime developers of a new inch-thick glass called "mosaic glass," or *betonglas;* he has installed handsome windows of this faceted glass over much of Europe and the United States. Although the architecture of many of the new French churches is too often only innocuous, the art has generally been magnificent. No other country has approached France in this excellence, or in the degree of joint designing by architect and artist.

In closing, the early postwar buildings of young French architects working in Morocco, Algeria, and Tunisia—away from the then hidebound mainland—must be mentioned. Much of this North African portfolio contains superior work.

1 UNESCO Building

Place de Fontenoy, Paris

Marcel Breuer and Bernard Zehrfuss, architects; Pier Luigi Nervi, engineer

The UNESCO Building—sired under monstrous, mean and harassing, political conditions—disappoints as an architectural monument. Excellent from the urban-esthetic standpoint in sensitively fitting a new construction into a difficult eighteenth-century *place,* and somewhat original with its Y-shaped main building, it is not altogether successful as a structure in space. At least the 8-story Secretariat is not; the attached, trapezoidal conference hall (basically the work of Nervi) is splendid inside and out. The main building, one gathers, was quite elegant in its unwrapped structure—"one of the landmarks of concrete construction in Europe"—but on completion it displayed such a welter of façade elements that the statement of the nicely rounded three-arm shape has been vaporized, particularly close up, under staggered vertical fins, elaborate horizontal trellises, and an unusual gray glass outrigging. Even the Cariocans at 23° south latitude do not need such elaborate sun-control measures! The brittle glass, particularly, detracts from the south façade. Furthermore, on the ground floor this (garden) façade sports an angular (where was Candela?) canopy to nowhere. An accent might well have been needed here but not one so obvious—or shallow. All of this is unfortunate because the basic planning and the basic building are excellent and of potentially handsome treatment. The conference wing, which abuts the garden side and is attached to the Secretariat at the south tip by a depressingly dark hall, harbors two assembly rooms, of which the Plenary Sessions Hall, seating 1,000, is absolutely superb. Here Nervi's concrete mastery is dramatically displayed in a pleated ceiling and end wall which are fully expressed inside and out. The dramatic folds of the inner wall of the Plenary Hall tend to render the speaker somewhat insignificant, but this is a detail, only, of a very impressive accomplishment. The exterior folds of the ceiling-roof are engagingly visible from the Secretariat. The other unit of the UNESCO group of three is the small (by now far too small) 4-story Delegates' Building standing free in the northeast corner of the site. Mirroring its great 8-story neighbor in near-identical façade treatment, it seems a little lost. Almost $200,000 worth of art was commissioned by UNESCO, some of it very good, some inadequate. Supposedly, 2% of construction costs was to be allocated to art, but this amount was conveniently reduced along the way. The Henry Moore in the garden, although it competes with its own base, fits well with the south façade of the Secretariat behind it. Noguchi's "sculpture" garden, between the Delegates' Building and the Secretariat, though charming and restful in spots, seems a bit artificial in its rather naked lack of traditional Japanese garden privacy. The huge

Picasso (29 by 32 feet) in the hall of the conference wing is probably the finest single work of art. Strangely, Picasso never visited the building, before or after painting! The Tamayo on the rear wall of the Plenary Hall is unconvincing in color and in the way it is "framed." The low Miro "walls" outside the link to the conference wing are very disappointing, for the artist's lively spontaneity is mired in the heavy bluish-brown of the background tiles. The 30-foot-high Calder, outside the other end of the conference wing, is fine, if a trifle small. Other works add lively touches in corridors, particularly on the seventh floor where the restaurant and bar are located. Much of the above description of UNESCO has, obviously, been critical. This criticism, however, stems largely from a letdown following the building's early bright promise. Even now, a straight-on elevation of the south façade is extremely handsome, indeed elegant; when one's eyes move up and to the right or left, however, the assured simplicity of the direct view gets confused in the clutter of sun-control appurtenances. This is a very important building; it is even a great one; but it is not, many feel, a very great one.

2 Exhibition Hall of C.N.I.T.

rond-point de la Défense, Paris-Puteaux

R. Camelot, J. de Mailly and B. Zehrfuss, architects; Pier Luigi Nervi and Jean Prouvé, consultants

This enormous exhibition hall—the Centre National des Industries et des Techniques—is technically daring and (within) visually exciting. Rising a bit west of the Pont de Neuilly, it terminates the axis that originates in the Louvre and proceeds straight down the Champs Elysées. From the exterior the building, poised lightly on its supports, resembles three conjoined divisions of a scallop shell. An equilateral triangle in plan, 710 feet on a side, it rises to a central height of 152 feet. Its great three-pendentive vault supposedly covers more than twice the area ever before roofed in concrete and provides 100,000 square meters of exhibition space. In the future the building will be joined by an ancillary hall for smaller exhibitions, congresses, etc. The vault was built like the wing of an airplane, with two thin "skins" of concrete, 5.9 feet apart, over a prefabricated frame. This provides lightness, flexibility in meeting wind pressure and temperature changes, greater fireproofing and sound insulation, and uses less material. The building is enclosed by three enormous walls of safety glass. Within there are five levels of exhibition space: a full triangular basement level, a balcony above this, a "main" floor

directly under the great vault and visually connected with the floors below by a hexagonal opening in the center, and two peripheral balconies above the principal floor. An interior view of the gigantic arc roof floating high above is breathtaking: one is enormously impressed by its effortless grace. An interesting, if sometimes unorientable, sensation, also characterizes the various upper exhibition levels. The exterior, however, is weak. Its window-walls, being flush with the edges of the vault, deny the vault visually, while the enormous rectangular boxes that break out from the lower sides of the window-walls appear as clumsy afterthoughts added to provide more space within.

3 Brazilian Pavilion, Cité Universitaire

avenue de la Porte de Gentilly at boulevard Jourdan, Paris
Le Corbusier and Lucio Costa, architects

Combining the talents of the two men who gave such encouragement to Brazilian architecture more than twenty years ago, this new student house constitutes a rich dish. It is particularly interesting in its location, being only a few hundred feet from Le Corbusier's famous Swiss Pavilion, finished in 1932 and recently completely renovated. The earlier building stands as a "classic" statement of cubic elegance, serenely poised on stilts above the open ground floor and the counterpointed curved stone wing. The new Brazilian house, at the east tip of the Cité Universitaire, is a bulkier edition of the Swiss Pavilion, but with the same general *parti* of elevated dormitory block (here five stories instead of four), and communal ground-floor rooms in a free-shape rear-projecting wing that "floats" under the main mass. Projecting somewhat incongruously beyond the east front are the director's quarters and the library. All east-facing student rooms have recessed loggias with pierced concrete grilles and brightly colored dividers à la Marseille. The slightly bowed west front has balconies concentrated at the center. The Brazilian Pavilion sits more heavily on the ground than the Swiss and has an awkward, almost medieval (the new Le Corbusier?) complication of supports. It is also more lush and (fortunately) more concerned with sun control than its older sister. Together, they are a fascinating pair.

4 Saint-Gobain Building

62, boulevard Victor Hugo, Neuilly (Paris)
André Aubert, Pierre Bonin and Marcel Marican, architects

As the largest and most recent company headquarters in France, this new building for the Saint-Gobain glass company (which has, incidentally, considerable holdings in the United States) tells us much of the recent French approach to office-building architecture. To begin with, it is very good, as up-to-date in the broadness of its thinking as any similar building in the United States. It has a fine parklike site, a gracious 7-story building (which handsomely demonstrates the company's manufacturing interest), an excellent detached "club" and cafeteria for the company's 2,000 staff members, and basement parking for 600 cars. The building proper with its two parallel wings boasts strict module construction (5.75 feet), prefabricated curtain-walls with floor-to-ceiling sliding windows of gray thermal double glass, slender enameled glass spandrels, acoustic ceilings, fiberglas insulation, a very interesting system of forced air supply rising between the glazed front and the transparent safety-glass set just behind the windows, and a unique system of demountable, hanging storage units attached to the movable glass corridor partitions. All interiors are flexible, attractive, and well decorated. The entrance hall with its panels of lacquer and "mosaic glass" bespeaks invitation. In sum, a flexible, advanced building, in spite of uncomfortable corners where the T-shape of the front wing laps and joins the rue Villiers section.

5 Marly-les-Grandes-Terres

Marly-le-Roi (10 miles W of Paris)

Marcel Lods and J. J. Honneger, architects; J. Beufé, associate

This "new town" for 6,000 inhabitants is one of the most interesting large housing projects in France; from the over-all planning point of view it is the best. On a lovely plateau of former farmland, overlooking the countryside and distant Paris, nine identical groups of three apartment buildings each have been laid out—with generous space all around. At the

88

south end of the development (which is approximately 80 acres in size) are a complete shopping center, a theater, schools, medical facilities, post and telegraph offices. One central plant provides all heat and hot water. One major road circumscribes the entire periphery of Marly, with no secondary roads harassing the site. Each apartment group possesses its own large parking area, with extra parking at the shopping center. No roads penetrate the interior; no car meets any pedestrian within the development; no child from any of Marly's 1,471 apartments crosses a street en route to school or to the center. This is as logical and commendable as it is rare: wonderful. The nine apartment groups that swim in Marly's large, flat, and almost treeless site are each composed of two long rectangular buildings, which are oriented

89

straight north and south, with a short building at right angles "closing" the group at its north end to form a neighborhood "yard," some 230 by 328 feet, for the more than 600 local people. The groups of buildings are identical except for slight variations in color treatment; the buildings in each group are likewise from a basic mold, even the short ones, and all are 5-story walk-ups—a hideous concept for families with children. A ridiculous (cf. other French developments) municipal height limitation of 15 meters (49 feet) prevented heights of more than five floors. A dulling repetition results. A series of 17-story buildings had been first proposed but was turned down by the authorities. The apartments were built with a considerable degree of prefabrication, and every effort was made to call on the latest techniques of both planning and construction. The fact remains, however, that they are not individually inspired buildings to gaze upon, nor does their uniform height and routine mutual relation provide spatial delight. Too much sameness—in wall texture, height, and sequential spaces—weighs on one. Fortunately, the shopping center suffered none of the restrictions (municipal, budgetary, and imaginative) that molded the apartment rectangles. This series of shops and offices is excellent, one of the finest in Europe after the Lijnbaan in Rotterdam. Built around a large open garden-court and smaller landscaped openings, it is well-scaled, attractive, and lively. Marly-les-Grandes-Terres speaks such excellence in basic plan, traffic control, and public facilities that it is a shame that its rationale is not finer.

6 Cité de l'Abreuvoir, avenue Eduard Vaillant, Paris-Bobigny
Cité des Courtilières, near Fort d'Aubervilliers, Paris-Pantin
Emile Aillaud, architect

These two somewhat fantastic housing developments are near neighbors both in distance and in statement of architectural philosophy. For architect Aillaud was determined that the sterile discipline of endless right angles and abstract geometry so prevalent in France would have no place in his work. Such rigid plans look fine on paper, but they can border on the inhuman in space. Aillaud sought instead a fluid approach, one that would take advantage of site features and one that would produce such an ever-changing visual variety that tenants would feel that the spaces were created for them rather than that they were created for the spaces. Aillaud pursued this variety both horizontally and vertically. At Bobigny, which comprises 1,500 apartments, he snakes a long, nearly con-

tinuous, sinuous line of 4-story walk-ups throughout the length of the development. This spine, so to speak, is roughly paralleled by a promenade of youthful linden trees. At the west end are placed the high buildings—13-story towers, some cylindrical, others three-pointed. The three-pointed plan also appears at the eastern end in a series of 3-story buildings (which are almost identical to the Gröndal apartments [q.v.] in Stockholm). Bent and staggered shapes are used in the odd corners. With a more limited vocabulary of building types and greater consistency in handling them, plus better road layouts and neighborhood groupings, there are impressive possibilities inherent here—as selected angles will show.

The Cité des Courtilières, between the Pantin Cemetery and the Fort d'Aubervilliers, contains apartments for 1,700 families and is similar in concept to Bobigny: Aillaud wanted to avoid parallel blocks and to create instead an ever-fresh series of spaces and perspectives subtly playing with sun and shadow. Here an extremely long (1 kilometer) 6-story band of housing winds and turns about a well (but newly) planted central park 10 acres in extent; all roads are outside the development, except one, which cuts through at the north end. Unfortunately, the long, sinuous housing appears a bit lonely and almost endless—and it is certainly homicidal to allow 6-story walk-ups. Happily playing against these at north and south are smart 13-story "star" blocks, with prefabricated wall-panels of enormous sizes. Neither Bobigny nor Pantin is altogether successful; each, however, is a fresh and stimulating entry into the housing field.

7 St. Agnes

Fontaines-les-Grès, Aube (12 miles NW of Troyes)

Michel Marot, architect

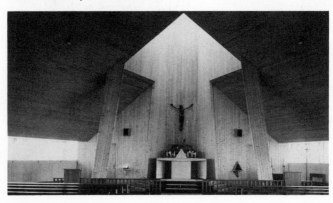

An unusual village church on the Paris-Dijon highway near Troyes. Although its interior is completely finished in wood, no boxlike atmosphere results, largely due to the triangular plan and the sharp pitch of the roof planes. The dramatic shaft of light over the altar gives a strong accent to the chancel. Windows are of white, gray, and yellow corrugated-glass set in rubber gaskets. The entrance has too many shapes and materials thrown at it to be altogether satisfactory.

8 St. Rémy

avenue de Lachapelle, Baccarat (33 miles SE of Nancy)
Nicolas Kazis, architect

A hard, self-consciously angular exterior and belfry might discourage the visitor to this church. Don't let it. For the interior is not only strong architecturally, it is bathed with colored lights from superb windows. In the center of the most famous glass-making town in France—the city whose crystal has been the pride of Europe for two centuries—this new church glows with glass of appropriate richness. Note that the light effect does not emanate from a constant clerestory, nor are the "windows" foursquare entities. Glass elements, with few major colors per "window," are composed into irregular semigeometric shapes. The lower bands of fenestration, lighting the side aisles, are of glass and concrete, molded—sculptured would be the better word—into impressive panels by François Stahly and Etienne Martin with A. Poncet and J. Delahaye. The over-all structure of exposed concrete is impressive and refined, weakened only slightly by a somewhat amorphous space about the chancel.

9 Notre Dame du Haut

Ronchamp, Vosges (13 miles W of Belfort)
Le Corbusier, architect

Coiling on its hilltop as though it grew from the very earth, dominating the countryside, and dominated in turn by the extraordinary projections of its shell-like roof, this strange form makes one churn within. Here sits no ordinary church, but a startling, yet deeply religious, statement. It is doubtful if a finer church has been built since Brunelleschi's 1446 Pazzi Chapel in Florence. Le Corbusier, its architect, was, appropriately enough, born just 42 miles to the south, across the Swiss border at La Chaux-de-Fonds. Built to replace an old church (a hideous one) that was destroyed in the war, the present Notre Dame du Haut culminates a long series of shrines that have topped this lovely vantage point—but never before with such majesty. One approaches it via a steep winding path, past a disturbingly prominent small inn for pilgrims. As one mounts the hill the impressive south side is increasingly—and tantalizingly—revealed, until one stands in front, stunned by the strangeness, the carefully orchestrated strangeness, of a great façade. Three elements dominate: a towering silolike chapel on the left; the bold projection of the brown concrete roof above; and the white wall below, a wall of pronounced batter, which turns out at the right end to meet—like the prow of a ship—its fellow wall from the east. This impressive south wall is diagramed with an irregular series of small square and rectangular windows, whose splayed re-

veals recall slits in pillboxes and fortifications—an analogy not
without reason considering the many previous churches on
this site which have been destroyed by wars and bearing in
mind that the famous, or infamous, Belfort Gap is less than a
score of miles away. The south façade, all in pure whitewash,
is punctuated at left by a brilliantly colorful enameled door
by Le Corbusier. The east side is occupied by the "outdoor"
church, which can serve as many as 12,000 pilgrims at once.
(The interior of the church proper has pews for only 50.)
Here are the outdoor altar and pulpit, in direct communication with the inside sanctuary which has a relic of the Virgin
placed in a "window" in the wall in such a way that it is
visible from the outside as well as the in. The tapered east
edge of the wing of the roof—Le Corbusier avers that the shell
of a crab inspired it—projects well over this outside chancel,
just as it does in front. The day-to-day entrance to the church
is not through the enameled door on the south side, which is
primarily for pilgrimages, but via a door in the north wall between two towered side chapels. On entering one finds an
interior totally sculptured in its shape and in its ability to
enwrap and make a participant of the spectator. Here one
finds no reference to known rooms; here, actually, are few
right angles or straight lines. For this is a wondrously plastic
shape, flowing and counterflowing, hiding and revealing—all
in an area of some 43 by 82 feet. Dominated by the powerful
underside of the roof, a soffit recalling a Biblical desert tent,
and ablaze with myriads of colors from myriads of irregularly
placed deep-set windows on the south, it is punctuated by

unexpected accents of vertical side chapels. Furthermore the room impels one to move about; it is not statically graspable. The windows themselves are so cunningly set that one can see only those opposite: one must move on to see the others, and as one does, new shapes and forms exercise their talents. This interior of all interiors in the history of architecture must be seen to be grasped and fully appreciated. A church, however, has a purpose far transcending that of being spatially exciting: it must serve as the House of God. Ronchamp not only does this, it carries a religious conviction and creates a religious atmosphere of the highest order. For many, it conduces more to individual prayer and worship than do the Gothic cathedrals, which though unequaled as monuments to God, do dwarf (as is their intention) the individual. Ronchamp is scaled to man: it is the greatest building of our time.

10 Church of the Sacred Heart (Eglise du Sacré Coeur)

Audincourt, Doubs (11 miles S of Belfort)
Maurice Novarina, architect

Although the architecture of this church is of slight consequence, the interior does provide a simple background for the glorious windows of the late Fernand Léger. Forming a constant width clerestory around the U-shape of the church, these seventeen windows depicting the Passions of the Lord are among the most scintillating to be seen today. Played off against the abstracted reality of Léger's thematic glass is the equally handsome, totally abstract glass by Jean Bazaine in the superb baptistery. The positive effect of this bright art is enormously cheering in Audincourt's dreary industrial setting. All planning to visit Ronchamp should make a slight detour to include this church.

11 Spa Pavilion

quai P. Léger, Evian-les-Bains (Lake of Geneva)
Jean Prouvé, M. Novarina and S. Ketoff, architects and engineers

As mentioned in the introduction, one of the most inquiring architectural-constructional minds in France today belongs to Jean Prouvé. In this airy pavilion, nicely situated in a park overlooking the south shore of the Lake of Geneva, Prouvé and his associates have achieved an easy, festive atmosphere well suited to the summer vacationers who come to Evian for the "cure," or a good time—or both. The pavilion is divided into three sections: a *buvette,* or bar, whence springs the famous water; a lounge in the center; and a "soft music" room at the far end. Services are placed in the partial basement. All four walls are of glass, permitting a free view of the lake and the well-tended park in which the pavilion sits. The particularly interesting structure is based on twelve modified T-shaped frames of steel, spaced 19.7 feet apart, freestanding and unencased within the room. An exposed cross-race gives lateral stability. A combination of steel, aluminum, and wood (fir) was used in the extraordinarily thin and widely overhanging roof, setting up problems of statics and expansion which were meticulously studied. The window-walls are set in the roof structure with the minimum of mullion showing. An engaging small building.

2 Le Couvent Sainte Marie de la Tourette

Éveux-sur-l'Arbresle (16 miles NW of Lyons)
Le Corbusier, architect

This staunchly virile pair of buildings constitutes a magnifi
cently positive reaction to the slick glass and shiny surface
now emasculating architecture. Concrete is the means, raw
potent concrete, the concrete of the twentieth century, bu
employed here with almost medieval strength of expression
Le Corbusier, the architectural apotheosis of our time, here a
in India has turned more and more to primitivism of state
ment in a framework of contemporary space. Gone from L
Tourette are the sculptured shapes and the fugue of window
so characteristic of Ronchamp. Rigid angles, a repetitiv
module, and a spartan directness—fitting the client—mark thi
retreat for 100 monks. Two units about a central court compos
the group: a U-shaped living, eating, and study building; an
a rectangular chapel at its open (north) end. Stepped dow
the steep slope of a hill—and enjoying a lovely west view o
the valley—the main building has three floors on the uppe
side and four on *pilotis* on the lower. The top two stories ar
devoted to narrow, ruggedly finished cells, cantilevered be
yond the floors below; library, instruction rooms, and a com
mon room are directly beneath. Refectory and kitchen occup
the lowest floor along the west side. The chapel is long, nar
row, and tall, with every angle a right angle. No direct ligh
enters the chapel, only the effect. The side altars, in low
annexes flanking the main altar, are illuminated via holes i
their ceilings; these project as boldly truncated cones an
cylinders above the roof, providing a strong interplay of soli
geometry. An extraordinary building.

13 Unité d'Habitation

boulevard Michelet, Marseilles
Le Corbusier, architect

The famous Unité—built amid tirades of every kind of abuse—
ranks as one of the pivotal buildings of postwar Europe an
is among our greatest contemporary monuments. Because
its extraordinarily powerful esthetic experience—one of th
most potent visible today—there is a nobility in Unité rarel
seen in any period, particularly our own. The richly tapestrie
sides of the building are masterful in their ingeniously com
posed interlocking unity—harmonic mathematics, Le Corbu
sier calls it. The use of primary colors (on the reveals of th
balconies) brings life to rough concrete. The molded shape
of the roof, though sculptured to esthetic ends, never stra
from function as regards services (ventilators, elevator hous
ings, etc.) and never sink to the obvious when shelter an
play areas for children are concerned. As the building, or

ented north and south, is raised 23 feet above ground on *pilotis,* the sun streams under it half the day, bringing visual joy and vitality to the shade (i.e., approach) side. Within, Unité displays planning ingenuity, spaciousness, and flexibility. The apartments penetrate the entire width of the building and are not simply grouped on the flanks of a central core. The 337 apartments for 1,600 people are of 23 varieties: from single rooms to accommodations for families with five children. The standard apartment consists of a 2-story living-room (15.75 feet high) and two bedrooms. The east-west orientation of the apartments allows cross ventilation and a view of the sea on one side and the mountains on the other—both important in this climate and setting. The double-height living-room and loggia are gracious and spatially liberating. Moreover, the ingenuity of the planning enables the central longitudinal building corridor to be eliminated on every other floor, cutting this waste area in half and simplifying and speeding elevator service. If the apartments' depth had been cut 30% (from 80 to 56 feet), and their width had been increased 50% (from 12 to 18 feet), the result would have been even more livable. The shopping "street" midway up the building—obviously somewhat arbitrarily placed there to give (as it does) a spirited façade accent with its *brise-soleil*—would certainly have enjoyed more customers from the neighborhood and have fitted more into the gregarious traditions of the Mediterranean market if it had been placed on the ground. The roof, as alluded to earlier, revels in a superb series of shapes and forms in space. Rarely in the history of architec-

ure has the top of a building been so rewarding both close up and as a distant profile. Most of the communal facilities of the tenants are here, including a small school, a gymnaium, and a meeting hall—all of which enjoy a superb view. The roof indeed provides a private air-borne piazza. Originally planned as only the first of six similar buildings on its site, this *unité* is the only one likely to be built here. A sister building at Nantes-Rezé (q.v.) is somewhat lumbering in appearance, while another sister in Berlin (q.v.) is lively in its color but cluttered at ground level. Extraordinary buildings all, indeed the finest multiple dwellings one is apt to see, but the greatest is Marseilles. Heroic.

14 School of Medicine and Pharmacy

boulevard d'Alès Marseille, Marseilles
René Egger, architect

A large, impressive first unit in a vast rebuilding and extension of hospital facilities in Marseilles, this school is located in a wooded, quiet area adjoining the Timone Psychiatric Hospital. It will be joined on its parklike site by a 700-bed teaching hospital. The plan is as straightforward and businesslike as the façades. A 3-story unit at the north end contains basic general rooms: large, fan-shaped cafeteria on ground floor; 1,000-seat auditorium directly above; 700,000-volume (potential) library on top. The main building directly adjoins: a long 7-story block containing all classrooms, with three parallel 5-story research-wings at right angles on the east side. In these wings, laboratories are placed on the north, offices on the south. The major part of the building was built on a module of 5.75 feet. The main (west) façade is protected from the low sun by fixed vertical concrete fins, while vertical and horizontal adjustable *brise-soleils* of aluminum shield the east side. This handsome, capable medical school is marred by a few heavy—or flashy—details, but in the main it is commendable. René Egger, its architect, has joined with André Devin and Jean Croizet in designing a 726-bed general hospital, now being completed in north Marseilles (chemin des Bourrély).

15 Chapel of the Rosary
Vence (13 miles NW of Nice)
Henri Matisse, artist

The architectural framework of the famous Matisse chapel is of slight consequence, inside or out—simple whitewashed walls and red tile roof in the Mediterranean vernacular. But the chapel's integration of the arts reaches the lovely. Here, probably for the first time in church history, one sees static art (stained glass and painted tiles) superbly fused with moving art (the priest's chasuble) and all done by the same master. In plan, the chapel consists of a modified rectangle; the sanctuary fills most of the far (west) end, and there is a small transept on the south side for the nuns. The altar is at 45°; thus the priest faces the transept and "nave" at the same time. On the south side fifteen identical slender floor-to-ceiling windows, six in the nave and nine in the transept, give light to the chapel. Two larger (and disturbing) windows are in the west wall behind the altar; though somewhat overscaled in pattern for the size of the room, their pure yellow, green, and blue panes add a most joyful note. The other two walls are decorated with black-and-white line-drawings fired on tiles, and an absolutely wonderful carved door, which was also designed by the master. As this is a private chapel for Dominican nuns, it is only open two days a week (generally Tuesday and Thursday). Check on these before visiting.

16 St. Joseph's Church
boulevard François I, Le Havre

Auguste Perret, architect; Raymond Audigier and Jacques Poirrier, associates

Whatever one may think about this extraordinary church—the late Perret's last work—one cannot ignore it, for it stands 350 feet high and can be seen 36 miles away. In effect, the church is a stupendous hollow shaft—rather interestingly reminiscent of an interspace rocket in profile. A large cube-shaped lower part supports the gigantic octagonal tower, which terminates in step-backs topped by a lantern and cross. The reinforced-concrete inner supports for this enormous tower cluster together and at ground level define the central altar and sanctuary in impressive fashion. The entire interior forms one breath-takingly lofty room. The building's powerful frame is revetted with panels of concrete grilles of typical Perret design. These are identical on both interior and exterior faces. Through these grilles, which are filled with glass by Marguerite Huré, pour strong bands of colored light. Seemingly dominated by the *idée fixe* that a monument is more important than a setting for worship, this rigid, didactic church should, however, be seen if one is in the vicinity.

17 Hospital

Saint-Lô (Normandy) (39 miles W of Caen)

Paul Nelson, chief architect; Roger Gilbert, Marcel Mersier, and Charles Sebillotte, associates

Not far from Omaha and Utah Beaches, where the Allied invasion of the Continent began, this 400-bed general hospital, replacing one destroyed during the war, rises as a memorial

to Franco-American understanding and sacrifice. It is also a product of a Franco-American architect, Paul Nelson, the United States Public Health Service, and the French Ministère de la Santé Publique. Its interest, however, lies far beyond this background: it is one of the most carefully studied hospitals on the Continent. Among its chief merits are (1) its "zoning" of subdivisions, (2) its horizontal and vertical circulation, and (3) its wonderful spheroid operating-rooms. The hospital proper is subdivided for patients requiring general care (including, on a special floor, maternity cases), those with contagious diseases (20 beds, isolated but connected), and tuberculosis patients (80 beds, on the eighth and ninth floors, and attached solariums). Outpatients and emergency cases have their separate entrances, as is standard practice. The main entrance hall, highlighted by a mosaic mural by the late Fernand Léger, is direct and friendly in scale—no puzzling, gargantuan, or formless room. Circulation from the reception desk is simple for patient or visitor, with separate elevators divided into conjoined banks for each. All patients' rooms have southern exposures, and there are no more than four beds to a room. The projecting floor slabs serve as a *brise-soleil*. All basic medical services for inpatients, outpatients, and casualty cases are on the main floor, filling a block to the north of the "bed house." Services (including kitchen) are all in the basement. Six novel egg-shaped operating-rooms, four on the main floor and two on the maternity —the most famous design feature of the hospital—provide complete flexibility of illumination for the surgeon. Experts consider this one of the best.

18 Unité d'Habitation

Nantes-Rezé (SW Nantes)
Le Corbusier, architect

Although this, the second *maison radieuse* has not the élan and majesty of the Marseilles prototype, it still rates as an impressive building. On the exterior, its differences are obvious: a completely regular fenestration-and-loggia grid on the west side (recalling early studies for Marseilles), and the same grid broken vertically by the stairhall on the east. Gone is the horizontal rhythmic *brise-soleil* that adds such visual spice and protects the mid-building shopping "street" at Marseilles. Gone, too, are the massive tapered *pilotis* that support the earlier building, replaced at Nantes by slender piers. The roof of the latter is also simplified: few sculptured shapes, instead, a crèche with walls of myriad small rectangu-

lar windows disported somewhat helter-skelter around their sides. Within, the most obvious difference between Marseilles and Nantes is that the famous duplex living rooms of the former—a Le Corbusier trade-mark since his Clarté flats of 1932 in Geneva—have given way at Nantes to single stories for all floors and rooms. The second *unité*'s 294 co-operatively-owned flats—the very existence of which is an affirmation of Le Corbusier's thinking—nonetheless form a virile building. If you cannot get to the Côte d'Azur, at least make it to the mouth of the Loire.

19 Notre Dame

rue du Chateau d'Eau at rue de Foncillon, Royan
Guillaume Gillet, architect; Bernard Laffaille and René Sarger, engineers

One of the largest new churches of Europe—it seats 2,000—this ovoid church is also one of the most interesting from several points of view. First, the construction: the frame is made up of enormous V-shaped concrete piers of constant width from top to bottom, 14.5 feet on center, with the open end of the V pointing outward. Between these self-supporting concrete enclosures are placed slender bands of windows, eventually to be of stained glass. Atop this framework, which is completely exposed inside and out and which dips slightly at the center, rests an inverted-dish, independent concrete

saddle-roof. The interior, whose main floor steps down 12 feet from the entrance, bristles with the vertical insistence of the V-shaped enclosing members. A narrow balcony-ambulatory cuts through the base of the V supports and surrounds the interior on two sides and the entrance. The second point of particular interest in Notre Dame is the esthetic. Although it is girdled by standardized, independent elements of prefabricated concrete, and although it is topped by a roof which does not—as did the Gothic—grow from the side walls but instead sits on them, the church in its over-all effect nonetheless strongly suggests much of the soaring spirit and the powerful verticality to which Gothic architects aspired. Exterior details of the entrance are self-conscious, almost casino-like, and within, the "dropped" effect of the main floor disturbs, but this remains a vigorous and imaginative church, one of Europe's most stimulating.

20 Covered Market

boulevard A. Briand, Royan
Simon and Morisseau, architects; R. Sarger, engineer

The badly bombed Royan on the Bay of Biscay—the city contained submarine pens throughout the war—has been largely rebuilt. The new church of Notre Dame is quite obviously the finest structure in town—and in all western France—but there are several other buildings worth seeing—including this

nearby sinusoidal paraboloid in concrete. Market functions demanded an unencumbered central space with ready access to supplies from the outside. In addition, the structure had to be economical. A set of thirteen counter-thrusting paraboloids, forming a circle 171 feet in diameter, establishes the periphery. These paraboloids develop "waves" as they extend toward the center, flattening and narrowing as they go, to become, in effect, arches. At mid-point the vault is 34.5 feet above the floor and 3.25 inches thick. The undulations of the market when seen from the street are effective, if a bit small in scale to terminate an important avenue. Within, the market exhibits a fine, workable space, unfortunately marred by artificial lighting that does all it can to mask the excellent structure from which it is suspended.

21 Industrial Complex and Housing of the S.N.P.A.

Route Nationale 117, Lacq (Pau), Basses-Pyrénées

J. de Brauer, architect of industrial section; R. A. Coulon, J. Maneval and Ph. Douillet, architects of Mourenx housing

In the foothills of the Pyrenees, halfway between Pau and Orthez and some 35 miles west of Lourdes, the Société Nationale des Pétroles d'Aquitaine, in 1951, discovered at Lacq a deep and mighty source of natural gas. To utilize this field—one of the most important in the world—a series of industrial complexes has arisen, some refining the gas for a variety of chemical uses, others drawing on it for a source of power. The widely spread out installation of the S.N.P.A. is the most elaborate and advanced of those thus far constructed. The S.N.P.A. has built both a refinery and a "new town" for its employees. The industrial complex comprises a central administration area, and factory area next to the railroad and Route Nationale 117. The service buildings (administration, laboratories, canteens) are of straightforward but undistinguished design (A. and P. Dufau, architects). On the other hand, several of the industrial buildings—at least those not made cosy by anachronistic fieldstone wall-panels—reach a high level of architectural excellence. The role of J. de Brauer, the architect of the industrial section, was to design various nontechnical shelters, to harmonize all constructions, and to give a clear-cut unity and optimum disposition to the various elements. The most outstanding feature is the magnificent

water tower, bell-swelling at the top, and visually echoed by nine huge refrigerating cylinders—the whole reflected in the filtration reservoir. As it is the dominant vertical accent of the area, the profile of the water tower is of course particularly important. Constructed of reinforced concrete throughout, the tower, because of its swelling shape, has a central access. This also obviates an unsightly exterior ladder.

To house the 4,000 people expected to be employed by the various new industries at Lacq, an entire new town has been built. As this number of employees corresponds to a total population of approximately 15,000, and as, in addition to housing, all normal urban facilities had to be supplied, the creation of this small city provided no little problem. The site consists of a slightly elevated, rolling terrain, off the main traffic routes and well screened by hills and forests from the smells of the various industrial plants to the north. The somewhat severely laid out civic center (more "northern" than Mediterranean) contains all public buildings and major shopping, and is surrounded by three multiple-housing sections. Beyond each of the latter are extensions composed of single-family houses and local shopping facilities. The central housing-zones are dominated by a total of six 13-story roughly square "point" houses, which give good vertical focus to each group while providing a type of living which many tenants prefer to the walk-up housing about them. Open space and pedestrian circulation have been capably worked out, and there is distinct separation between foot and automotive traffic. Space between buildings is good, but as almost every building is at right angles to or parallel to its neighbor, the flow of space becomes stiff and static. Furthermore, greater following of terrain would have been beneficial throughout, both visually and constructionally. Mourenx's plan is more that for a flat site than for one deployed over the junctions of even low hills.

22 St. Pius X Basilica

Cité Religieuse, Lourdes
Pierre Vago, chief architect; Eugène Freyssinet, engineer

Built as a church to shelter 22,000 pilgrims for the centennial of Lourdes, this enormous underground basilica is one of the most impressive concrete structures in France, a close cousin of Morandi's automobile exhibition hall in Turin (q.v.). The multitalented Vago did not want to impinge on the limited open space in front of the small existing church, or on the grotto, so he sympathetically let this great construction into the ground and covered it with lawn, although the water table from the adjacent Gave River greatly complicated the foundation and waterproofing. If possible, all ceremonies are held above in the open, but if the weather is unfavorable—rain, too cold, too hot—the basilica is used. Its plan resembles a somewhat flattened oval; it is 660 feet long and 265 feet wide. Twenty-nine ribs, or double arches, of prestressed concrete are attached to a central spine to form the basic structure. Their spring point, being 33 feet in from the outside walls, permits access ramps to be located along each side. The V-shaped supporting sections of the arches, the heavy member taking the thrust of the central span and the smaller that of the side aisle, make a dramatic forest of concrete surrounding the entire periphery. The whole interior attains, indeed, the impressively awesome. With the altar in the slightly depressed center, good visibility is assured.

Berlin 1-3

● Hanover 4

● Münster 6   ● Bad Salzuflen 5

Bottrop 7
    ● Gelsenkirchen 8
    ● Bochum 9
    ● Düsseldorf 10-14
    ● Leverkusen 15
    ● Cologne 16
Düren 17

● Frankfurt 18

● Hasloch-am-Main 19

Mannheim 23-24
Saarbrücken 20-22   ● Heidelberg 25

● Stuttgart 26-28

● Ulm 29

● Munich 30-31

GERMANY

50   100   150 M

50   100   150   200   250 K

GERMANY

Germany's recovery from the unbelievable destruction of modern warfare has been phoenixlike. From prostrate urban chaos, from catastrophic financial destitution and agonizing moral reassessment, this energetic nation has in a decade achieved one of the strongest positions in Europe. Its postwar building has been sometimes brilliant and sometimes disappointing—depending to a large extent upon what category of building one examines. Tragically, one can definitely state that the extraordinary planning opportunities war so gratuitously provided have been almost totally rebuffed. Hanover and Hamburg have done some farsighted urban reorganization, but few other cities have to a significant degree. As the German architect and critic Alfons Leitl says, "The fiasco of German urban reconstruction may well be a source of grim satisfaction to those prophets who went unheeded" (*Landscape*, Winter 1955–56).

Germany was the great contributor to the development of modern architecture from the early 1900's to the 1930's. Peter Behrens's Turbine Hall, built in Berlin, in 1909, has been termed "the first piece of modern architecture" (J. M. Richards, *Modern Architecture*). Only two years later Walter Gropius introduced multistory curtain-wall construction in his Fagus Works in Alfeld. The influence of Gropius and the famous Bauhaus he designed (1925) and first directed remains of singular importance. In 1929 Mies van der Rohe, who has since probably influenced the design of more new buildings than any architect who ever lived, produced his still unsurpassed Barcelona Pavilion. These men with Otto Bartning, Wassili and Hans Luckhardt, Ernst May, Eric Mendelsohn, Hans Poelzig, Hans Scharoun, Bruno and Max Taut, Martin Wagner, and others formed a core of dedicated, advanced thinkers—and doers. Has such a kinetic group of architects ever before been witnessed at one time and in one country? The United States is indeed fortunate that Gropius and Mies, the two greatest German architects of our day, found intellectual refuge here and that both directed architectural schools in this country.

But during the Hitler years of 1933 to 1945 modern architecture was strictly *verboten* in Germany. That much of merit has been achieved since that time is doubly creditable, for the older architects remaining in Germany could not carry their achievements into what should have been their peak years, while an entire generation of younger men was educated away from the contemporary approach. The very lack of progressive, well-rounded teachers today is one of the factors plaguing German architectural education: the older professors are too old—and too often still steeped in *heimatstil*—the young have not sufficiently matured. Furthermore, the now older public—from which come the present clients —was systematically educated against modern architecture.

In the last decade, however, an extraordinary volume of new work has been done. The new churches, primarily those in the Rhine-Ruhr area, are the most forward looking in the world. No other country can touch the new German churches in quality or quantity. Some of these churches have exhibited a too restless search for novelty, but the finest are masterful. The theaters and opera houses, in a land where theatergoing is a highly developed pattern of life, are likewise impressive; they are easily the most stimulating in Europe. And the development of schools has proceeded on a wide and inquiring basis, reflecting deep thought in human, psychological, and environmental aspects as well as straight pedagogic and architectural expression.

There then follows a miscellany of building types, some fine, some not always distinguished. Among the latter will be found an unprepossessing assortment—and scale—of low-cost housing. Along the fringes of the smaller cities and towns this usually takes the form of steeply roofed detached single and double houses deployed like toy villages in a picture book. Totally unimaginative and second-rate. Inside the cities multiple housing is of a better cast, but it rarely reaches the level seen throughout Scandinavia, England, and Italy. Indeed, much of it represents no advance over the better housing of the 30's. All of this is doubly regrettable when one recalls the exciting Weissenhof housing experiments in Stuttgart in 1927, when Le Corbusier, Behrens,

116

Gropius, Mies van der Rohe, Oud, and others pioneered new solutions to low-cost housing. And in Ernst May's early work in Frankfurt, especially Römerstadt (1925–31), wall-sized prefabricated concrete panels were used—a technique too rarely employed in Germany today. Even the new Hansa Viertel (Interbau) in Berlin (q.v.) does not enjoy the success or vitality of Germany's far earlier housing experiments.

There are a great many new twenty-odd-story office-blocks throughout Germany, particularly in industrial areas. The majority of these are only well-built, competent "Middle Style" towers; a few, however, do approach the scintillation of their counterparts in Milan. Some of the large factories, many of which have headquarters in these towers, are also of a superior cast. For one thing, factory architecture is more "technical" than "esthetic," hence, one might say, more to the Teutonic temperament; for another, industrial architecture was just about the only form of building free from "supervision" from 1933 to 1945, so that there has always been a splendid tradition of fine work in this field. After all, modern architecture in Germany started with a turbine hall!

The architecture of public pleasure and purchase—cafés, bars, hotels, shops—is almost universally heavy-handed, rarely reaching the delightful lightness of touch and unaffected gaiety found in such buildings in Denmark and Sweden, or the imagination and artistic creativity found throughout Italy.

Painting, sculpture, and graphics (as these arts relate to architecture) are too often rigid and self-conscious. However, in government-supported buildings considerable encouragement is given all arts. Legislation requires that 2% of the cost of constructing such buildings be devoted to the arts. This is a wonderful law: would that it obtained in the United States!

With several noted exceptions, there has not been the general daring or experimentation one might expect in postwar German work: Italy and France have been far more progressive. In some respects, German architects and engineers have been so busy building that they have not had time to think! When on occasion they have searched for new building means and expressions they have been highly successful. Their most significant

117

achievements include the thin-shell-concrete pioneering by Ulrich Finsterwalder and Franz Dischinger, the pre-stressed bridges of Fritz Leonhardt, the straight-cable bridges of F. Schreier, experiments in structural-tube construction, and the absolutely wonderful tent shelters by Frei Otto.

In conclusion, one can say that in spite of a certain heavyhandedness and a monument complex, in spite of a too great addiction to the rigid straight line in design, and despite a too unimaginative client potential, an increasing amount of excellent new work appears in Germany. Some of it is the finest to be seen; much of it is put together with a competence and thoroughness matched only by the Swiss.

1 Interbau (Hansa Viertel)

Tiergarten, Berlin
various architects

The Hansa quarter was constructed in 1957 as permanent housing for the Berlin International Building Exhibition, or Interbau. Remembering—in part—the meaningful lessons of the famous 1927 Weissenhof development in Stuttgart, Berlin also called on a collection of many of the world's greatest architects. Aalto, Le Corbusier, Gropius, Jacobsen, Niemeyer, Stubbins, Pierre Vago, and others from abroad joined Wassili Luckhardt, Paul Schneider-Esleben, Hans Schwippert, and a strong German contingent. Unfortunately Berlin did not also call one man, Mies van der Rohe, to be again the firm synthe-sizer he was thirty years earlier, when he welded together a similarly varied group of international architects at Weissen-hof. The weakness of Interbau lies first in its poor basic plan and second in its somewhat unavoidable appearance as a "collection of buildings" rather than as the "unity of build-ings" it should be. However, from the talent-loaded panel of many of the world's greatest architects has come a fascinating —if at times short-of-expectations—group of some forty build-ings housing 3,000 people. These buildings range from single-family houses to multistory high blocks. Although each unit is well situated and planted, the problems of street pattern, traffic, parking, and shopping are not well solved. It is inex-cusable, for instance, to have a main traffic artery bisect the development at grade level. Interestingly enough, many of the buildings are very handsome from one position but do not

118

turn the corner well. Or they have—to recall Mark Twain—a Queen Anne front and a Mary Anne behind. One of the nicest single bits of design is Werner Düttman's delightful small library and kiosk. Both churches are frightful.

2 Congress Hall

Tiergarten, Berlin

Hugh Stubbins, Jr., architect

Poised on its elevated platform like a gigantic yet sprightly lepidopter, this building serves both as symbol and as shelter. As a tangible symbol of intangible freedom of speech, it is possibly even more successful than as an auditorium for 1,250 people. The prime purpose of this permanent adjunct to Interbau is to speak freedom to the world—significantly the building is well within sight of East Berlin—and like dual megaphones back to back it opens willingly and broadly to do just that. Tucked (coerced?) beneath the protective wings of its great saddle-roof lies the working rationale—the auditorium, exhibition area, and services. A bit of confusion is in evidence here, in plan and in structure, for the interior is not the pellucid space the roof might indicate, nor is the nestling of the auditorium under this roof as satisfactory as early models predicted. However, the general esthetics of the building excite, while the structure (which was done in association with Severud-Elstad-Krueger) is impressive. This is formed by two "leaning" arches butted together at base and held at top by a compression ring.

3 Unité d'Habitation
Reichssportfeld (off Heer Strasse), Berlin
Le Corbusier, architect

The third of Europe's *unités,* this superb 16-story apartment
with 557 flats was built as part of Berlin's Interbau of 1957.
Because of its size, however, it was located 6 kilometers (3.7
miles) due west of the Hansa Viertel, where it enjoys an excellent site overlooking the former Olympic grounds. In basic
form it more nearly follows Nantes-Rezé than Marseilles, but
in surface treatment this Berlin edition asserts a personality
of its own, one that sings with a joyful and vivid use of color
which produces enormous vitality. Both earlier *unités* use
color on the partitions that divide apartment units, but
neither uses it so extensively, or on the intra-apartment
spandrels themselves. The result here, though approaching
an intensity that threatens the form itself, is vibrantly alive.
At the ground level the approach and public rooms are
hacked to unrelated bits—indeed, Le Corbusier brought suit
against the design changes—and within, the finishes and corridor lighting are poor, but the exterior apartment levels
flash stimulation. Concentrate on the positive features—and
forget the weaknesses.

121

4 St. Martins

Badenstedter Strasse, Hanover
Dieter Oesterlen, architect

This church, constructed to replace a nave destroyed by war, is handsome both without and within. The old tower was still standing, and the new church has been sympathetically related to it. The frame of the new building, of concrete "bents," is fully expressed. Between these supports, walls of concrete block have been used as enclosure, with small (perhaps too small) panes of glass between the horizontally staggered ends of each block. Thus a glareproof light floods in from all sides; two large floor-to-ceiling windows of agreeable stained-glass provide accents at the chancel. Along the south side of the church, a lateral balcony is airily suspended from the concrete frame. The sanctuary wall, which is of sculptured brick, is commendable in theory but too fussily carried out, producing antagonistic interests behind the altar.

5 Sanatorium

Wüstenerstrasse, Bad Salzuflen (just off the Autobahn, 53 miles W of Hanover)

Harald Deilmann, architect

A large and well-thought-out complex. The sanatorium, which treats patients with heart and circulatory troubles, comprises two basic sections: a low service and dining-kitchen wing and a 10-story block for 231 patients. This latter, angled into two unequal divisions, has double rooms for ambulatory patients in the main arm and single rooms for

bedridden patients in the adjacent cant. All rooms face southerly and the single rooms have balconies large enough to receive a bed. A marked discrepancy in scale between the two arms of the main unit, and indeed, between the "bed house" and the service wing mars this basically handsome hospital.

6 City Theater

Neubrückenstrasse, Münster

Harald Deilmann, Max von Hausen, Ortwin Rave and Werner Ruhnau, architects

This 960-seat theater is one of Europe's very finest and is unquestionably its most imaginative. Interesting diagonal placement arose through the wise wish to incorporate into the new building the ruined walls of the bombed Romberger Hof. This nostalgic and fitting souvenir is surrounded

123

by the glass-enclosed foyer and the attached restaurant—both of which are gracious and festive—and hence though it is open to the sky, it forms an intimate part of the interior visual scene. The capacious and handsome areas for public circulation, which are ideal for social promenading, are also glass enclosed and are ablaze with light in the evening, producing a lively atmosphere, even for passers-by. The interior of the main auditorium has a fantastic ceiling of 1,200 lights—an "optical" ceiling below the structural one. Roof structure, acoustic measures, sprinklers, and other utilities can thus be left exposed above the lights. Together with the intimate, compressed shape of the auditorium and the bright purple of the seats, these lights make a sumptuous over-all effect. Theater, opera, and concerts can be presented.

7 Holy Cross Church

Scharnhölzstrasse, Bottrop (NW of Essen)
Rudolf Schwarz, architect

One is introduced to this church by a swirling, striking stained-glass "infinity" by Georg Meistermann. This covers the entire front, and is even more positive and colorful from within. On passing this joyful abstraction and entering the nave one is greeted by a painfully realistic "eye of God," balefully focused on every sinner present. Except for the clinical detail of this eye, the church is strong and commendable.

Its tapered shape concentrated on the altar, its exciting exposed-concrete framework in front, and its unbroken side-walls of brick are all excellent.

8 Theater

Ebertplatz, Gelsenkirchen

Werner Ruhnau, Ortwin Rave and Max von Hausen, architects

A striking theater brightly set down amid the smog and gloom of the Ruhr industrial area. The U-shaped auditorium and the entrance lobby—which envelops the auditorium on three sides—together form an over-all rectangular block two and a half stories high. The high flat façade of the entrance is entirely glazed from floor to ceiling and the "U" auditorium is itself wrapped with glass (to keep lobby noises from the audience), producing sparkling results, particularly at night, when the whole is ablaze with lights. The 1,050-seat auditorium, although a bit heavy architecturally, is extremely advanced from the theater point of view, delivering a noted intimacy between actors and audiences and having great flexibility in the stage and backstage areas. The rapport between actors and audiences is cleverly intensified by having a continuous ceiling-height for auditorium and stage, and by treating the auditorium walls, the ceiling, and the movable proscenium with a matte-black finish so that when the house lights go off, walls are "obliterated" and the actors are thus projected forward. A smaller, experimental, playhouse adjoins the main theater.

9 Christ Church

Am Rathaus, Bochum
Dieter Oesterlen, architect

Repairing—or reconstructing—or starting afresh—with war-shattered churches poses one of architecture's most difficult problems. If, as here, a nave has been leveled, yet the tower

remains, it is a clear confession of bankruptcy in religious architecture to build another nave just like the old. Oesterlen has conquered a difficult task at Christ Church, creating a nave that obviously belongs to the ancient tower but just as obviously belongs to the 1960's—a highly commendable achievement. On the outside, the angles and diamond shapes of the walls and roof tie in with the Gothic tower. Within, the play of planes and the excellent natural lighting—to say nothing of the glass—produce an admirable setting for worship. One of the best of the new churches.

10 Phönix-Rheinrohr Building
Jan Wellem Platz, Düsseldorf
Hentrich and Petschnigg, architects

This metal-sheathed 22-story building takes a fresh look at the skyscraper image. Instead of coming up with one prismatic box, the architects divided the 14,000 square feet of office space needed into three roughly equal conjoined slabs. A striking effect of monumentality is thus achieved. Furthermore, this division is just as flexible as a regular rectangular plan because each slab is one column bay in depth. The middle bay, which is slightly wider than the two flanking ones, contains all vertical circulation, toilets, and services. In addition, at each end it provides half the amount of office space possessed by each of the side slabs; thus the office spaces in all three sections are equal. The two outer slabs, asymmetrically placed against the central core, are separated from it by single-loaded corridors their entire length, and enjoy column-free construction to facilitate mobility in partitioning. The structural framework—like that in the new and not distant Mannesmann Building (q.v.)—is of tubular columns, not rolled-steel shapes. A garage for 200 cars occupies two floors of the basement. The basic thinking in generating the tripartite shape was absolutely brilliant, and the resulting building is certainly one of the handsomest skyscrapers in Europe. One could only wish that such detailing as its curtain spandrel had more character and that the stainless steel sheathing the end walls expressed the floor joint with greater finesse.

11 Mannesmann Building

Mannesmann Ufer, Düsseldorf
Paul Schneider-Esleben, architect

A superior office block for the Mannesmann Steel Company, this building breathes easily between a park on one side and the Rhine on the other. A certain élan is given the building by the definite statement and treatment of the ground floor, an air that is emphasized by the round tubular-steel (instead of the more normal box-shaped) supports, and by the slightly dropped canopy on three sides which extends into a marquee in front. The building has an unusual structural system for a building of this size, its entire outside frame being composed of 56 large tubular columns, 5.9 feet on center, to which the steel box-girders for the floors are hinged. Vertical circulation, toilets, and storage form a compact core attached to the north wall, freeing a U-shaped office space, uncluttered by columns, with views east, south, and west. One of the trimmest office blocks, esthetically and structurally, to be seen, it is interesting to recall that in 1908 Peter Behrens designed the original Mannesmann Building, to which this new one is adjacent.

12 Hamiel Garage and Motel

Grafenberger Allee at Sohn Strasse, Düsseldorf
Paul Schneider-Esleben, architect

An imaginative, indeed entertaining, 4-story, 500-car garage on the north edge of the city. It consists basically of a precise glass box, 119 by 269 feet, with a widely overhung roof on the two long sides. Automobile access and egress ramps, 14 feet wide and at an angle of 14.5°, are suspended on steel rods from the projecting concrete roof-beams on the long flanks. These ramps have a toothed surface and can be heated in icy weather. Because the walls are of glass, the motorist, as he enters or leaves, can readily see approaching cars; at night these glass walls are ablaze with light. Complete service facilities are located in the basement. At the entrance a well-designed 22-room motel with a small restaurant is perched on stilts above the work area.

13 St. Rochus

Rochusmarkt, Düsseldorf
Paul Schneider-Esleben, architect

On the exterior this is one of the finest rebuildings of an old church to be seen in Europe. The pseudo-Romanesque, homely, but affectionately regarded, old tower was all that remained after bombardment. To rebuild the nave as it was originally constructed in the late nineteenth century was obviously to make a fake of a fake. The architect therefore chose a form whose simple metallic smoothness and geometry would set off the rusticated stone of the old tower. By careful proportions and sympathetic relationships he set up an architectural counterpoint that vibrates in space and actually makes the old tower far more significant than it ever was. The interior, though spacious and pleasant, is not as distinguished as the exterior, being amorphous in shape, and with its constant-height clerestory, glaring.

14 The North Bridge (Nordbrücke), Düsseldorf; *F. Schreier, engineer*

Footbridge over Autobahn, above Düsseldorf; *F. Schreier, engineer*

Severin Bridge, Cologne; *Gerhard Lohmer, architect, with Gutehoffnungshutte Sterkrade AG, engineers*

The three bridges shown here are striking examples of new bridge-building in Germany. Note that each is based on the straight cable, as opposed to the catenary, which is more normal for suspension structures. As a result, each has a visual tautness hitherto almost unknown. The thinking and daring exemplified by these bridges constitute one of the most refreshing facets of German reconstruction and building, which, with few exceptions, has been routine and timid.

The two bridges at the top opposite are by Ing. F. Schreier. The first is Düsseldorf's handsome, flat-deck Nordbrücke, the twin 131 foot high pylons of which support a clear middle span of 853 feet. At the end, and as a fine counterfoil to the straight lines of the bridge proper, the bicycle and pedestrian paths peel off the main roadway and descend in broad sweeping 360° curves to the ground. Splendid. The smaller bridge (middle photograph) is an elegantly designed unipod footbridge; its "bent" supporting mast, asymmetrically placed, soars airily above the roadway. The top extension of this mast—beyond the call of duty—is dubious but graceful. Note that the cables do not uphold the bridge platform itself, but a frame from which the footpath is cantilevered. This bridge was originally used in the West German pavilion at the Brussels Fair of 1958. It is equally impressive here in its permanent berth over the Autobahn just north of Düsseldorf.

The bridge at the bottom opposite, designed by Gerhard Lohmer, architect, and Gutehoffnungshutte Sterkrade AG, engineers, is an extraordinary span in midtown Cologne. Its sole support—suggested by the architect—is an A-shaped frame asymmetrically placed between the river banks. It thus has less than half the structure of the normal suspension bridge; this is particularly fortunate here, for twin pylons would seriously mar the downriver view of the nearby cathedral. The bridge deck is supported by straight cables gathered at the closed top of the A-frame and fanning from it on each side. The ramps on both river banks are of prestressed concrete.

15 Christ Church

Stresemannplatz at Erzbergerstrasse, Leverkusen-Bürig
Hentrich and Petschnigg, architects

One of the several churches in Germany where form follows
form, but still an imaginative expression. The clearly articu-
lated geometry of the structure is particularly successful. On
the exterior, the white concrete Y-frames stand out firmly
against the blue glazed-brick of the enclosing walls; within,
these concrete supports are topped by an admirable space-
frame roof-truss. It is unfortunate that the seeming demands
of consistency forced clear glass all about the church's six
walls, for such glass causes a glare in front.

16 St. Maria Königin

Goethestrasse at Leyboldstrasse, Cologne-Marienburg
Dominikus Böhm, architect

The shape of this church is a simple square of little import.
However, the glass wall that sheaths its south side belongs
to the finest in contemporary church art. Made with a near-

monochrome palate of grayish green, and with abstract panes
of leaf and trunk shapes, recalling the park setting beyond,
this superb window is a glorious tribute to the late Dominikus Böhm, one of the fathers of the new church movement
in Germany. The baptistery is almost invisibly attached to
the church proper by a clear-glass nexus. Note the red Lally
columns supporting the roof.

17 St. Anna

Annaplatz, Düren
Rudolf Schwarz, architect

A mighty church—one of the most impressive in Europe today. It is bounded in an L-shape by two great walls of stone—
stone reclaimed from war's rubble—topped by a raw-concrete
roof, and illuminated by commercial glass-brick. The ingredients of St. Anna are not prepossessing. However,
Schwarz has achieved the most splendid atmosphere of
strength and holiness in his design. Entering under the low
pilgrimage-foyer, one is thrown against the rising, unbroken
height of the nave in shattering fashion. Behind the simple
cube of the freestanding altar, a symbolic tree of life is let
into the wall and can be seen both from without and within.
The general massiveness of the nave is set off by the airy,
delicate, metallic lights. The sternness of the exterior will be

softened in the future by the addition of a belfry
and a baptistery in back. The interior will remain u
—it is magnificent.

18 St. Michael

Rotlintstrasse at Gellertstrasse, Frankfurt

Rudolf Schwarz, architect

On the exterior, this church resembles some great ship plowing through eternity. Within, it is a bold and mighty refuge, purposefully disdaining any contact with the outside world. Walls are solid; windows are of glass blocks placed as a high clerestory. To this quasi fortress—this retreat from the world and its cares—Schwarz brings an atmosphere of almost celestial peace and withdrawal. The modified double-ellipse of the plan, pointing the four directions of the compass, has been used in Germany since the late Renaissance, but never before with such simple dignity and power. The altar, being placed well forward, can be used by the priest from any of three sides, to face congregations in the main nave, or on either side.

19 St. Joseph

Hasloch-am-Main (W of Würzburg)
Hans Schädel, architect

This charming little church in a tiny village on the Main River has little consequence without. Its interior, however, is of refreshing simplicity. An excellent statue by Julius Bausenwein is precisely placed: rarely has contemporary sculpture complemented contemporary architecture so handsomely. The altar and other fittings are likewise well done. Note that the natural light, which is well concentrated at the altar, comes from an invisible source; only the effect is seen.

20 Maria Königin

Kohlweg at Zweibrücker Strasse, Saarbrücken
Rudolf Schwarz, architect

A strong, strange, and—in a way—quite wonderful church. Fortresslike in external appearance, it effuses an inner strength and a statement of power. The plan consists of four arms, each half-ovoid in shape, attached to a square central crossing, making a modified Latin cross. Vertical quarter-ovoids are sliced out of the towering walls of these arms as they meet at the crossing; these sections are fully glazed, producing as a consequence a great intensity of focus at this point. The altar is located at the crossing—the point of greatest concen-

tration of illumination. The approach to the nave rises from a lower level, which though cramped and confusing at the entrance, leads up to the main floor by two stairways that throw one into the fabric of the church in a spatially dramatic fashion. The attached church-school has a dubious medieval quality.

21 St. Mauritius

Moltkestrasse, Saarbrücken
Albert Dietz, architect

St. Mauritius is distinguished by two excellent features. The first of these concerns the problem of approaching a church: one pushes open a door and enters most churches too abruptly, and one leaves too shatteringly, with no visual or spiritual preparation. Here, however, one is introduced to the church by an entrance forecourt and cloister. The forecourt allows one time to prepare psychologically to enter (or leave); the twentieth-century cloister gives one a protected yet open shelter for strolling. The second fine feature of St. Mauritius is found in the superb south wall of *betonglas*—inch-thick chunks of glass set in concrete. Being faceted on the outside, this glass has an ever-varying jewellike intensity of sparkling beauty. Designed by Prof. Boris Kleint, the glass was made in Chartres by Gabriel Loire.

22 St. Albert

Jägersfreuder Strasse, Saarbrücken
Gottfried Böhm, architect

With a single oculus pouring forth a dramatic—and glaring—light, St. Albert exhibits one of the most theatrical naves in recent church architecture, a lineal descent of the Baroque. Although overly dramatic within and overly complicated in structure without, the church should be experienced. Its strongest point lies in the excellent relation, in plan and in space, of the congregation to the sanctuary; the pews are

grouped respectfully about the altar, which is pushed well forward under the oculus. Flying buttresses of concrete dominate the exterior, from these the roof is supported by cables. The buttresses meet and bend into the roof to form a cage about the altar. Note the fine semidetached baptistery.

23 National Theater
Goetheplatz, Mannheim
Gerhard Weber, architect

The National Theater in Mannheim has had its important name in this theater-conscious city for some two hundred years. When the former building was destroyed during the war, plans were undertaken to build a new one. In 1952 an invitation competition was held, and though the design by Gerhard Weber won, the project that attracted the most international attention was the famous "universal space" submission of Mies van der Rohe. Weber was obviously influenced by Mies's basic scheme when he arrived at his final design. The theater's lovely location, a full block surrounded by trees, had one grave fault: an enormous above-ground air-raid shelter that (supposedly) could not be removed. Thus the entire stage-level was raised a full story above the square and over the shelter. A basic requirement of the problem was to provide for two theaters: one, primarily for opera, seating 1,200 spectators, and a smaller one, of experi-

mental nature, seating up to 600, or when used as a lecture hall, 870. Administration, shops, and storage were already satisfactorily housed nearby and did not have to be included. Prof. Weber devoted the entire central section of the ground floor to a gay, glass-encased lobby with snack-bar and coatroom. The square outside with its flowers and other plantings thus becomes an extension of the lobby's glass-lined interior. Even the paving of the square carries through this part of the building. Services take up each end at ground level. Above the lobby floor and placed at opposite ends of the building are the two theaters. These are reached by broad but lengthy stairs, which at intermission make possible the multilevel see-and-be-seen interval so relished on the Continent. The theaters are placed back to back so that their stages share a common work-area in the center. Of the two, the smaller is the more provocative, for it provides a highly flexible, straightforward space capable of adapting to many experimental uses. Although the larger auditorium—and the exterior of the building also—are of stiff, somewhat graceless design, this numbers among Europe's more interesting theaters.

24 Trinity Church

G 4 Block, Mannheim

Helmut Striffler, architect

An unusual building technique combined with a stern and compelling interior atmosphere makes this one of Germany's original and successful new churches. The technique is based on a freestanding concrete frame enclosed by a new system of small panels (approximately 2 by 3 feet each), some solid, some partly glazed. These *betonglas* and concrete panels were made in Chartres by the famous (and ubiquitous) Gabriel Loire. Varicolored light filters through them on all sides, giving a sparkle to the impressively somber interior. Even as one enters, this light casts a luminous pattern over the floor. The over-all interior, though powerful, is not as fine as selected sections. In plan the church swells outward in the middle to provide extra seating capacity on feast days. Note the unusual—and questionable—exposed vertical fluorescent lights attached to pew ends.

25 Trade School (Handelschule)

Römerstrasse, Heidelberg
F. W. Kraemer, architect

Nestled against the hills and around the corner from the famous university, this altogether admirable trade school makes a worthy addition to historic Heidelberg. Its great merit lies in the spatial interplay of its several units—instead of one huge cube—and in its subtle and effective use of

color. The school is divided into two separate but attached groups: a large 4-story vocational-school, on stilts, and a lower business-school which is built about a garden court. The compact quality of the former and the more relaxed atmosphere of the latter reflect the curriculum and age group of each. Excellent planting can be seen throughout. This is one of the finest buildings in postwar Germany and possibly the best trade school in existence.

26 The Romeo and Julia Apartments

Haldenrain Strasse at Schozacher Strasse, Stuttgart-Zuffen-hausen

Hans Scharoun, architect; Wilhelm Frank, associate

The great Hans Scharoun, one of the pioneers of modern architecture in Germany, has, since the war, pursued a fascinating and highly personal path. Rejecting completely the cubic geometry that has characterized far too much building—such geometry being rarely more than a thoughtless box-enclosure of assorted functions—Scharoun has sought an expressive, at times extravagantly expressive, statement of planes and spatial series. Little of his work has thus far been built, but his design for a primary school in Darmstadt, his competition-winning plans for the City Theater of Kassel and his recently completed school in Lünen (10 miles north of Dortmund) have not been without their effect on

German architectural developments. This new apartment group in Stuttgart obviously suggests the obstreperous—and the provocative. There are not many buildings, old or new, with such anthropomorphic characteristics—even to names. The towering 19-story, compact, erect "Romeo" is happily paired by a low link to the shorter (13-story) but broader and curved "Julia." "Julia" (see photograph) is headed in nine different directions at once from its basic U-shape, but each of these expresses an apartment grouping, and each apartment is well planned. (It is interesting to compare in this regard Aalto's not overly dissimilar building now under construction in Bremen; its apartment plan resembles a fanned hand of cards.) A total of 200 co-operatively owned apartments are contained in this Stuttgart group, with restaurant, shops, and services on the ground floor, and a garage in the basement. There is more here than meets the casual eye: "But, soft! what light through yonder window breaks? It is the east, and Juliet is the sun."

27 Concert Hall (Liederhalle)

Berlinerplatz, Stuttgart
Adolf Abel and Rolf Gutbrod, architects

A puzzling, mixed-up complex: no one connected with its design knew when to stop. In spite of its spatial ambiguity and jazzed-up appearance, however, rewarding features ap-

pear. These are best seen in its plan and its flexibility. The main hall provides a multipurpose room that serves as theater and concert hall most of the time. As such it accommodates 2,000 people, of which 830 are in a balcony that sweeps down to the main-floor level on each side. The lower part of the auditorium, having a flat floor and removable chairs, can readily be adapted to assemblies, fairs, exhibitions, and other functions, even including banquets. To facilitate this latter use, when as many as 1,000 can be seated, the kitchen that serves the regular, permanent restaurant is directly adjacent to the main auditorium and on the same level. The large-scale banquet use of the auditorium has been very helpful from the financial standpoint. In addition to the main, multipurpose hall, there are two smaller theaters, accommodating 400 and 750 people; each has its own stage.

28 Television Tower (Fernsehturm)

Degerloch, Stuttgart

Fritz Leonhardt, architect and engineer

Rising some 500 feet above the highest hill of north Stuttgart, the observation floors and restaurant atop this smartly turned concrete tower enjoy a heady view of the entire countryside. Including the open-web steel mast, the total height is 708 feet. The tower structure is of reinforced concrete 35.5 feet in diameter and 12 inches thick at its base, and tapers to a 17-foot diameter and 7-inch thickness at top. It is serviced by two express elevators. Well worth a look, particularly from on high at sunset.

29 School of Design (Hochschule für Gestaltung)

near Fort Oberer Kuhberg (off Grimmelfinger Weg), Ulm
Max Bill, architect

This unique school, though designed and built with the most spartan economy possible, is sensitively spread and keenly grouped over the lovely hills southwest of the cathedral city of Ulm. Carrying on the traditions of Gropius's famous prewar Bauhaus, the four-year term of the Hochschule für Gestaltung is basically concerned with educating 150 pupils as specialists in industrial design, architecture, and visual communication. The rough and severely finished —sometimes unfinished—buildings are not appealing in detail, primarily because of their minimal character, but the flow and variety of their interior spaces is excellent.

147

30 Ministry of Pensions (Landesversorgungsamt)

Hess Strasse at Lothstrasse, Munich
Wassili and Hans Luckhardt, architects

An altogether admirable building—from its unusual yet logical layout to its bright vermilion spandrels sparkling in the sun and played off against the green of the grass. Its basic disposition provides four slightly boat-shaped low wings on the ground floor; these are reserved for the public. Straddling them at right angles and lightly poised above them is a 3-story staff-only administrative section 328 feet long. The building's design arose through the desire to have no steps, elevators, or confusion for the aged and infirm who visit it. Coming into the glass-lined entrance hall, which is well embellished with art, even the stranger can readily find his way. Each ground-floor wing has a central toplighted corridor off which open well-glazed offices. One of Germany's brightest new buildings.

31 Maxburg Rebuilding

Lenbachplatz, Munich

Theo Pabst and Sepp Ruf, architects

A wise and wonderful incorporation of the old into the new. The ancient (late-sixteenth-century) tower of the Graf Maxburg fort was all that remained following bombardment. In the competition proposals of the two architects (who later joined forces) this nostalgic souvenir was not only retained, it was also expertly tied by a glass nexus to the new office-block, setting up the liveliest of architectural counterpoints. Furthermore, the tower is not just a pleasant—but dead—accent, it actually serves as a staircase for the new structure. This building constitutes but one of five new units in the Maxburg rebuilding; the five vary in height and are loosely and pleasantly deployed around a generous open court. Although not distinguished individually, away from the street their group effect is that of a delightful urban oasis full of unexpected charm.

149

Athens 1-2

Andros 4

Glyphada 3

Heraklion 5

GREECE

GREECE

Greece gave architecture its name, and Greece took architecture to heights that are still unequaled. However, the Greek architect of today has until recently found only limited opportunities for satisfactory practice. At times he has been overawed by the sublimity of his classic inheritance—an inheritance still parlayed too strongly in the architectural school—and on other occasions he has been thwarted by the austerity economics of his country. As Georges Candilis, a very clever Greek architect now working in Paris, has said: "Pour un grec qui veut être architecte, le plus difficile c'est de se débarasser de l'emprise de son milieu" (*L'Architettura*, No. 33).

Actually, surprisingly good work is now being done, and though none of this possesses luminous significance, several items are worth a look. One of the rewarding features of the architectural situation in Greece is the prominence given to competitions: they are held for most important official buildings (National Gallery, Technical University at Salonica, etc.). Nearly all of the published winners have been well chosen and hold fine promise, but one recently victorious design for an orphanage was distinctly dismal. The Greek government has embarked on an extensive progam of building motels and hotels throughout the mainland and the sublime Greek islands. All of these are, or should be, very comfortable; several are fine architecturally. (Note especially the Triton Hotel at Ándros, shown below, the Xenia at Mykonos, and the motel at Igoumenítsa on the coast near the Albanian border, all three by Aris Konstantinidis.)

The most dynamic man in contemporary Greek architecture and planning is the talented C. A. Doxiadis. His headquarters (illustrated later) are in Athens, but his work extends over much of the Near East, and of late, to the United States, where he has offices both in Washington and Cambridge.

The recently born Greek architectural magazine *Architectoniki*, though at times loaded with appalling villas, has been doing a commendable job. One of its finer periodic features investigates the wonderful "plastic" forms found throughout the architecture of the Greek islands, that Mediterranean vernacular which excited—and had such a tangible impact on—Le Corbusier. Its "back to fundamentals" approach can refresh and delight us all. No trip to Greece is complete without visiting at least one of the isles.

1 United States Embassy

Vasilissis Sophias Boulevard at Macedonon Street, Athens

The Architects Collaborative; Walter Gropius, partner in charge; H. Morse Payne, Jr., associate (Paul Weidlinger and Mario Salvadori, structural engineers; Pericles Sakellarios, consultant)

The overseas postwar architectural program of the U.S. State Department has produced the most brilliant series of official buildings constructed by any country in the world. These buildings are almost universally fine; some are scintillating. In giving them "a distinguishable American flavor" while bearing in mind "local conditions of climate and site . . . local customs and people, and . . . the historical meaning of the particular environment," U.S. architects have not only achieved successes from Bangkok to Oslo, they have liberated modern American architecture itself from the doctrinaire prism that had been a too-facile answer to almost every architectural problem. Among the embassies that promise to rank with Edward Stone's almost ethereal building at New Delhi is this one now being finished in Athens. Gropius says: "Our aim was . . . a building which should appear serene, peaceful and inviting, mirroring the . . . political attitude of

United States. Also, the design should abide by the classical *spiritus loci* . . . but in contemporary . . . terms" (*Architectural Record*, December 1957). Of all embassies abroad, that at Athens obviously had the most demanding design problem. However, Gropius and his associates have acquitted themselves well of the challenge of the Parthenon, paying proper respect but not genuflecting. The Embassy, which is of square plan and has a square and open central court, rests on a well-terraced platform. Planting, pools, and sculpture (by Harry Bertoia) handle the changes in levels invitingly. The ground floor, one third of which remains happily open, is given to consular offices; the upper two floors are devoted to embassy activities. A structural section through the building reveals its most unusual architectural feature: a heavy roof-girder resting on and extending well beyond two columnar supports, one on the outer periphery of the square, the other in the court. These are spaced 19.7 feet (6 meters) apart. The 2-story block of embassy offices is tucked-up under this frame (the side walls actually are hung from it), the roof of which projects as a gigantic *brise-soleil* 6 meters on either side. Vent spaces at the points where the roof projections meet the office block allow for air circulation; the roof itself is of double construction for further insulation. All exterior framing is revetted with the same *café-au-lait* Pentelic marble that was used in the Parthenon and Thesion. Gropius's desires for the Embassy have obviously materialized —it is serene, peaceful, and inviting.

2 Doxiadis Associates Building

Syndesmou Street 24, Athens
C. A. Doxiadis, architect

This assured building, the finest office-block in Greece, provides headquarters for the extraordinary Doxiadis Associates. With the craggy Lycabettus looming up on one side and Athens and the distant Acropolis on the other—the near vs. the far, nature vs. man—and yet with a location that is both quiet and convenient to downtown Athens, the building is perceptively located. Divided into two basic units, it is joined by lower floors common to both. The 7-story main section (on the uphill side) houses the Doxiadis offices, while the smaller block now serves as the Athens Technological Institute but will be taken over by Doxiadis in future expansion. A garage occupies the basement; the reception area and an assembly hall take up the ground floor, which has a cafeteria and kitchen on its mezzanine—these facilities are shared by

Doxiadis Associates and the Institute. Classrooms are above in the Institute section, and office space above in the Doxiadis block. A square grid of 75 centimeters (2.48 feet) was used throughout. The large windows can be shielded from the sun by adjustable-slat roll blinds in vertical tracking.

154

3 Astir Beach Resort

Glyphada (11 miles SE of Athens)
E. Vourekas, P. Sakellarios and P. Vassiliadis, architects

Situated around a charming cove, within a half hour's drive of Athens, and distinguished by generally very good architecture, this 72-acre motel, dancing-restaurant, and beach resort has been enormously popular. The restaurant, at north end (nearest Athens), has its own entrance and can thus be used without entering the resort grounds. Beach facilities are divided into two sections—three courts of cubicles, which are let by the day, and a number of staggered ranks of elaborate cabana-bungalows (100 in all), which can be rented for short or long terms. The two sections are separated by the entrance to the beach area, which also contains a small series of shops and a large and attractive snack-bar. The cubicles are outstanding architecturally, with slightly bowed plywood roofs, excellent detailing, and good clean lines. Roof vaults extend forward beyond the changing cabins to provide agreeably sheltered, shaded porches. End walls—of narrow random slabs of ashlar marble—are not in character, but the over-all design of the cubicles is, nonetheless, first-rate. The cabanas, though pleasant, are not as fine. Astir is well worth the drive from Athens—and take your bathing suit.

4 Triton Hotel

Ándros (island E of Athens, reached from Piraeus)
Aris Konstantinidis, architect

Ándros, one of the largest (it is 23 miles long)—and the northernmost—of the Cyclades, was dedicated by the ancients to Dionysus. Appropriately enough, it was one of the first islands that the Greek government selected to receive a new hotel. The wine is still pressed there, and the excursion required to sample it locally has been made thoroughly agreeable by the presence of this splendid little hotel. It consists of a bedroom wing and a set-back dining-room-kitchen group, with a sheltered dining-terrace between. There are 26 bedrooms altogether, with a total of 44 beds; 14 rooms directly overlook the bay. Each room is well planned, and nicely, but simply, furnished; almost all have attractive private loggias. The architecture is unaffected and direct and rests easily above the rocky breakwater in front. The whole building is sympathetic and thoroughly well done. Be sure to have a reservation before leaving Athens-Piraeus.

5 Low-cost Housing

Heraklion (Candia), Crete
Aris Konstantinidis, architect

Heraklion, or Candia, as the Venetians called it when it was under their domination from the thirteenth to the seventeenth century, is the largest city in Crete, and the center for exploring the magnificent second-millennium B.C. ruins at Knossos just south of the town. The city was heavily damaged by the Germans during the early part of the war, but considerable reconstruction has taken place (and a comfortable new hotel has been built). Housing has been the city's foremost need, and this group of 63 minimum-cost dwellings on the outskirts of town has filled an important gap. The dwellings, which are for workers, are 2-story row-houses in block lengths varying from five to seven to fourteen units. A living-dining room with separate kitchen fills the ground floor of each house; the top floor has two double-bedrooms and a bath. Framework is of reinforced concrete. The brick-panel fill is stuccoed and painted in lively colors, which recall Greek fishing boats: white is used for the structure, blue for the lower floor, and red or yellow for the top. The upper floor overhangs the lower to provide a semisheltered porch and to shield the ground-floor windows from the sun. The upper windows are protected by wooden slat blinds, which, being hinged at the top, can be either closed flat or pushed out to any angle desired. The entire development, despite its minimum cost, has been realized with imagination. One's only objection lies in its ridiculously rigid layout.

ITALY

Corte di Cadore 32
Ivrea 17-18
Redipuglia 31
Milan 19-28
Sauze d'Oulx 16
Trieste 30
Turin 13-15
Padua 29
Genoa 12
Pescia 11
Larderello 10
Chianciano 9
Francavilla 8
Rome 1-5
Pozzuoli 6
Matera 7

50   100   150 M
50   100   150   200   250 KM

ITALY

Italy is the only land of ancient splendor which has never died: in two and a half millenniums it has only napped occasionally—to awaken again to artistic triumphs. It is wide awake now. Architecture in today's Italy has a vitality, an exuberance, and a statement of personality that make it both unique and wonderful. Italy also plays host to more architectural horrors than any country this side of the U.S.A., while its land usage is almost unrelievedly shocking.

Modern architecture developed more slowly in Italy than in the rest of Europe. For one reason, the rather brittle austerity of the early modern movement did not sit easily with the more lush Italian philosophy and inheritance; for another, the Italians have always exported, not imported, culture. The significance of the early but tragically short-lived "futurist" projects of Antonio Sant' Elia, who died in the first World War, is only now beginning to be recognized. Sant' Elia, along with Boccioni, the sculptor, Balla, the painter, and a few other kindred souls issued a "futurist manifesto" in 1912, calling for a culture and environment based on the potentialities of the future, and not on apings of the past. The cities of tomorrow which Sant' Elia drew up were extraordinarily prophetic. If he had lived beyond his twenty-eight years, our cities of today might well be better.

When Fascism came on the scene, modern architecture was getting a firm grip in several of the north European countries, and as it represented "youth" and "progress," Mussolini initially encouraged its development in Italy. But megalomania crept in, and promising beginnings degenerated into pompous neoclassicism—except in a series of brilliant expositions and a few isolated buildings such as Terragni's Casa del Popolo in Como (Via V. Emanuele II), the health colony at Legnano by Banfi, Belgiojoso, Peressutti and Rogers, and Gardella's sanatorium on Via Burgonzio in Alessandria. With the end of the war, Italian architecture—along with almost everything else in Italy—burst into the most dynamic and dramatic cultural *risorgimento* of modern times.

For well more than a decade following the war, contemporary Italian architecture was the brightest, most imaginative, and most stimulating in all Europe. In many respects it still is. But the exciting freshness, "rationalism," and clarity of architectural statement that characterized most early postwar work is now giving way to a conscious indeterminateness of form and a strong expressionism among some—but fortunately not all—practitioners. "Neo-liberty" the Italians themselves call it; "the retreat from modern architecture," others add. It might well be argued that this is simply architectural evolution in Foçillon's step-pattern and that the Italians are architectural bell-wethers—as they have been so many times before. A growing neomedievalism and an antipellucid school certainly loom evident in the United States for instance.

In any case, the architectural situation in today's Italy certainly differs from that of several years ago. Some will be intrigued by this, some left cold; some will find refection, others will feel that much of this new work is overrationalized and "dowdy," to use a word recently applied to a prominent Turin example.

The dominant figure in Italian architecture is unquestionably the architectural engineer Pier Luigi Nervi. His gloriously poetic conquests of space are among the greatest constructions of the twentieth century. Nervi is a giant in a land not unfamiliar with giants. As his forebears 1,900 years ago first hurled concrete over then-unheard-of spaces, so Nervi by adding small steel-rods to ancient Rome's pozzuolana cement likewise stuns us today.

After the unequaled works of Nervi, the most interesting building types in Italy are exhibitions, museums, shops, and memorials, some housing, and large structures such as the Rome railway station, which is the finest in Europe. Strength is thus found in two extremes—the engineer-architect and the artist-architect—reflecting, one might say, the Roman sense of structure and organization and the Renaissance synthesis of the arts. The social (*not* society) architect gets passed over except for the bit of first-rate housing mentioned above. Few schools, hospitals, or public buildings of merit will be found.

Fairs and exhibitions, notably Milan's Triennale and its yearly Industrial Fair, are always wonderfully imaginative in Italy, the most stimulating to be seen. They were thus

160

even in Fascist days, when more substantial architectural efforts were closely prescribed. Museum building, remodeling and installation, after a long period of horrors, has recently surpassed anything done elsewhere. As Bruno Zevi, the brilliant Italian architect and critic, wrote in the *Atlantic Monthly* (December 1958): "We had been accustomed to museums conceived architecturally on a monumental scale, a shell into which the works of art were inserted at a later stage. But now this concept is being reversed: the works of art themselves create the architecture, dictating the spaces and prescribing the proportions of the walls. Each picture and statue is studied for the best possible view: it is then set in the necessary spatial quantity." In addition to the museum work of Albini and B.B.P.R., shown later, that of Gardella and Carlo Scarpa is outstanding. Gardella's Gallery of Modern Art in Milan (Via Palestro) and Scarpa's Castelvecchio Museum at Verona (Corso Cavour) and Palazzo Abbatelli Museum at Palermo (Via Alloro) are distinguished installations.

Shops and restaurants will not be treated in the descriptions of individual buildings; they are too subject to ruination. However, even the casual observer will discover many of merit throughout Italy. The most modest coffee-bar will sport some original work of art, often very good.

Memorials have been notable in Italy since Etruscan days. The "Monumental Cemeteries" of Milan and Genoa are phantasmagorias of crowded tombs. They must be seen to be believed. However, some stunning work has appeared in them of late, generally representing collaboration between architect and sculptor. Again, this is a field in which Italy is unequaled.

Finally, housing must be mentioned as among the outstanding basic building types. Through INA-Casa, Italy has done remarkable work in all sections of the country: from entirely new communities of attached houses in rural areas to multistory apartments in cities. Individual farm-building has also been implemented, particularly in sparsely inhabitated, depressed areas. One of the most significant features of new minimal-cost housing in Italy can be seen in its regional variation and regional concern for the cultures, social patterns, and work habits of the

161

immediate district. Without such sympathy, new housing, no matter how great an improvement over old, might well have been looked upon with a certain wariness in underdeveloped areas, where "authority" was long, and rightly, regarded as suspect. Among the many fine developments throughout the length of the peninsula are: the Olivetti housing at Ivrea, by various architects; La Falchora in Turin-Falchora, by Giovanni Astengo and associates; the Bernabo Brea estate and the Via Isonzo housing in Genoa, by Daneri, Grossi-Bianchi and Zappa; the Cesate development, 8 miles north of Milan, by Albini, Albricci, B.B.P.R., and Gardella; "Ca Granda Nord," Milan, by Vittorio Gandolfi; San Basilio, near Rome, by Mario Fiorentino; the Tuscolano development in Rome, especially the unusual one-story "Mediterranean" houses by Adalberto Libera; fine housing by Luigi Cosenza in Naples; the Barra development in Naples, by Carlo Cocchia; and the work of the Caronias in Palermo. La Martella Village, near Matera, epitomizes much of this work; it is illustrated later.

Other outstanding Italian contributions to contemporary architecture are anonymous; they may well be endemic. They are (1) the wonderful working relations and mutual appreciation of architects, sculptors, mosaicists, and muralists, and the employment of such artists for almost every type of building, including bars and butcher shops; (2) a keen awareness and expression of structure in building (the "bones" are increasingly prominent in contemporary Italian building and are in many cases the design dominant); (3) an absence of the clichés so monotonously dragged across the U.S. with every new issue of the architectural magazines (Italian architects—for better or worse—think for themselves); (4) an appreciation of the richness and vitality of materials, and a fertile imagination in using them; and (5) a great knowledge of and respect for architectural inheritance, but no aping or bowing to it such as is still found in France and England.

Against these splendid credits, the following debits occur: abysmal planning, often in the building, almost always in city and suburban developments; a lack of social consciousness and responsibility; shocking lack of upkeep, especially in housing (there would be more ex-

162

amples of such work in this book if upkeep had been better); poor public architecture, and in particular, poor schools (since the war only 25,000 schoolrooms of the more than 130,000 needed have been built); and a liberty that too often becomes license.

Modern Italian architecture is, like that in the United States, an architecture of very high peaks amid a morass of mediocrity. But, with a public that enthusiastically "reviews" new buildings as it does new plays and books, with several fine professional schools, and with three searching and refreshingly outspoken architectural journals—which are on the top layer of every newsstand—the ambience for the Italian architect is highly stimulating. Milan alone is frenetic: energy with taste, vitality with perception (usually!). And though Rome has its "Hollywood" school—stroll through the Parioli district—so do most countries of the world. If occasional lacunae occur, as indeed they must everywhere, Italy in the present, as in the past, always excites, always overpowers with beauty and achievement, and always leaves the beholder richer for the experience.

P.S. to the motorist in Italy: The documents of the Touring Club Italiano, Corso Italia 2, Milan, are the most useful one can have; the new three-part *Guida Rapida* is invaluable, with or without a reading knowledge of Italian.

1 Fosse Ardeatine

Via Appia Antica, Rome
Aprile, Calcaprina, Cardelli, Fiorentino and Perugini, architects; Francesco Coccia and Mirko, sculptors

Among the great memorials of Europe and among the very finest works of postwar Italy is this noble monument outside Rome. In its sarcophagus lie the bodies of 335 Italians barbarically murdered by the Germans in reprisal for the loss of 32 storm troopers killed in an explosion. The unfortunate men buried here—none of whom had anything to do with the bombing—were herded into these caves and shot; the entrance was then blown up. The basic design of the memorial leaves the scene of the disaster intact. Outside, the architects have put an enormous sarcophagus with a lid seemingly floating in the air. The whole area, which is entered through superb gates by Mirko, has been enclosed by a simple,

163

mastabalike wall. A weak statue of three bound men accents the entry. One proceeds to the caves, then by a rude earth tunnel bursts into the sarcophagus itself, an area 25 by 50 meters (82 by 164 feet). Protecting this great communal grave of identical tombs, and supported above it by three blocks on each side, hovers the concrete slab of the roof. This brilliant understatement, this mortifying contrast of the horrendous caves with the simple burying ground, this restraint when heroics might be expected, make the Ardeatine Caves a deep emotional experience.

2 Termini Station

Piazza dei Cinquecento, Rome

Montuori and Calini, chief architects; Castellazzi, Fadigati, Vitellozzi and Pintonello, associate architects

This magnificent railroad station is of interest for two reasons: the fact that the fourth-century B.C. Servian Wall forms a very positive part of its design, and the grand manner and élan of its entry. Incorporating the 2,300-year-old wall into the fabric of the station—the profile of the wall is mirrored in the structure of the entrance and forms a visual part of the station's interior—reflects Italy's genius in preserving its distinguished heritage, and in logically wedding it to the new. The juxtaposition of the ancient wall and the sparkling new station emphasizes as nothing else could the cultural roots and the never-dying cultural vitality of Rome. The entry proper sweeps passengers in from the piazza and de-

posits them in the *galleria* and on the train platform, both on the other side, with a magnificence of movement that Bernini himself would have loved. The *galleria* is so attractive that it serves as a spontaneous core for its part of Rome. With the exception of the fenestration of the lengthy (760-foot) office-block atop the entry, and the design of the prewar wings on either side, this is the most exciting railroad station in Europe.

3 Palazzo dello Sport
Via Cristoforo Colombo, E.U. 42 Grounds, Rome (SE of city)
Pier Luigi Nervi, engineer; M. Piacentini, architect

A great sports building and a technological and (on the interior) esthetic triumph by Nervi, the master of prefabricated unit concrete. Built for the 1960 Olympics and beautifully integrated into the grounds originally prepared for the never-held Rome Exposition of 1942, this nobly capped arena seats 16,000 people. With its small brother, the Palazzetto (q.v.), it provided covered Olympic stadiums that will probably never be equaled in elegance and pleasure of seating. One's exterior impression of the Palazzo wavers, for the structure of the building is lost behind the reflective wall of glass wrapped about it. However, Nervi's sensitive mastery asserts itself when one enters. Note that the supports for the access to the upper tiers of seats and the exterior columns supporting the roof edge are leanly sculptured, not just inexpressive and graceless rectangles. The weblike inverted-dish dome, which

in one leap of 100 meters (328 feet) spans all seats, is made of the small-scale lightly reinforced prefabricated concrete elements for which Nervi is so famous. The entire roof was put together with great precision yet with great speed and economy. Enormously impressive within.

4 Palazzetto dello Sport

Viale Tiziano, Rome
Pier Luigi Nervi, engineer; Annibale Vitellozzi, architect

Whereas the great Palazzo dello Sport dazzles with its technical daring, the Palazzetto seduces with a gemlike civility. Moreover, it commences its charms on the outside and carries through within; thus a far greater and more expressive structural unity develops here than in the larger arena. The building is topped by a shallow dome, 194 feet in diameter, which rests airily on the 36 prominently exposed Y-shaped supports that carry its thrust into the ground. The Y-piers are sharply canted to be tangential to the dome, and the eave is rippled for greater strength. The effect from within of the angled break between supports, the concentration of ribs from the dome nervation, and the view of the upper end of the external Y-piers is potent. The dome was made of 1,620 beautifully precast concrete coffers in 19 different sizes; the largest is the pie-shaped piece at the eave. As with the dome of the Palazzo dello Sport—and many of Nervi's

other large roofs—the underside of the dome exhibits a harmonious and meticulous diagram of concrete thrusts. Total roof thickness, including insulation and membrane waterproofing, is 4.75 inches. The arena holds 4,000 people for tennis and basketball and 5,000 for boxing and wrestling. There are few who would deny that this is the most beautiful sports building in the world—inside and out. The Flaminio Stadium by Nervi and his son Antonio stands just east of the Palazzetto and should also be visited.

5 Leonardo da Vinci Airport

Rome-Fiumicino (16 miles SW of Rome)

Amedeo Luccichenti and Vincenzo Monaco, architects (Andrea Zavitteri, associate architect); Riccardo Morandi, engineer

Virtually within sight of the fourth-century B.C. ruins of Ostia Antica, which in ancient days served as the port of the capital, Rome's new international airport is dramatically situated vis-à-vis old and new. Punic Wars and jets are cheek by jowl. Architecturally, the airport's main building comprises a great central hall—superbly engineered by Morandi—which with two lengthy corridor-wings on either side stretches a total of 600 meters (1,970 feet). To the right as one faces the entrance are the separate flight building and control tower. The central building occupies three levels: the lowest

167

level is used for baggage and services; the main floor (reached by automobile ramp) for passenger traffic; and a suspended mezzanine for airline offices and a restaurant. This main unit expresses a virile personality lacking in the somewhat "international" modernism of the corridor wings and flight building. Its strength derives from its boldly stated reinforced-concrete frame and its light steel roof, the angled box-shaped beams of which alternate with bands of glass. The other elements are capable but not outstanding. Unfortunately no weather protection is afforded the passengers as they enter or leave their planes.

6 Olivetti Factory and Services

Via Domiziana, Pozzuoli (8 miles W of Naples)
Luigi Cosenza, architect

Above the ancient Pozzuoli—where the Romans found ingredients for their concrete and established a flourishing city 2,000 years ago—Olivetti commissioned a wonderful industrial grouping as a key plant in extending industrialization to the south of Italy. This complex is gloriously situated on

168

a hillside overlooking the Bay of Naples, with Ischia and Procida near its feet and the Sorrento peninsula rising in the distance. Cosenza has incorporated this contact with nature into his design: not only to make work here as pleasant as possible from the standpoint of creature comfort—as in all of Olivetti's enterprises—but also to dignify the working man as a human and not just an industrial unit. If, on occasion, workers look up from their tasks to enjoy the lovely view, this is precisely what Olivetti and Cosenza had in mind. Such is not a waste of time, but a closer tying of the worker to the pleasures of his job in an industrial ambience that is in pointed contrast to the factory maw that endlessly ingests human cogs. Higher production at Pozzuoli than at the parent factory in Ivrea fully bears out this philosophy. The group here has more the atmosphere of a hillside school than that of a high-precision manufacturing-establishment. The administrative office is set back from the road, with adequate parking alongside and an apprentice school beyond. Behind rises the main plant, built in a 2-story cruciform shape; manufacturing is on the ground floor, and assembly and inspection are above. On the west side are social services—library, cafeteria, kitchen, etc.—with an adjacent building for dressing rooms. On the north border are placed the warehouses and powerhouse. Ample expansion was foreseen in the original plans. This complex represents a new and very human concept in industrial architecture.

7 La Martella Village

Via Timmari, Matera (Lucania)

Ludovico Quaroni, architect (F. Gorio, M. Valori, P. Lugli, and L. Agati, associates)

The problem of the rehabilitation of the *Mezzogiorno*, the depressed south, continues to be Italy's most urgent and most resolutely undertaken operation. Its symbol of effort might well be said to be this admirable village near Matera. A small inland city above the "instep" of Italy, Matera has been known for many centuries for its soft stone hillsides, into which thousands and thousands of caves have been cut. Until recently, 15,000 people occupied over 3,300 holes in its vicinity. As many as 7 members of a family lived in one grotto—with the donkey sleeping beside them! Such caves are always damp, and almost always sunless and airless. Few had any exterior opening other than the front door. With United States Counterpart Funds and UNRRA-Casa's help it was decided to move the most destitute people from these horrors and to set them up in a new village outside of town but in close connection with their farmland. This sparkling village resulted. Planned with the most minute attention to the needs and traditions of the people who were to live there, people with a very strong sense of dignity and a group pride even in poverty, this self-contained community achieves a laudable sociological and architectural solution in spite of the economy of its means. The neat single and double houses, with separate quarters for the farm animals, are of stuccoed local stone. Together they form neighborhoods of friendly length—reflecting the communal groups of the caves—and these in turn focus on the village center with its shops, meeting hall, church, schools, etc. There is no formal statement of architectural greatness in La Martella; it is nonetheless a model for the rehabilitation of underdeveloped areas. Whatever problems it has encountered are found in general economics, not specific urbanism.

8 San Franco

Piazza San Franco, Francavilla al Mare (5 miles SE of Pescara)

Ludovico Quaroni, architect

Carrying on the tradition and function of dominating the profile of a town, which had been the estate of the destroyed church that previously stood on this site, this new building rests sensitively on its ridge overlooking the Adriatic. The mass of the church proper sympathetically echoes—but does not copy—the shapes and forms of the houses at its feet, and as a consequence, it is thoroughly and properly at home in its environment. The campanile, though fine in essential statement and in location, is filigreed at the top with unfortunate details. The corpus of the church provides a single high, laterally swelling room, with a varyingly deep side-aisle. A good entrance under the low part bursts into the lofty nave after a few steps. Streams of light flood down from the four windows placed high under the broad roof. The roof, clearly stated as a structural entity in sectional drawings, is lost in the "wrap-around" treatment of the ceiling. The altar stands well placed and free in front of its "ambulatory," but a

171

window directly behind causes an unfortunate glare. The side aisles of the church provide retreats for individual worship as opposed to the corporate quality of the nave proper.

9 Spa and Casino

Viale Baccelli, Chianciano Terme (47 miles SE of Siena)
Pier Luigi Nervi, architectural engineer; Mario Loreti and Mario Marchi, architects

Not far east of the interesting towns of Pienza and Montepulciano are found some of the most famous mineral springs in Italy. These have recently been refurbished by new buildings, of which the most spectacular is the casino shown in photo. An incredible concrete sunflower, of breath-taking size and beauty, hovers over the floor in one of the most superb geometric manifestations known to architectural engineering. The room itself, in its shape and details and in its visual support of the helianthus, is commonplace, but the lovely ceiling is a thing apart. Made of prefabricated concrete panels, it was put together with astounding workmanship.

10 Volcanic Gas Steam Plant

Larderello (20 miles S of Volterra)

Belching hot gases and looking like something out of Dante via Doré, these impressive hyperbolic cooling-towers generate electricity from the internal rumblings that have shaken and scarred this region of Italy for centuries. South of Volterra and halfway between Siena and the sea, the rumpled, rather desolate landscape bubbles and shoots forth vapors of from 200 to 350 Fahrenheit degrees. Though these have been known for hundreds of years, they were never put to more than local use until the end of the last century. At that time, besides extracting boric acid, sulphur, and other chemicals, small beginnings were made in converting the gases to electricity. Since the war an enormous expansion in these power facilities has been undertaken; they now produce industrial kilowatts on a significant level for all of central Italy. The hyperbolic towers, in addition to their importance as imported-fuel savers in an almost resourceless country, are certain to impress esthetically all who drive by. Though stock forms, they are indeed striking in space.

11 Covered Market

Piazza del Mercato, Pescia

Brizzi, Gori, Gori, Ricci and Savioli, architects

Halfway between Lucca and Pistoia, and not far from the famous Montecatini Spa, the small town of Pescia erected this masterful covered market, where its famous flowers and its asparagus and other vegetables are sold. The market's soaring scalloped shell of concrete, poised lightly on lateral supports, hovers like a great umbrella weightlessly and effortlessly over its 75-foot span. There is a pared-to-the-bone statement in its expression and a sculptured refinement in its shape. The roof of the market, which covers an area roughly 75 by 230 feet, consists of a thin, open vault; its lateral thrust is borne by five arch-buttresses on either side. At the four corners, splayed buttresses transmit the diagonal thrusts of top and side forces into the ground. The roof is made of contiguous reinforced hollow-tile arcs (of rectangular section), concreted top and bottom to make them watertight. The use of reinforced tile beams, both flat and arched, is very popular in Italy, as they are easily fabricated and installed, inexpensive and light. The entire market is open, except for administration, toilet facilities, and storage for merchants, which are in closed wings on either side.

12 Museum of the Cathedral Treasury

San Lorenzo Cathedral, Piazza San Lorenzo, Genoa
Franco Albini, architect

Albini's touch—he does the most elegant interiors in Italy—is shown at its most sensitive in this tiny museum under the courtyard of San Lorenzo. Measuring less than 43 by 46 feet, it has a flow of space in and out and around its small rooms that approaches the transcendent. The cathedral possesses a number of very valuable works of art—including, reputedly, the Holy Grail—some of which are still used in

various ceremonies. Thus direct connection with the church
had to be maintained. To give the art a proper atmosphere
of preciousness Albini contrived a series of four varyingly
sized "cylinders," similar to Mycenaean tholoi, in each of
which only a few objects are displayed. These cylinders open
off a highly irregular central anteroom, and the contrast between this irregularity and the geometry of the display rooms
generates one of the design elements that make this museum
significant. One enters each of the cylinders via a small
somewhat medieval door; these doors heighten the "treasury"
atmosphere. The imaginative display of the works inside each
cylinder varies subtly according to the size and character
of the objects. As the museum is underground, only one of
its rooms has daylight—a central dramatic oculus. Albini's
nearby Palazzo Bianco Museum (Via Garibaldi), although
housed in an existing building, and hence of less spatial interest, should also be seen.

13 Italia 61 Pavilion

Corso Polonia, Turin

*Pier Luigi Nervi and Antonio Nervi, engineer and architect;
    exhibitions under direction of Gio Ponti*

This stupendous structure along the Po River somewhat south
of the famous exhibition buildings by Nervi and Morandi
graphically demonstrates that Nervi's triumphant conquests
of vast spaces are by no means limited to small-element prefabrication, or for that matter, to domes or vaults. Furthermore, steel as a major material in its own right is used here
by Nervi for the first time. This enormous building (which
covers an area larger than St. Peters in Rome) celebrates
dually Italian labor and the hundredth anniversary of the
unification of Italy. A competition was held for its design
and was won (unanimously) by the Nervis, father and son.
The liveliness of the submissions of the runners-up—Mollino,
Bordogna and Musmeci; and Nicola and Rizzotti—shows how
fertile other minds are in Italy. The project posed enormous
problems of space, speed, and subsequent use. Nervi's
solution, one of great flexibility, proposed a gigantic square
hall, 520 feet on a side, upheld by sixteen towering cross-
shaped piers each supporting a square roof-section. The
resulting building provides a main floor and mezzanine, with
a square central bay, 191 feet on a side, which is open to an
over-all inner height of 82 feet. The mezzanine is carried
separately by its own supports. The sixteen great columns
support square steel roof-slabs 131 feet on a side—steel was

used because it is quicker to erect. Each bay of slabs is separated from the others by a continuous "grid" skylight 2 meters wide. The great mushroom columns are structurally independent. Adjustable exterior *brise-soleils* protect the south and west façades. A prodigious and wonderful building.

14 Palazzo delle Esposizioni

Corso Massimo d'Azeglio, Turin
Pier Luigi Nervi, engineer

This is the finest exhibition hall since Paxton's Crystal Palace in London more than a hundred years ago. In it are held the many annual displays for which Turin is noted. Built to replace war-damaged buildings, its two units, the great Room B and the smaller but more lyric Room C, are superlative structures. Room B had to be built with the utmost speed, so Nervi, in this, his first major postwar design, turned to pre-

177

fabricated reinforced-concrete, small-unit construction. These elements, which could be made right on the site, are triangular in shape, 14.75 feet long by 5.25 feet high. Thirteen of them are needed to make the 190-foot-long arc between the great "flying" buttresses that receive them. The nine center units are glazed, admitting ample daylight. Fluorescent artificial lights are also attached to these units. A semicupola, 131 feet in diameter, terminates the far end of Room B. This resembles nothing so much as the underside of a *Victoria Regia* Waterlily in concrete. Room C, which measures 164 by 214 feet, is not as majestic as Room B, but it is more sensuous and more totally graspable as its entire framing rises ex-

posed on all four sides of the beholder: one almost feels a part of its elegantly stated structure. Here, in Nervi's hands, concrete becomes an alive and vital material, not just an ingredient to make the usual series of rectangular beams. The main vaulting of Room C, supported by four weightless arches, rises to a clear height of 45 feet, and like the roof of the semicupola was constructed with a formwork of prefabricated diamond-shaped elements. After these panels were in place and the reinforcing laid between, concrete was poured from above to make the roof. When set, the form was stripped off, leaving a marvelously smooth undersurface and a weathertight top. This building has few equals in our time.

179

15 New Automobile Pavilion

Corso Massimo d'Azeglio, Turin
Riccardo Morandi, architect and engineer

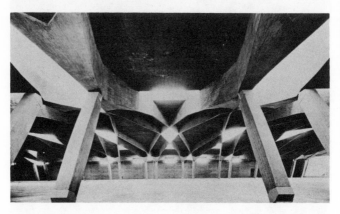

A powerful adjunct to Nervi's adjoining exhibition halls, by
a man whose talents are far too little known in the English-
speaking world. It is, of course, difficult for anyone to match
structural wits with Nervi, but Morandi has done just this
with his triumphant building. To preserve the park in which
this new unit is located, the entire hall, which is 496 feet long
by 236 wide, was put underground. Its position, shape, and
framing will immediately recall Vago and Freysinet's somewhat similar structure at Lourdes (q.v.). Morandi used
prestressed-concrete beams to roof his great room, criss-cross-
ing them in dynamic fashion and supporting them within the
hall by paired inclined columns. These tilted supports,
roughly square in cross section and capped with steel at each
end, give an accent of herculean strength to the interior.
Twenty-two skylights permit natural light. A ramp and
drive lead into the south end; thus automobiles can drive
directly onto the exhibition floor. A covered passage connects this new building with Nervi's main exhibition hall.

16 Ski Lodge

Lago Nero, Sauze d'Oulx
Carlo Mollino, architect

This ski lodge, high (its elevation is 7,500 feet) in the Alps
west of Turin, and almost in sight of the French border, is
one of the most three-dimensional buildings in modern Italian

architecture. Difficult to grasp frontally, its design encourages one to walk around the lodge, as one would walk around a piece of sculpture. This anti-Renaissance development, this shunning of the perfect single façade in a search for a free-

standing building with four faces that are equally fine and mutually dependent is very refreshing. The lodge consists of an arrival and departure section on the ground floor; restaurant, bar, lounge, and south-oriented terrace on the main floor; and dormitories and rooms on top. The terrace in front is a spectacular element of the design, jutting like the prow of a ship into the sunshine and view of the ski slopes. If it has been properly maintained, this is an expressive three-dimensional building, attractive winter or summer.

17 Dining and Recreation Hall for Olivetti Workers

Via Jervis, Ivrea
Ignazio Gardella, architect

Gardella—with Franco Albini—is the most sensitive, civilized, and elegant of Italian architects, and he has been for well over twenty years. His revolt against Fascist rhetoric and monumentality was clearly stated in his tuberculosis clinic at Alessandria (1936–38), and it has been maintained ever since. His work never clamors for attention as a masterpiece for all to admire; rather, it grows from given conditions and requirements and is fitted into its setting as graciously as possible. This newly finished recreation center and cafeteria for Olivetti workers, located on a hillside directly behind the main factory, is one of his finest buildings. Roughly hexagonal in shape, the 3-story main building settles into its park-

181

like situation with admirable grace, letting the landscape and trees dominate wherever possible. The dining rooms occupy the top floor, providing seats in the cafeteria for 1,800 and table service for roughly 500. Beneath flows a complex of lounges, coffee-bars (space is even provided for dancing), writing rooms and a library, game rooms and a television room. Tennis courts and dressing rooms are adjacent to the east, a new theater to the north. Could any lunch hour be more catered to? Other new Olivetti buildings are being erected all the time in Ivrea. Among the most interesting of these are an extension of the main factory by Figini and Pollini along the Via Jervis (Figini and Pollini also did the original plant in 1939–42); a very recent, and interesting, "social service" building by Figini and Pollini directly across the street from the main factory; another factory (along the Strada Statale 26) by Eduardo Vittoria, and a handsome

study-center (behind the first industrial grouping) by this same architect. Adding these to earlier "social care" buildings and housing (q.v.), no other corporation in Europe, and no corporation in the United States, can point to such enlightened and farsighted concern for products, environment, and employees.

18 Housing for Olivetti Workers

Canton Vesco, Ivrea
Nizzoli and Fiocchi, architects

The housing and facilities that Olivetti has built for employees in Ivrea, a depressing town an hour north of Turin, are the finest company buildings in Europe. In the group shown here, a bit west of the town, we have a rare ex-

183

ample of units that are felicitously related both to each other and to the whole. Two parallel north-south blocks of four floors, staggered by the angle of the side road, are closed in composition by a 3-story building oriented east and west. The three together make a well-proportioned and well-disposed open court in the center of which are a planted yard and a low play pavilion for the children. The ground floor of the unit facing the street is devoted to services and two wide access passages. These openings allow one to see through the front building across the court to the others, tying the group together. An excellent use of color distinguishes them all. This has been imaginatively confined to the broad bands of the "inner" balcony-walls and to the bases of the two north-south units. The "outside" walls—the walls that receive the beat of the hot sun—are all white; the buildings are thus unified by the generic light color but given individual personalities by the colors of the inner panels. Apartment planning falters: kitchens are cramped, no storage or closets are provided, and the balcony access interferes with privacy. But from the visual and urban standpoint this is excellent housing.

19 Pirelli Building

Piazza Duca d'Aosta, Milan

Gio Ponti, architect, with Antonio Fornaroli, Alberto Rosselli, Giuseppe Valtolina and Egidio Dell'Orto; Pier Luigi Nervi and Arturo Danusso, structural advisors

The keenly anticipated, 33-story Pirelli block near the Milan Central Station is meaningful in both esthetics and structure.

Gio Ponti—the contemporary "Universal Man" in his multi-faceted talents—was determined that the building for Italy's great rubber company would not be another elongated vertical stack to which one could add and detract bays and floors without impinging on appearance. He wanted a "finite form" that would stand as a finished product. To complement this design approach, somewhat Euclidean in its implications, the architects and engineers sought an equally determined structure. The multicube frame of steel was obviously out: it had no feeling for statement, being simply additive. With Nervi and Danusso the solution reached was a brilliantly novel double-vertebrate structure of reinforced concrete 416 feet high. From its two great transverse spines, which are placed 79 feet apart, and which taper as they get higher, the unimpeded floors are cantilevered. In plan the building provides a double-ended boat-shape, with services and storage behind the blank, angled end-walls, and well-lighted, columnless office space between. Unfortunately the exterior has not lived up to its initially sparkling promise. Nervi's epic concrete frame became absorbed within the skin instead of projecting lightly on the exterior as an elegant taper—as in the model. Furthermore, the early delicate façade treatment gave way to a weighty horizontal division of routine spandrels and windows. In spite of the above, however, the boat-shape reveals constantly fresh perspectives as one walks about, and its basic thinking and structure will keep it among the impressive skyscrapers of our time.

20 Office Building

Corso Europa, Milan

Luigi Caccia Dominioni, architect; Agostino Agostini, associate

Clear, clean, and elegant, this is possibly the finest small commercial building in Europe. Free of cliché, it asserts with obvious refinement what a sensitive hand can produce even with a downtown office-and-apartment block. The building's untroubled smoothness and conspicuous understatement make it doubly welcome in the architectural hurly-burly about it. The ground floor is entered by a somewhat puzzling labyrinth of arcades, but the floors above are serene in their clarity. The building shown here is one of twins, the second being separated from the earlier by two old *palazzi.*

21 Torre Velasca
Via Velasca at Corso di Porta Romana, Milan
B.B.P.R.: Belgiojoso, Peressutti and Rogers, architects

The Torre Velasca is a puzzling, even an irritating building, but not one to be brushed off casually. Its rationale evolved

from the twofold desire to fit the skyscraper into the *mise en scène* of Milan's Gothic pride, the Cathedral, some 1,000 feet away, and to express the bifurcated division of the building into offices on the lower floors and apartments on the upper. Furthermore, as this was to be a 26-story tower, freestanding in the profile of the city, it had to be designed as a three-dimensional entity—from side to side and from top to bottom. The reinforced-concrete frame of the building merits particular attention (Arturo Danusso was its engineer). The architects wanted to have the peripheral structure on the outside of the enclosing walls, as this would not only facilitate interior subdivisions but would also blend more sympathetically with the exposed construction of the Gothic cathedral. This frame was enclosed with prefabricated masonry panels of narrow width, but unlike the regular, rigid patterning of fenestration typical of virtually all tall buildings, the windows and wall sections here vary according to the needs and expressed desires of the individual clients. To many critics, both within Italy and without, the Torre Velasca seems to be an overrationalized design. It has been called "the world's only do-it-yourself skyscraper." But, lump it or like it, take a look!

22 Monument to Those Fallen in Germany

Cimitero Monumentale, Via Cerésio, Milan
B.B.P.R.: *Belgiojoso, Peressutti and Rogers, architects*

A refined and evocative open-frame cube commemorating the many, many Italians who died in German concentration camps. Like Rome's Fosse Ardeatine (q.v.), it eschews histrionics and the obvious. In plan, section, and elevations a Greek cross—a cross whose proportions were reached via a golden section—this fragile framework epitomizes the geometric approach to memorials. The outside "walls" are hung with abstractly disposed panels of white and black marble on which are engraved such sentiments as "Blessed are those who suffer persecution for the cause of justice." A glass case in the center holds a prisoner's bowl containing earth from the notorious Mauthausen in Austria. Twisted about the center framework with a thornlike symbolism, a strand of rusted barbed-wire presents an almost unbearable contrast and poignancy to the mathematics of its setting. This is a disturbing memorial, which by its purity, its prison bowl, and its rusty wire calls forth a whole philosophy of life and death.

23 Olivetti Headquarters

Via Clerici, Milan

Bernasconi, Fiocchi and Nizzoli, architects

Although a bit strident for its piazzetta, this seemly head-quarters possesses distinction inside and out—as do all Olivetti products. The main building consists of eight floors of offices on top of a ground floor given over to the entrance and to exhibitions of the firm's wares. A 4-story wing projects at right, and another, similar, wing is anticipated for the left. As the entrance side faces the hot southwest sun much of the day, it is protected by vertical exterior aluminum *brise-soleils,* which are adjustable in groups; the northeast side—perhaps the finer of the two—having little sun, needs only a simple overhang to shield its ranks of windows. The office space within is completely flexible. Note the art on the ground floor.

24 Castel Sforzesco Museum

Foro Bonaparte, Milan

B.B.P.R.: Belgiojoso, Peressutti and Rogers, architects

The rehabilitation of the 2-story museum in the five-hundred-year-old Sforza *castello* has more to offer the distressingly fusty museums of the world than any structure to be seen elsewhere. Here is no warehouse of art, with identical case after identical case filled with near-identical objects and parading drearily through selfsame rooms. Here ancient art and artifacts become excitingly alive and fascinating to experience. Why do the objects here have so much more pertinence and visual satisfaction than their contemporaries on display in New York, London, and Paris? The answer, of course, lies in brilliant and sympathetic installation. Belgiojoso, Peressutti and Rogers—obviously working with satisfactory funds—have tailored the rooms and displays to complement the character of the art: each room has a personality of its own; each related grouping achieves an expressive entity. Every detail has received sumptuous care, in relation to itself and its neighbors and to the room. This is just as characteristic of the austerely handsome setting for Michelangelo's "Pietà" as it is for medieval armor. In some cases perhaps too much care (and money) has been spent: some of the objects are not as fine as their installations; sometimes installation overly dominates, and occasionally visual indigestion results. In the main, however, this is the finest large display of ancient works in the museum world.

25 Matri Misericordiae Church

Strada Provinciale Varesina at Via Trieste, Milan-Baranzate
Angelo Mangiarotti and Bruno Morasutti, architects; Aldo Favini, engineer

In an industrial suburb of northwest Milan rises this highly inquiring and exciting church. Donated by private funds and accordingly unfettered in its approach, it offers both esthetic and technical rewards. So that a degree of privacy and a "preparation" space could be realized in the flat neighborhood, a low wall encircles the entire church. The stations of the cross are placed, in this private "court," not in the church itself. Because of the high water-level in this area the main body of the church had to be elevated, with only a small chapel, sacristy, and service rooms on the ground floor. The church proper, usually entered from below, is very unusual structurally, having only four supports for its entire roof. These in turn carry two heavy cross-beams of concrete on which rest six prestressed, longitudinal X-shaped beams, made up of 30 prefabricated units approximately 1 meter long. This roof structure rests completely independent of and structurally

detached from the enclosing walls, which, in their turn, are also of technical interest. They are made of a double wall of glass with 1-inch panels of translucent foam plastic in between. A nonglare diffused-light thus suffuses the interior (compare the Madonna of the Poor), while the insulating factor of the panels is so high that even the summer heat of Milan leaves the church agreeable. Potted plants, gaudy banners, plastic figures, and other assorted bric-a-brac now mar the sanctuary that stood so clean and attractive when first finished.

26 Madonna of the Poor

Via Alessio Oliveri at Via Baggio, Milan-Baggio
Luigi Figini and Gino Pollini, architects

The unfinished "warehouse" exterior of this church seems harsh, even repellent. The finished interior is, to many, likewise brutal, but it nonetheless proclaims an extraordinarily potent statement of thinking, deep thinking, in religious architecture. Figini and Pollini, who were among the very first modern architects in Italy and who did significant work as far back as the early 30's, wanted to create a mystic atmosphere in this church, with a subdued, meditative glow of light in the nave and a deluge of light in the chancel. Further, they wanted to achieve this play of illumination by indirect means and with no visible source. The nave is thus lit by an over-all

low-level of light from small panes fitted into the concrete-block walls. The presbytery, in contrast, is flooded with light from unseen windows placed in the ceiling of its high "tower" over the altar. The frame of the church is of raw concrete, daringly—and effectively—emphasized by the pierced cross-beam in front of the chancel. The altar is set forward in an open hexagon so that the priest faces the congregation during the service. This low "enclosure" will eventually be covered with murals; its present trappings and plants are shoddy substitutes. The crypt beneath the chancel is simple, strong, and impressive. Whether one likes it or not, this powerfully conceived and realized church should be seen.

27 Marchiondi Institute

Via Noale 1, Milan-Baggio
Vittoriano Viganò, architect

An apotheosis of the "New Brutalism," this rehabilitation school outside Milan has raised a storm of comment, pro and con, in Italy and abroad. It was built to replace a dingy in-town home for abnormal and difficult boys, and financed partly by private, partly by public, funds. Many of the determinants of its design were supposedly as much psychological as architectural. A total contrast to the prisonlike, confined atmosphere of the old was of course sought first. Thus the new is based on "free hospitality," contact with nature,

193

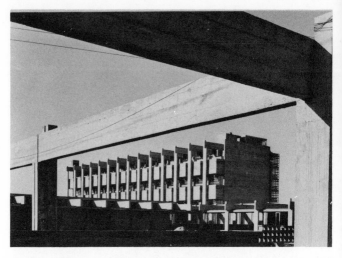

open layout and "transparent" buildings. The major part of the project has now been completed, and in assessing it one must find an obvious difference between the Italian and the U.S. or Scandinavian attitudes about what constitutes a friendly, hospitable building. It is unquestionably fascinating: craggy, powerful, assertive, it demands attention. Whether or not one agrees with the success of its intent or with the often involved elaborateness of its means, this compelling building belongs among the seminal structures of recent Italian architecture.

28 Apartment Hotel

Via F. Corridoni 22, Milan
Luigi Moretti, architect

With a clean, unflinching statement, the pure and elegant mass of this apartment block rises serenely above the architectural rabble that surrounds it. An apartment hotel, run generally on short-term rentals, it serves both working men and women. The former are housed in the 14-story block shown opposite, the latter in a 6-story unit placed at a slight angle. Connecting the two is a low entry with public rooms, restaurant, shops, and laundry. Allowed only single-room apartments of one window each—a restriction that permitted little façade interest—Moretti skillfully divided the tall major mass into two identical abutting buildings, and these he visually subdivided at the short end by the strongly ex-

194

pressed vertical line of the halls and their windows. By these means he achieved four elegantly proportioned slabs instead of one ponderous mass. In plan the buildings are straightforward, competent structures. The individual apartments are very well worked out, with a clever compactness that provides bath and limited kitchen facilities as well as closets and storage. Both buildings are faced with small (1 by 1.5 inch) white glass tiles.

29 Small Warehouse

along Padua-Venice highway, Padua

Angelo Mangiarotti and Bruno Morassutti, architects; Giovanni Morassutti and Aldo Favini, engineers

This shed for steel parts for a hardware firm—one of its several new units—has a significance beyond its own admirable realization, for it graphically shows the wonderful Italian inquiry into the design and structure of architectural problems no matter how seemingly insignificant. Industrial architecture has here been raised to a very high plane. The basis of this imaginative building lies, first, in a resolutely scaled frame of reinforced concrete—recalling, incidentally, current Japanese work in this medium—and second, in the quality of its roof. For this roof is no routine span, but an ingenious system of hexagonal steel pipes, 197 feet long, 3 feet in diameter, and 13.7 feet on center. The top halves of these transverse beams project above the roof line, giving an undulating effect to the profile. Let into the beams are a series of cylinders topped by hemispheric Plexiglas caps, which admit natural light and shelter the source of artificial. As the great hexagonal cross-beams are glazed at the ends, the artificial lights shine through, and the roof frame therefore glows after dusk, producing a remarkable feeling of lightness. The side walls are of glass and corrugated sheets of aluminum, some fixed, some sliding, and of concrete block. Highly creative.

30 Boys' Town

Trieste-Opicina

Marcello D'Olivo, architect

Just off the autostrada and nicely situated outside Opicina, a village in the northern suburbs of Trieste, this unusual—and controversial—group of buildings arose over a period of eight years. The Frank Lloyd Wright influence, so desperately evident in the over-all plan and in the design of the restaurant, which was the first building, evolved into a more personal expression as time went on. Maturity becomes especially evident in the printing shop, which though of little pretension on the exterior, reveals an interesting structural system. This

is based on four square, slightly separated, prestressed parasols of concrete, three of them 46 feet square, the other 69 feet square, grouped regularly about a smaller, lower square that acts as the communication core of the group. Each square workshop is devoted to a particular phase of printing. The dormitory, whose considerable length is well broken by strong vertical fins, is raised a story to provide a covered yet open space at ground level. The school block is attached to the dormitory and canted at one end. The church—in sketch form—has almost a Mayan quality in section, and a very dubious futuristic bell-tower. Full of faults—among them inexcusable Wrightian "decorations"—this nonetheless numbers among Italy's most interesting examples of so-called Organic Architecture.

31 Sacrarium
Redipuglia (SW of Gorizia)
Giovanni Greppi, architect

On the rocky countryside of northeastern Italy, near the Yugoslav border and between Gorizia and Monfalcone, rises Italy's finest monument to the dead of World War I. Here 100,000 "Unvanquished" lie in a series of platforms stepped up the hill that overlooks this tragic plain. At the entrance to this wide and terraced hillside is the monolith that contains the body of the Duke of Aosta, the commander of the valorous Third Army, and directly behind are the tombs of his five generals. Then in an impressive sweep of twenty-two enormous steps are buried the bodies of the 40,000 known dead. The unknown are grouped around the chapel located under

197

the three Crosses of Calvary at the top. Each grave on the regimented terraces of the hill has a bronze plaque bearing the man's name and organization, with the word *Presente* repeated as a frieze across the top. Although of dry restraint, this is an impressive necropolis.

32 E.N.I. Vacation Village
Corte di Cadore (9 miles SE of Cortina d'Ampezzo)
Eduardo Gellner, architect

For a number of years—since well before the last war—many Italian firms and industries have admirably engaged in building vacation "colonies" for their employees. To these, mothers and children and sometimes whole families can be sent for vacations at minimal cost. Among the most extensive—and successful—is this superbly situated village, which will eventually have accommodations for 6,000. With a backdrop of the breath-taking Dolomites, this provides a winter and summer vacation paradise for employees of the Ente Nazionale Idrocarburi. The "village" consists of a central social and shopping center with a number of residential zones grouped about it. The center contains all the group functions, including a hotel, church, school, health clinic, etc. The residences are single-family houses of varying sizes, all extremely well planned and designed. They are deployed over the mountainside in zones of 60 to 80 houses, accommodating 350 to 500 people. A fine feeling of entity identifies each subdivision. While Gellner's buildings in nearby Cortina are somewhat involved and overly complicated, in this vacation village he has achieved superb results. A sociological monument and excellent architecture.

Lulea 27

Borgafjäll 26

Jyväskyla 12

Säynätsalo 13

Imatra 11

Lillehammer 4

Mora 25

Gävle 24

Järvenpää 9

Gravberget 5

Turku 8

Kotka 10

Oslo 1-3

Fors 23

Helsinki 1-6

Eskilstuna 11

Hanko 7

Orebro 12-13

Stockholm 1-10

Linköping 17

Oxelösund 16

Gothenburg 14-15

Aalborg 14

Växjö 20

Aarhus 12-13

Orrefors 18

Helsingör 11

Karlskrona 19

Malmö 21-22

Humlebaek 10

Copenhagen 1-9

SCANDINAVIA

50   100   150 M

50 100 150 200 250 KM

SCANDINAVIA

The four northern countries—with a total population well less than half of France's or Italy's—have been the architectural paladins of the modern movement for thirty years. Sweden, Finland, Denmark, and—at a distance—Norway have had for years a greater private and official acceptance of the logic and beauty of modern architecture than any other countries in the world.

Contemporary architecture arrived like a bombshell in Scandinavia with Gunnar Asplund's famous Stockholm "Expo" of 1930. It has remained there ever since—with the usual hiatuses and obliquities expected in times of rapidly changing mores and techniques, to say nothing of wars.

With pioneers like Sven Markelius and the late Gunnar Asplund in Sweden, with a genius like Alvar Aalto in Finland, and with a man of the elegance and imagination of Arne Jacobsen in Denmark, a high level indeed can be expected. It should be pointed out, however, that the architecturally sensational rarely appears in Scandinavia. Often, especially in Sweden, the contribution will lie more in a neighborhood or group of buildings than in individual structures. And in all four countries it is the over-all average of competence which will impress one, not a few masterpieces amid mediocrity, as on the Continent. Furthermore, this broad plateau of attainment is not confined to the major cities: it is usually visible in the villages as well. Modern architecture is the accepted way of life and building, and it has been thus for years. Wherever one goes in Scandinavia one will find a relaxed pleasure in architecture, a delightfully human scale—not bombastic, not self-important—and a very deep respect for nature and architecture together—not in competition, not via a triumphant bulldozer. This bespeaks an educated, mature approach to life and to shelter.

NORWAY

Norway has been busy getting on its postwar feet, and as a consequence, its building until the last few years has been—like most of England's—primarily in an austerity mold, with the emphasis on housing and industrial construction. Even before the war, however, contemporary architecture in Norway never had the degree of acceptance—or achievement—found in the other Scandinavian countries. In many respects this can be explained by the fact that Norway's 1,100-mile-long mainland and its 150,000 islands are so barren that they are almost 70% uninhabitable, and so rumpled that, instead of large centers tied to world communications and ideas, scores of small villages developed. Then, from the early part of the last century until the first part of this, Norway was under the domination of Sweden, and before that it was ruled by Denmark for over four hundred years. It has thus had little opportunity to develop an architecture of importance in the past, and little time to do so in the present.

Norway's considerable contributions to the arts have been made by individuals like Ibsen, Grieg, and Munch; architectural contributions, which demand technical—and national—resources, and international germination, have been lacking. As a consequence only a limited amount of distinguished recent architecture appears in this charming country. Several very good beginnings have been made, and the hump has been passed, but it will be some time before Norway produces a large volume of significant new work. Norway's most brilliant man in the field of architecture, engineer Fred J. Severud, is now in the United States and is a consultant to many of this country's most progressive designers.

1 United States Embassy

Drammensveien 18, Oslo
Eero Saarinen, architect

Occupying a tight, triangular lot opposite the grounds of the Royal Palace and at the top of one of Oslo's main streets, this new embassy was built on a very demanding site. Saarinen acquitted himself well with its restrictions, producing a hard, even severe, building but one that is nonetheless striking and full of character. There is nothing but architectural muscle showing here, in spite of the plasticity of the fenestration and outside walls. These walls are structural elements, not mere curtains. The façade material, which was masterfully produced locally—as a result, a whole new industry was

started in Norway—is artificial stone made from pulverized green-black local granite and labradorite. With an in-and-out pattern of projections and recesses, the polished outside surfaces reflect light from the sky on the shade side, producing a changing checkerboard of shiny lights and darks—vitality even when there is no sun. The building proper has four stories and a basement. In the center—in High Renaissance style—is a full-height main hall, which is in the shape of a parallelogram and has circulation halls about it on all upper floors. A brick grille encloses this on two sides, and vertical teak fins enclose it on the other two; these warm accents are welcome in Oslo's northerly climate. A pool, 5 meters square, embellishes the center; it is hoped to have a piece of sculpture in it later. The United States Information Agency's library, with space for 20,000 books, occupies the front of the building on the second floor. In the basement, in addition to garage and services, there is a flexible 116-seat auditorium from which seats can be removed for receptions. John Engh and Henrik Kiaer were local associate architects.

2 Government Office Building

Grubbegaten and Henrik Ibsens Gate, Oslo
Erling Viksjø, architect

A northern variation on a theme by Le Corbusier, imaginatively carried out with pertinent contributions of its own. A competition for the design of the building was won by the architect in 1939, shelved by the war, changed—and much improved—over the years, and finished in 1959. The resulting 15-story all-concrete block on stilts, with semi-egg-crate fenestration on the sides and blank end-walls, exhibits a

203

striking and provocative feature—one that offers tantalizing possibilities for all users of concrete—in the pattern and decoration sandblasted onto its concrete structure. This, indeed, hatched a new art technique, and Carl Nesjar, who executed the designs, became a new type of artist. Dressed in rubber suiting, which completely covered his head and body, to protect him from air-blasted dust, Nesjar at work looked more like a well-armed invader from outer space than a brilliant artist. On the exterior the most prominent art-work covers the blank end-walls. The architect had the strength —guts might be more descriptive—to decorate these 15-story walls by carrying the floor levels through and filling the panels with abstract patterns repeated every other floor, the whole being realized as thin linear pattern. Very successful. On the interior the stairhalls are similarly decorated by a number of artists, including Picasso, who was reportedly very interested in such sandblasting. New techniques in concrete—especially with choice of aggregates—had to be created to allow full possibilities of such blasting. At times (as on the ground floor piers) this form of decoration gets out of hand, but in the main it is not only well and imaginatively done but full of promise for future development. There are a number of other good details throughout the building—and some which get involved and fussy. The most unexpected are the window spandrels of narrowly proportioned wood set in a pebbly concrete honeycomb. (Wood is cheaper than steel in Norway.) Although the building itself proves provocative in many respects, its location in a historic, very crowded section of mid-town Oslo appears questionable. Being commissioned for the government, it would seem that the new official center (of which this forms only the first unit) would perhaps have had far finer civic possibilities if placed along the Oslofjord.

3 Økern Old People's Home

Økernveien and Nordalveien, Oslo
Sverre Fehn and Geir Grung, architects

This long low handsome building, beautifully situated on a small plateau overlooking the capital, is a model of its kind. In plan it consists of three double-loaded main-wings joined top and bottom to make a symmetrical building around two open courts, with a separate, but similar, staff block for 33 parallel to the main unit. The central section contains reception, dining room, and kitchen—which rises higher than the sides and which is top lighted and ventilated—and a rank

of 9 bedrooms. The other two double-corridor wings contain bedrooms on each side, with service in the center, and a monitor roof bringing natural light and air to the halls. Across the bottom, looking outward, are 30 single rooms, while across the top, opening onto the courts, are the public rooms. In all, a total of 128 elderly people are accommodated, two thirds in single rooms. The courts are beautifully scaled as regards their width relative to the height of the low enclosing building, and are furnished with large reflecting-pools, which in twilight especially, add to the delight of the glass-bound public-rooms. Furthermore such enclosed courts are useful for a breath of fresh air in the Norwegian winters, when the unshielded hillside site of this building often is swept by the wind. Although a bit resolute in its statement outside, this is an extremely handsome building, municipally commissioned, one of which Oslo's town fathers can be proud.

4 Folk Art Museum

Maihaugen Park, Lillehammer
Sverre Fehn and Geir Grung, architects

Some 115 miles north of Oslo, at the head of the largest lake in Norway, lies one of the wonderful Scandinavian open-air museums of folk architecture and art. The largest such museum in the country, it has an outdoor collection of ancient provincial architecture; its new building (pictured) houses costumes and artifacts, an auditorium, and administration. The positive forthrightness of the new building and its raw concrete expression reflect the structural directness of the vernacular wood buildings about it. Other than glass, no shiny or polished materials were used. The new building steps precisely down the sharp contours of its site in three sections: a small wing, which contains storage and shops, on the uphill side; then the conjoined main museum, basi-

cally one very attenuated block that can be subdivided at will; and below, a separate but attached administration-block. The whole museum hugs the ground and is tied to its setting. In winter the bands of white concrete and the flat roofs piled with snow produce a highly indigenous effect, but in summer, it should be noted, the unrelenting great length of the main unit and administration building seem somewhat ill at ease against the domestic scale of the vertical pine backdrop.

5 Village Church

Gravberget (120 miles NNE of Oslo, 25 miles E of Elverum)
Magnus Poulsson, architect

Buried in the forest of a large lumber concern, and resembling an architectural bell-buoy in a sea of trees, this small church by the late Magnus Poulsson, recalls the romance of the forest. The exterior—a splendid statement of geometry, crisp and expressive—is sheathed on both roof and wall by the fish-scale shingles found on so much of the older architecture of Norway and Sweden. The interior is far too cosy for the international visitor, although undoubtedly it serves its isolated, local community admirably. The broad planes of the outside are chopped into small pieces within and are elaborately painted with traditional motifs. The exterior is excellent.

SWEDEN

Sweden's outstanding single contribution to contemporary architecture lies in its usage of urban land. This is unquestionably the most advanced in the world. Stockholm, indeed, has the most extensive planning and housing workshop to be found in any city anywhere. As city extension and urban rehabilitation are the most urgent architectural-planning problems facing—but barely touched by —most of the world, the lessons of Stockholm are of transcendent importance. In 1904 the city commenced a program of land acquisition and ownership which has been continued to date. Having thus for over half a century purchased virtually all the available land they could afford, the Stockholm planning authorities have now achieved the enviable, indeed unique, position of extending a city of 1,000,000 into unspeculated greenery on all sides. Stockholm, and to a lesser extent Gothenburg and Malmö, have been able to follow, since the mid-thirties particularly, a planned, if at times not brilliant, slum-free expansion as they have burgeoned.

The Vällingby-Hässelby-Blackeberg section in west Stockholm, the new Farsta in south Stockholm, and Kortedala in Gothenburg, all of which are illustrated later, are exciting testaments to Swedish land policy and land usage. No country does it better, or on such a large-scale basis.* However, lest the impression be given that

* Several other developments are worth a look, in parts at least, and generally more for their milieu for decent living than for startling architectural excellence. In Stockholm: Torsviks, on Torsviksvägen, Lidingö, by Ancker, Gate and Lindegren; Rei-

the system is immaculate, and that the housing itself is always distinguished—generally it is only pleasant—one has just to visit Biskopsgården in Gothenburg (housing 25,000 people) or Lorensborg in Malmö (2,500 apartments). Both are shocking.

In a different urban regard, there are those who question the wisdom of the new monumental commercial core of quintuplet 18-story skyscrapers for the very center of Stockholm (Hötorget). Although the subway system runs under its feet, and roads are being widened, and a 700-car garage placed under the new buildings, the decision to plant this great new density in an already impossibly tight section of town seems more than dubious. With the power of the city to get industries and offices *out* of town, the cramming of this concentration into a viewless, joyless, jam-packed area seems puzzling. The individual buildings (not all of which are completed), though done by five different architects, follow closely the undistinguished design of the first unit.

On the strictly architectural side—architecture and urbanism are fortunately rarely divorced in Sweden—the Swedes, along with the Finns and Danes, have achieved the highest general level of design in the world. Although this level is only occasionally punctuated with genius, it is almost never sullied with horrors. One might say that it has produced civilized cities with civilized buildings for civilized people. In many respects the high-water mark for individual buildings in Sweden was reached in the late 30's and early 40's. This "classic" phase produced such outstanding buildings as the concert hall (interior) in Gothenburg (Götaplatsen) by Nils Einar Eriksson; Asplund's law courts in the same city (Gustav Adolfs Torg) and his supreme Forest Crematorium (q.v.) in

mersholme, by H.S.B. Co-operative (dull buildings but wonderfully preserved island site in harbor); eight 17-story "point" houses at Näsbydal, Töby (7 miles north of city), by Vattenbyggnadsbyrån; the upper part of Gärdet (above Askrikegatan—more than 20 years old but still nice); terrace houses, Gröndalsvägen, by Backström and Reinius; parts of Danderyd (north of city); and parts of Älvsjö, Karrtorp, and Gubbangen (south of city). In Gothenburg: Guldheden, Guldhedsgatan (impressive in extent, but otherwise fairly routine buildings about pleasant shopping centers), and Järnbrott (southwest of city), both laid out by the Town Planning Office. In Malmö: Ribersborg, Limhamnsvägen (old, but well situated); and Sorgenfri, Sorgenfrivägen, by Jaenecke and Samuelson.

209

Stockholm, one of the great monumental works in our century; the delightful museum in Linköping (Vasa Vägen) by Ahrbom and Zimdahl; Markelius's elegantly simple pavilion at the New York World's Fair of 1939; and the theater in Malmö (q.v.), still one of the finest in Europe. This period also produced a number of very fine schools—probably the most forward looking in the world at that time—by Paul Hedqvist and by Ahrbom and Zimdahl. Bridges, too, were outstanding. In the immediate postwar period—which affected Sweden a good deal more than has been realized—municipal investiture produced a bureaucratic leveling and "statism" in architectural expression. As a result, with the exception of the large-scale developments mentioned, there was a certain lack of excitement in Swedish architecture until recently. Sweden could undoubtedly profit from another Asplund (1885–1940)—as could any country. In the last several years, however, a crop of talented younger men has arisen and is beginning to infuse new life, imagination, and experimentation into one of the most fertile fields in contemporary building. Anders Tengbom's technical-training school outside Stockholm, Carl Nyrén's church in Vällingby, Ralph Erskine's ski hotel in Borgafjall, and Engström, Landberg, Larsson and Törneman's chapel at Gävle—all discussed later—are top-flight buildings.

In closing this general preamble on Sweden's architectural contribution, health and medical care should be mentioned as two related facets of building; both are of considerable social importance, although not radiantly distinguished architecturally. The Swedes are world leaders in health and well-being and in medical facilities. They have built scores of cleanly designed sports centers and buildings all over the country, from such notable prewar buildings as Hedqvist's lovely Vanadisbad (Sveavägen, Stockholm), Ahrbom and Zimdahl's Eriksdal Hall (Ringvägen, Stockholm), and Westman's excellent indoor pool at Lund, to the multitudinous (but less distinguished) ones of today. The two great Stockholm hospitals are also important—and provocative in that their architectural philosophy is diametrically opposed: one great block for one versus numerous scattered buildings for the other. They are the Southern Hospital (Ringvägen) by Hjalmar Cederström, an enormous structure overlooking Ärsta Bay; and the Karolinska Hospital (Uppsalavägen at Karolinskavägen) by Sven Ahlbom and Carl Westman, a series of separate units sympathetically placed amid trees. In addition, Sweden has commenced an extraordinarily extensive—and enlightened—series of homes for the aged (who in Sweden, as in the rest of the world, are rapidly increasing in number). Over 400 of these homes have already been built; 180 more are under way or in the planning stage. This is magnificent for a country with only seven and a half million people. The best of the recent geriatric homes are by Reinius and Bäckström near Stockholm (Elfviksvägen, Lidingö); by Boustedt and Heineman in Munkedal (70 miles north of Gothenburg); and by Åke Lindqvist in Finspång and Motala (two towns west of Norrköping, in south central Sweden).

Note to the Tourist: Every few years Stockholm, Gothenburg, and Malmö each put out local guides—in English —to modern architecture. These are available in many bookstores, or the branch Svenska Arkitekters Riksförbund, at reasonable price. The Stockholm guide is by far the most complete, but with 230 buildings, each with stamp-sized photographs, it is not very selective. It does, however, have an excellent map.

1 Vällingby

Bergslagsvägen (via Drottningholmsvägen), Stockholm
Stockholm Town Planning Office; Sven Markelius, chief planner, with various architects

This new "town section"—not satellite city—in west Stockholm has more lessons to offer the cities of our times than any other development yet built. It shows to a beautiful degree how the suburbs that increasingly envelop the world's cities can be well-planned, parklike, viable centers, and not haphazard accretions strangled in transportation, mired in shopping, and frantic for enough schools and public facilities. Every road, every building location, every need for Vällingby's 23,000 inhabitants, was minutely planned before ground was broken. It is the embodiment of Sweden's intimate relationship between architecture and the land on which it stands. Virtually all the major decisions in the molding of Vällingby were good

ones: strict preservation of the landscape and trees; free
planning in space with fingers of green everywhere; separation of pedestrian and motor traffic; direct rapid transit to
the center of the city; full cultural and entertainment facilities; a great variety of housing types; one central plant for
heat and power. One can quarrel with minor decisions—
especially with some of the architecture—but the basic concept and its execution are superior.

One of the planning commission's basic decisions was to
give Vällingby a modified commercial, business, and industrial base that could employ up to 25% of the resident population. This was to prevent it from becoming a dormitory
suburb. Another decision was to give it a size exceeding that
of any new development in Scandinavia. In addition to its

own resident population, which, as mentioned, numbers 23,000, Vällingby provides a shopping, amusement, and employment center for 60,000 more people grouped about it in Hässelby and Blackeberg. All of these communities are directly and quickly tied together and to the city proper by a rapid transit (which becomes a subway downtown) and by a net of express roads. In addition, they are intimately related to the Grimsta Forest recreation area, about which they form a crescent with Lake Mälar the southern border. The development of the great Hässelby-Vällingby-Blackeberg area represents a magnificent concept and is a superb testimonial to the foresight and virtues of municipal land acquisition and planning.

Vällingby's centrum (by Backström and Reinius) combines commercial, amusement, and cultural activities for 80,000 people. It is built directly over the rapid transit and over the service roads for its 70 shops. No trucks are ever in sight. Automobiles, too, are confined to the periphery of the centrum. One of the now acute weaknesses in the design of the centrum is the lack of sufficient parking: since the center was first laid out the incidence of automobile ownership in Sweden has skyrocketed. (It is now the highest in Europe.) One still shops undisturbed by cars, however, and the centrum can be reached from most parts of the development without having to cross a single street. The designers of the shopping section, not content with making the ground on which one walks merely safe from cars, have also made it festive and gay. Circles of fountains convolute with circles of mosaics and are taken heavenward with spheres of rampant lamps. Vitality here is almost fairlike, and the general atmosphere, highly conducive to spending. The centrum radiates that elusive quality of downtown animation that is essential to the success of a suburb. It is important to note that this does

not stop after dark. Parts of the centrum are too rigid; the large illuminated signs are obnoxious; the theater, cinema, and clubrooms too crowded together; but the main achievement here is excellent.

Another of the basic decisions in planning Vällingby was to have a concentration of 10- to 12-story apartments grouped about the centrum. This places the greatest number of people not only near the shopping but next to the rapid transit station. Many of the special flats for old people are here too. For families with children, for those who welcome more intimate contact with nature, and for those with automobiles, there are walk-up apartments, row houses, and cottages farther out. Being by many different architects, the design quality of the various housing groups varies considerably. Among the better are the "point" houses by Hjalmar Klemming (Kirunagatan and Grimstagatan), the cross-shaped smaller units by Paul Hedqvist (Mörsilsgatan), and the new row houses along the northern edge. Vällingby has many faults but it is nonetheless the most faultless of new urban developments. Don't miss it.

2 Västerort Church

Vällingbyvägen 186, Vällingby, Stockholm
Carl Nyrén, architect

A brilliantly original and exciting small church—the finest
single building in all Vällingby and one of the most impressive church interiors one will see anywhere. A potent, theatrical play of natural light from an inconspicuous skylight
above the sanctuary provides the focus of the design. To
avoid a subterranean character, this skylight is supplemented
by a low band of glass giving onto a garden along the left
side and by a window placed high at right rear. Excellent
general illumination is thus produced. The whole interior is
of angled planes of raw concrete, with a sculptural quality in
antithetical contrast to the sculptured feeling of Ronchamp,
which was achieved with soft curves only. Interestingly
enough, when Le Corbusier visited Vällingby several years
ago this was the only architectural item that reportedly
evoked his admiration. The church was built for a group
belonging to the Swedish Mission Society, largely a Lutheran
organization, but permission for a separate church-building
could not at that time be given in the development of
Vällingby. It therefore had to be built as an adjunct to an
11-story apartment house (also by Nyrén), with mission
offices occupying the ground level of the apartment. A small
church on a small site attached to a towering building posed
a difficult design problem as regards identity for the church.
Nyrén largely overcame this by angled walls and sharply

canted roof, which he played against the rectangularity of the apartment behind, composing these elements for maximum three-dimensional effect on the church's tiny triangular site. No matter what approach one takes, the church, though small, has thus an identity. The interior, which normally seats 180, but which can expand into the office area via folding doors, was arrived at by means of extensive model-studies. Its final shape recalls folded hands. The excellent crucifix with its "Eye of the Needle" is by Fritz Sjöström. A powerful and wonderful interior, and an index of new religious thinking in concrete.

3 Farsta

Agestavägen (via Nynäsvägen), Stockholm
Stockholm Town Planning Office, planners; various architects

Farsta, at the southern terminus of Stockholm's rapid transit, bears many comparisons to Vällingby, its companion large-scale extension of the capital. Farsta's population is to be 35,000 (somewhat larger than Vällingby's 23,000) when the development is completed. Its centrum is very close in size and facilities to Vällingby's, and like it, serves neighboring communities as well as the local population. Gubbangen, Hökarängen, and Sköndal, plus shoppers from even farther out, will bring the total population served by the core to over 60,000. Heeding the need made almost desperate at Vällingby, Farsta will accommodate almost four times as many cars about its shopping center. And the great, ugly acres of autos are just as much a problem in Sweden as in the United States! At least they might have been divided by lines of evergreens (in both countries). The design of Farsta's centrum was carried out by Backström and Reinius, who also did the one at Vällingby. Interestingly enough, Farsta represents the "negative" of the earlier approach, for it is built basically around an open square of lozenge shape, whereas Vällingby's open area is largely wrapped around a solid square block of buildings. The Farsta piazza *parti* works well for the department stores and shops that face it, but tends to isolate the long flanks of shops and offices which will eventually spread out from this heart. All shops and offices are serviced from beneath via sunken roads. The rapid-transit station terminates one end of the plaza. The housing—not of an inspired mold—contends with far rougher terrain than at Vällingby. It concentrates 45% of the population in 3-story walk-ups and 23% in single-family housing, higher figures for these types than is normal in Sweden. Rooms and apartments, furthermore, are wisely larger. A sizable strip for light, clean industry has been set aside along the main approach road. The whole community will be heated by an atomic energy plant.

4 Gröndal Apartments

Gröndalsvägen and Sjöbjörnsvägen, Stockholm
Backström and Reinius, architects

These low-rental apartments are situated on a bare and blustery site overlooking Stockholm's harbor area. This the architects have transformed into a honeycomb plan of small sun courts—each painted a different color—protected from the wind. Besides the wind protection necessary and the economies realizable with a "star" unit, the architects sought a solution away from the constant straight-line pattern that determines too much housing. They felt in this case that it would be nice to come home to one's own "yard," bright with color and intimate atmosphere. As can be gathered from the aerial photograph opposite, the basic unit is a three-armed shape that can generate an almost unlimited variety of combinations to fit specific conditions of site or grouping. Each arm contains identical apartments of living room, kitchen-dining room, bedroom, bath, and large storeroom. The space between wings is

217

sufficient to prevent a shut-in sensation or too much noise reverberation. At Gröndal there are 216 units altogether, the group along the street containing shops on the ground floor. The success of this human, very intimate scale has led to a similar scheme by Backström and Reinius (Rosta Estate, Hagagatan, Örebro) and to copying by both French and American architects.

5 Skogshem (Employees' Training School)

Elfviksvägen, Yttringe, Lidingö (Stockholm)
Anders Tengbom, architect

An elegant and harmonious group of buildings: Swedish architecture at its most sensitive and characteristic. Beautifully situated amid ample trees on the edge of a small bay (north shore of Hustegafjärden), far out in northeast Lidingö, this "college" serves superintendents and young executives who come here for bush-up instruction and to learn new techniques. Its three main buildings are oriented toward the south, stepped down a slight hill, and grouped to form an open court. On the right, as one approaches, lies the hostel for students; in the center, and set back, the teaching and assembly unit; and on the left the 2-story reception and dining-room-kitchen block. The 2-story hostel has single rooms with bath for 70 students. Its simple, largely built-in, ash furniture was designed by Sven Kai-Larsen. The walls of the building, canted out as solid planes and alternating with the window returns at right angles, produce a saw-tooth effect of brick and glass. This breaks the length of the building, fits its profile into the pine-girt setting more graciously, and provides privacy for the rooms. The classroom block has two medium-sized (30–40 seat) lecture rooms, and a number of smaller discussion rooms, in addition to a large central assembly-lounge. The reception building contains office, sitting rooms, library, and services on ground level, with dining room and kitchen above. Two smaller units, for personnel, and a heating plant complete the complex. With its superb landscaping, keenly sensitive relation and grouping of the main buildings—note the angle of the long hostel, bent (but not at right angles) to state a spatial relation with the teaching building—and with its precise detailing and use of brick, copper, and wood, this is one of the finest new buildings in Scandinavia.

6 Forest Crematorium

Sockenvägen (via Götgatan and Nynäsvägen), Stockholm
Gunnar Asplund, architect

The Forest Crematorium is one of modern architecture's great buildings and a magnificent memorial to its designer, who died shortly after it was completed. If there is to be a "monumentality" in contemporary architecture, it can begin with this, a truly poetic conception. The extraordinary impact of the crematorium derives not alone from the building, but also from its superb setting; both were created by the same man. The gentle, silent hill, the rising grade that the great cross and chapel surmount, are partly built-up so that the utmost accord will prevail between structure and background, between geometry of building and freedom of nature. The ap-

proach to the crematorium traces up this gradual ascent, past the burial plaques, the cross, then the small chapels, and into the covered court in front of the main chapel. Here the relation of architecture to nature, the defined to the infinite, becomes most moving. Here the eye rests on the peaceful wood to the south, the small hill in the setting sun to the west, or turns to Joel Lundqvist's expressive sculpture, soaring heavenward through the open center of the court. Behind this symbolic sculpture lies the main chapel. This chapel, which can normally accommodate 300, is closed off from the court in front by a bronze-and-glass door that can be lowered into the ground. With this massive gate removed, the whole court becomes part of the interior, and hundreds can attend services. Unfortunately the interiors of the main chapel and the two smaller ones are not of the superlative caliber of the exteriors: their hesitancy, their lack of clarity and unity, remain in puzzling contrast to the assured serenity of the front. Behind, reached by a rear road, are the cremating chambers and services. Deeply impressive.

7 Trade-union Center (Folkets Hus)

Barnhusgatan, Stockholm

Sven Markelius, architect

This complex package, with theaters, congress halls, assembly halls, meeting rooms, and restaurant—backed up by a previously built office adjunct on Vallingatan—is one of Stockholm's

more fascinating buildings. Occupying a distressingly confined lot in an older section of Stockholm, its situation, though not prepossessing will, it is hoped, spark the rehabilitation of much of the neighborhood. (Just as New York's Lincoln Center will rejuvenate its west-side surroundings.) The Folkets Hus consists basically of a collection of meeting rooms, varying in capacity from 25 to 1,524. Because of the marked difference in grade between the two streets on which the building faces, the major assembly rooms are stacked and "interleaved" above one another for the entire central part of the building. The smaller rooms, many of which can be thrown together, are concentrated on the street façades. Sven Markelius first attracted the world's attention with a theater-concert-hall (at Hälsingborg in 1932): this new complex should carry on his epochal earlier experiments—it is his finest work.

8 Royal Gymnastic Institute
Lidingövägen 1, Stockholm
Wejke and Ödeen, architects

Gymnastics and physical instruction occupy an important part in all Swedish education; this institute was built to train young men and women as athletic instructors. Located directly behind the stadium built for the 1912 Olympics (on Valhallavägen) it uses these outdoor facilities. In addition to its own separate gymnasium buildings shown here, the group includes an administrative building with offices, museum, and

221

dining room, and, to the right, a building for experimental physiology. Thus all the facets of physical fitness, including research problems, can be studied. Architecturally, the gymnasiums are the only important units. These, although built of the most common materials, attain on the outside a distinguished, almost classic simplicity and refinement. The interiors of the gym halls are filled with exercise bars and equipment. A balcony corridor runs along the side with a full balcony (useful for instructors) at the end. Dressing rooms to the north are low, permitting cross ventilation in the gyms. The entrance hall and lounge in the administration building show good uses of wood. Lamps and furniture were designed by the architects.

9 Swimming Bath and Sports Hall

Bergslagsvägen 78, Bromma, Stockholm

Åke E. Lindqvist, architect

The Swedish athletic facilities, found throughout the entire
country, are almost always keenly designed. The new combination of facilities shown here (Åkeshovshallen), though
not shattering, is worth a look in the swimming pool area.
Placed so that it would be readily available to the nearby
grammar school, it provides in the building nearest the street
eight bowling alleys and services in semibasement, and men's
and women's locker rooms, showers, and a Finnish bath on
main floor. Behind, and rising above the butterfly roof of the
front building, are the main swimming pool building with
pool 85 feet long, and, at right angles, a small building containing another pool half this length. The outdoor sun-bathing
terrace, framed by these wings on two sides and by a grove
of oaks on the other two, achieves a pleasant atmosphere.
Beyond stretches a garden area for play and further sunning.
The interior of the large pool building is festive, with gay
lighting fixtures and a bright mural. Its fenestration, however,
is far too small in scale; it is better on the smaller wing. The
sports hall, which lies to the right, has four gymnasiums on
its main floor, and in its basement, the central locker room
and four small convertible rooms for boxing, table tennis, etc.

223

10 Stockholm's Parks

Stockholm Park Department
Holger Blom, chief architect

The parks in Stockholm are twentieth-century urban parks specifically designed to serve today's population in today's city. They are free and delightful space organizations whose function is antifunction. They are the foil to the mechanistic buildings they interpenetrate: the escape from the cramped apartment, the busy school, and the factory. There are parks for the old and for the young, for the mid-city and for the water's edge. The parks in Stockholm are not merely a collection of extraordinary green fingers tying the outlying countryside to the very center of town; they are part of the Swedish concept of life—a concept that demands contact with the freedom of nature in order to offset the indoor restrictions of man. The Stockholm parks and their furniture have no peers either in Europe or the United States. After experiencing them on foot, take a boat ride around the city and see from the water how even industrial areas are landscaped and comely. When there are no natural park opportunities, smartly designed movable flower pots, seasonally planted, are put at strategic corners. Among the better centrally located parks in Stockholm are Kungsträdgården, with pleasant snack restaurant, off Hamngatan; Berzelii Park at Nybroplan; Humlegården, with delightful "play sculpture" by Egon Moeller-Nielsen, off Karlavägen; and those along Norr Mälarstrand.

11 Fröslunda Centrum
Skogstorpsvägen at Sturegatan, Eskilstuna
Jon Höjer and Sture Ljungqvist, architects

A delightful residential and shopping center for 7,000, just south of the industrial city of Eskilstuna (79 miles west of Stockholm). Not only highly pleasurable to walk about in, the group has a clever and effective combination of building types, and ingenious multiple-use buildings. The main square

225

provides the key element with its L-shape "closed" by a squarish low block of shops on the diagonal corner. Full of lively urban know-how, it plays smartly with changes in level and textures, pulled together with just the right vertical accent by the 13-story apartment-house canted along the long arm of the L. The square defines a clear, easily grasped, easily orientable space. One knows at all times where one is and which way is out—and the ways out are agreeable ones, through trees, flowers, fountains, and sculpture. Beyond the main square lies the "garden" square, bounded by buildings on the east, the school on north and west and the "combination" (public cinema, school auditorium, and assembly) hall on the south. This adaptable building is also used by the National Theater, and, with the seats from its flat section removed, for dances and parties. It connects directly with the café and bakery on the pivotal corner of the main square, and from thence under a marquee with the other shops and the tall apartment unit. The public restaurant in the mezzanine of this apartment shares kitchen facilities with the school's second-floor dining-room overlooking the garden court. The school's woodworking and handicraft shops are used by the district's youth center at night. Beyond lies the semienclosed court of the school proper, with general classrooms at far end. Four 4-story apartment-blocks are grouped easily along the south side of the Centrum. An admirable urban development.

12 Water Tower

Hovstavägen, Örebro

Sune Lindström and Poul Kühl, architects; Vattenbyggads-byrån, engineers

The highly pleasant, and rapidly growing, city of Örebro, 127 miles west of Stockholm, has here produced an imaginative, entertaining solution to a difficult civic problem. Not only is this tower acceptable on the skyline, but with its panoramic aerial restaurant and gazebo, it rates as the prime attraction of the area. Furthermore it furnishes a striking example of prestressed concrete. The inverted conic top was poured on the ground to facilitate placing the reinforcing and to reduce scaffolding. The entire weight was then lifted by 32 hydraulic jacks while the stem was being cast beneath! The stem contains a spiral stair and two lifts, with television mast above. The restaurant-observation terrace is 150 feet wide, with a total above-ground tower-height of 190 feet. The tank capacity is approximately 250,000 gallons. A keen look at a pesky problem.

13 Baronbäckarna Housing

Hedgatan, Örebro

Ekholm and White, architects

In basic planning concept this is the finest "family" housing development in Sweden. Some 1,227 one- to six-room apartments are grouped around and open onto a loose but connected series of U-shaped courts, and these in turn encircle a large central coppice. All automobiles and garages are confined to the outer periphery, so that the open central area becomes an uninterrupted park and recreation ground. The small "yards" or courts at the same time take on the character of miniature piazzas where the children can safely play, neighbors meet and chat, where mother strolls to nearby shopping, and father returns from work. Considerable family life takes place in these, especially in warm weather, as the entrances to all apartments are on the yard side. In the winter the courts afford wind protection. So that mothers can keep watch over their children playing outside, all kitchens, living rooms, and balconies open onto the neighborhood courts. All bedrooms, on the other hand, open outward for greater privacy and less disturbance. The horizontal ratio between building height and yard width is such that there is no visual feeling of confinement, nor does noise reverberation become excessive. Parking, shopping, schools, kindergartens, laundries, and other services are integrated to make the development largely self-contained. Careful studies of colors were made at Baronbäckarna: on the approach, or outer, side, green, chocolate, and mulberry are among the hues used to differentiate the various "yard" sections. The inner yards, however, are all light gray and white, but with gay colors on the balconies. From the outside one is thus automatically steered to one's apartment grouping by a strong statement of color; within, the calm gray and white produce a feeling of unity and space, the accents of color on the balconies giving the necessary quiet vitality. Partitions between bedrooms are largely movable and can thus be adjusted to suit changing family conditions. Sensitive thinking throughout, and brilliant planning.

14 Kortedala

via Almanacksvägen, Gothenburg
Gothenburg Town Planning Office and various architects

Kortedala, an enormous, solely residential suburb just east of Gothenburg, has both positive and negative qualities. Its most obvious virtues lie in its land-usage, its strict preservation of nature, and its excellent landscaping. The great variety of accommodations available, from row houses to tower blocks, is also good. This not only produces more stimulating visual

results, it lets a family choose the type of living it prefers. The chief fault of Kortedala lies in the fact that it has little neighborhood quality, for one "coreless" apartment group follows another with too few community buildings as focal points. Other weaknesses lie in the insufficiency of its local shopping facilities, and in the quality of the architectural design of most of its units. (Each section was done by different architects.) In general the buildings are competent but undistinguished. However, the five 12-story triangular blocks (by Brolid and Wallinder) grouped around a traffic-free park and recreation ground are interesting if only because their denticulated balcony-edges restore to the profile of buildings an importance and interest almost lost today; these edges vibrate against each other in spirited fashion. The triangular plan of the blocks allows more sun on all sides than would a square.

15 Nya Ullevi Stadium

Skånegatan and Levgrensvägen, Gothenburg
Fritz Jaenecke and Sten Samuelson, architects

A rhythmic, flowing roof-line—the high swoops rising to mark the greatest depth of seats—distinguishes this imaginative stadium near downtown Gothenburg. The widest roof-span is supported from above by cables hung from two 174-foot-high concrete pylons, eliminating the need for intermediary stanchions. The remaining roof-section was easily cantilevered over the narrower banks of seats. Thus, as the protective roofing envelops the ovoid of the stadium, keeping the while a constant rake, it rises and falls in handsome wave-formation. The roof consists of a steel frame carrying lightweight concrete panels. The stadium accommodates 54,000 people, almost half under the roof, and has the novel feature of seats only (for 22,000) along the better half with standing room only (for 32,000) on the opposite side. Though the supporting masts for the roof cables (and for the artificial lights) seem unnecessarily rigid and angular, the stadium is good. In addition to football (i.e., soccer), other field sports, ice hockey (in season), and small-car racing can also be accommodated. The same architects have done a somewhat similar, but smaller stadium (31,000 capacity) in Malmö on John Ericssons Vägen.

16 St. Botvid's Church

Kyrkogatan, Oxelösund (SW of Stockholm, near Nyköping)
Rolf Bergh, architect

Perched on an escarpment overlooking its small fishing village and the Baltic, this commanding concrete church stands as a beacon by land and by sea. Its exterior is strikingly handsome, the openwork upper part recalling a bell buoy, while the splayed walls of the lower section visually anchor the whole to its rocky site. The tower carries a sympathetic echo of the bold structure of the traditional Swedish timber belfry —one of the most fascinating facets of wood engineering in Scandinavia. This is good, very good, and the church's square plan readily fits the building onto a site visible from all sides. However, on the interior, boldness is replaced by confusion, clarity of statement by finicky detailing. The elaborately sculptured backdrop behind the altar is hectic and distracting—a quiet, hand-woven Swedish tapestry would have been far better. The pulpit is angular and far too complicated, and the tinselly lighting fixtures are of a different breed altogether from the architectural statement of the room. Notwithstanding these inappropriate interior embellishments, the church, for its exterior, still merits an eight-mile detour if one is driving south from Stockholm.

17 Folkets Hus

Ågatan (behind Cathedral), Linköping
Sven Markelius, architect

This unusual combination of trade-union center (left), apartment block (center), and small office-building (right), plus restaurant, cinema, and four substantial meeting and club rooms, is diagonally opposite Linköping's thirteenth-century Cathedral. Its location, adjacent to one of Sweden's great historic monuments, posed a problem that Markelius, with that sensitivity found in most progressive Swedish architects, went out of his way to solve by keeping his building as quiet and respectful as he could, neither imitating the old nor compromising the new. Such a regard for the space and buildings about one is of course not limited to Sweden—nor to Italy, where the best men also practice it—but it appears too rarely in the U.S.A. The whole character, scale, and lack of insistence of this *folkets hus* is calculated to enable the building to fit gracefully into its setting. If it does not startle one, it is thus a success. The interiors, less inhibited than the exteriors, are more spirited. The decoration of the various public rooms—from the colorful theater, which seats 667, to the more subdued meeting rooms—closely relates to their functions. Interestingly enough, Markelius not only designs buildings such as this, but the fabrics that enliven them, and often the cities in which they are located (Vällingby). "All the same kind of problem," he says.

18 Orrefors Exhibition Hall and Museum

Orrefors (26 miles NW of Kalmar)

Bengt Gate, architect

The tourist motoring down the east coast of Sweden will find it worth while to detour from Kalmar to see the factory (ancient) and showroom (very new) of the famous Orrefors glass. The new building provides a simple but pristine background for the wares it shelters, and though based horizontally and vertically on a module of 4 meters (13.1 feet) it achieves a fine play of spaces in small size. The entry (1 unit deep) leads to the completely glazed exhibition room (5 units), where current production is displayed. The tiny museum (2 units long) at far end is totally enclosed except for one door and clerestories high on either side. The building is 2 units wide throughout and 1 high, with ceiling of redwood and floor of grayish-brown polished limestone. The glassware in the first hall is displayed both in the open and in cases, while that in the museum is all in cases. The showcases in both are elegantly designed: note, for instance, the use of threaded rods to support the shelves—far more flexible and attractive for glass than the intruding mechanics of pegs or hooks. The designer, appropriately enough, is the son of the late Simon Gate, until recently one of the great Orrefors artists. The architect visiting Orrefors will be invigorated by the newly expanded lamp division next door. A trip to the nearby (13 miles) Kosta Glass Museum, designed by Bruno Mathson, is also worth while.

19 Gullberna Mental Hospital (Gullberna Sjukhus)

Karlskrona (SE Sweden)
Lars-Erik Lallerstedt, architect

Most of the twenty major buildings that make up this mental hospital are not individually distinguished. Indeed the majority of them are quite fusty. However, its new concept of handling the mentally ill and the resulting architectural expression of this, plus the reasonable design of the central buildings, mark it apart. Restoration of the sick, not prison-like confinement, forms the essence of the hospital's philosophy. To this end there are no fences around the grounds and no gates; a group of small-scaled buildings traced through the trees and overlooking the water from a splendid unspoiled 125-acre site proclaim the hospital's creed, the "open door." Twelve near-identical buildings, six for males and six for females, can accommodate 800 patients. The men's and women's quarters are placed on opposite sides of the central public buildings. Tunnels connect all units. Staff quarters are located beyond the work and patient areas to the west. The central area comprises four buildings; three are connected to make a slightly splayed-out U-shape, which is semi-closed by the fourth. These buildings are for administration, medical treatment, assembly, and occupational therapy. The "square" they form is excellent in scale and landscaping, and is so designed that it creates a feeling of well-being and "belonging" for the disturbed people who pass through it. This is enhanced by a series of craft shops, beauty parlor,

235

and a café (shown in photograph), each of which is an element of therapeutic treatment. Kitchen and utilities are placed in separate buildings behind the central administration.

20 High School (Nya Läroverk)
Norra Esplanaden 2, Växjö
Åke E. Lindqvist, architect

A high school for 850 pupils in a progressive town in south-central Sweden with several unusual features—including a divertingly shaped auditorium (see photograph), and a basic classroom division into "subject rooms." The school authorities and the architect claim that 21 special rooms used for one subject only would in effect equal 30 multiple-use classrooms. These they put in small 2-story, squarish pavilions attached by glazed passages to the main school body. Each pavilion has three corner-classrooms, toilets, and services on the ground floor, and four corner-classrooms above. These pavilions give onto a large combination entrance hall, coatroom, and lobby—which is used for dances and parties on occasional weekends. The auditorium also opens off this central lobby, and is reached by two flights of stairs. Seating 600, the auditorium doubles as the town's concert hall and theater, the school lobby and cloakroom then being used by the public. A 4-story block containing lunchroom, kitchens, and

236

technical classrooms occupies the west side of the entrance building, with a double gymnasium at right angles. Though the architecture of the individual units is not brilliant (the "lapping" of the auditorium being ill resolved) and the planning is a bit formalistic, there are constructive ideas in this school.

21 City Theater

Fersensvägen and Rönneholmsvägen, Malmö
Helldén, Lallerstedt and Lewerentz, architects

This excellent theater for Sweden's third city is one of Europe's most important. Among its admirable points are its location at the head of a main street, next to a park, and the advantage taken of this position. At night the façade glows with light shining down the avenue, making the lobby and elevated promenade highly effective advertising media. The whole ground floor of the front part of the theater is devoted to entry and coatroom, one's seat ticket serving also as one's hat check. No mad rush, no elbows. A restaurant, open to the public throughout the year in addition to serving as a popular intermission snack-bar, adjoins the entrance at right, with access both from the theater and the pleasant square in front. Above the entry, reached by two generous staircases, stretches the glass-fronted promenade. This is full of space, Orrefors chandeliers, sculpture, plants, and elegant ladies. No wonder the theater is popular! The auditorium seats 1,200 normally but can be reduced in size by pulling out flexible walls of wood hung from undulating ceiling-tracks. Although the relation of the projecting stage to the auditorium is not as advanced as it is in more recent German theater experiments, the audience maintains good contact with the actors. An intimate theater, seating 104, is placed to the right.

22 Crematorium

Östra Kyrkogården, Sallerupsvägen, Malmö
Sigurd Lewerentz, architect

A personal, strangely moving crematorium by one of Asplund's former associates. This design is no ordinary turn of architecture: its effect stems from no shallow emotionalism, nor is its religious overtone the product of borrowed clothes. In a flat, dreary cemetery at the east end of the city, a subtle and disturbing pair of chapels have been built, each stone and board of which has been minutely studied. The most impressive achievement is found on the exterior, where the spatial relationships between the two buildings and their double-angled open porches (somewhat suggestive of north Italian barns) change and charge with every step. Very stimulating. Note, too, how finely every detail has been expressed, from the alternately locked granite-panel revetment on the supporting columns to the size and coloration of the thin stone in the walls. The two interiors, unfortunately, are not of this same sensitive caliber. They are dignified, but they do not proclaim the architectural profundity characteristic of the outside.

23 Cardboard Factory

Fors (N of Avesta and Krylbo, 107 miles NW of Stockholm)
Ralph Erskine, architect

The arresting features of this handsome factory stem primarily from the temperature and humidity demands of its industrial process in a cold climate. Cardboard is made with straight-line machinery, which in this case reaches 426 feet, during which length the water-carrying pulp undergoes various chemical treatments, pressures, suctions, and heat. In the process, enormous quantities of moisture have to be removed from the pulp and machines, and exhausted from the building. As this is done by hot air, a ruinous condensation would result in the cold Swedish winter unless special pains were taken to avoid it. The means employed by Erskine are evident on both the exterior and interior, and he has made the most of their esthetic possibilities. The long line of the mass of the building is broken near the mid-point by the extensive ventilating machinery. The air intakes, turned down against snow and rain, are carefully placed in the reverse curve of the wall. Within the building, the whole roof was built double to form an enormous hot-air duct so that condensate would not drip on the machinery below. The suspended ceiling, slightly bowed, is made of aluminum to reduce weight, upkeep, and cost, and to increase light reflection, for which purpose it is especially effective in winter when there is snow on the ground. The frame of the building is of concrete on 15-foot bays; walls are of yellow brick.

24 Crematory Chapels

New City Cemetery, via Rikshuvudväg 10, Gävle
Engström, Landberg, Larsson and Törneman, architects

Nestled in, almost invisible in, an unspoiled pine forest 2
kilometers west of town, these conjoined chapels form an impressive example of Swedish architecture. The architecture
is anti-architecture: a few broad horizontal planes floating
aerially over a series of vertical planes, the whole in sympathetic partnership with nature, visually and materially. The
exterior seeks out the forest, brings it into its courts and
partakes of it, while from within the continuous clerestory
brings a backdrop of natural trees into rooms whose lower
two-thirds are lined with rough-cut trees. Lally columns support the roof, and the band of clear glass joins vertical and
horizontal with a minimum of mechanics. A quiet atmosphere
of peace and eternity suffuses the whole. There are three
chapels altogether, each approached from a different side.
The two larger (the bigger to the right) have open court-
yards in front surrounded by pine revetted walls, which also
frame the lower section of the main building. These yards
have small waiting-rooms along the outer side, and these are
separated from their private court by only a plate of glass.
Several trees were left in each, and together with the admirable texture of the paving, they make these garden "preparation" spaces quite serene. The interiors of the large chapels
are simply glazed and heated extensions of the courts themselves. Pews, altars, and lamps—all designed by the architects—form the only furniture. The pews reveal a sparse and
appropriate angularity; but the lamps are hard and unsympa-

thetic. A service block, with crematory mechanism in the basement, connects the chapels. A wonderful building.

25 St. Michael's Chapel

Cemetery, Mora

Borje Blomé, architect

For all going to Dalarna, the lovely "heartland" province of central Sweden, the village of Mora (220 miles northwest of Stockholm) has two architectural attractions: Anders Zorn's famous open-air museum (Gammalgård) of ancient vernacular architecture, and this recent cemetery chapel. The chapel block, which actually contains a main chapel and a small ancillary one, is joined by an arcade to the caretaker's house and office. The cemetery lies behind. The chapels can be entered directly through two confusingly and unnecessarily symmetrical front doors, but the most pleasant approach is via the garden court and arcade. The exteriors are of secondary consequence—although the court is spatially pleasant— but the interior of the large chapel is very handsome. This is dominated by a magnificent mosaic cross, by Gert Marcus, "vibrated" across the sanctuary wall. Made of black, gray, and white tessarae, it not only achieves an eloquent statement in itself, it also shows how architect and artist can, and should, work together. Note that the altar is not behind the catafalque in front of the mosaic cross, but at one side, where it is bathed in direct light.

26 Sports Hotel

Borgafjäll (near Dorotea), Lappland
Ralph Erskine, architect

Its magnificent relation to its wild setting—it snuggles as "ground sculpture" in the terrain—its bold, original lines, and its use of local materials make this mountain hotel a model of organic imagination. In winter the hotel is one of South Lappland's most popular ski centers, enjoying snow for about eight months of the year. For the intensive, almost never-dark summer it is an excellent fishing and hiking resort. The architect sought the "protection" of the ground and the snow —as does the wildlife in these parts—in designing the building. He wanted it to grow out of the ground, to be a part of the landscape. He even had windscreens built at strategic points so that the wind would blow snow into sculptural forms complementing and emphasizing the gigantic ground-sculpture aspect of the whole. Inasmuch as the hotel is located over 70 miles from the nearest town and railroad, it was built almost exclusively of the district's own materials. There is, however, no rustic or folksy quality about it. The building is divided into two main sections with public rooms at one end and bedroom accommodations for 70 to 80 people at the other. Basic material is heavy timber, for insulation, availability, and looks, with the kitchen block in masonry, for fire protection. All furnishings were designed by the architect. Though at times the interiors get unnecessarily complex, this is an imaginative work.

27 Shopping Center

Storgatan at Kungsgatan, Luleå
Ralph Erskine, architect

Located less than 70 miles south of the Arctic Circle, this shopping center is the reverse—and perceptively so—of the loose confederation of shops that makes up commercial complexes in more temperate zones. In essence it might be said to be a warm, friendly, gigantic shell, with a variety of inner levels and spaces lined with shops, where the customer will find a welcome protected from outside rigors. Furthermore, to encourage visits even when buying is not an objective, amusement and cultural attractions are also incorporated. The first stage, which includes many of the shops, has now been completed. Though one is almost assailed by the variety of shapes, surfaces, and signs within, the over-all atmosphere suggests so much of an arctic "oasis" that already this has become a core for the city. When finished, it should develop into a lively enclosed piazza producing an entirely new concept of social life in the far north.

Finland is by many considered the most architecturally interesting country in Scandinavia, and one of the finest anywhere. In spite of the meagerness of its resources—agonizingly strained by wars and postwar reparations—and in spite of its lack of wealth, its small population (4,400,000), and its extreme northern position (the country parallels Greenland and Alaska), Finland's architects have made enormous contributions.

The country's first designer of note, the late and distinguished Eliel Saarinen (1873–1950), made his mark initially with his famous Helsinki Railroad Station (1910–14), still one of the notable monuments in that city. However, after his entry in the *Chicago Tribune* competition of 1922 won second prize—and enormous acclaim—Saarinen visited the U.S., settled here, and shortly after commenced the impressive Cranbrook School at Bloomfield Hills, Michigan. His son, Eero, born in Finland in 1911, is now one of the topmost leaders in American architectural development, achieving even greater distinction than his father.

The most famous architect Finland has produced is Alvar Aalto, the dean of its contemporary architects and its northern star. The youngest of the great masters of our time (he was born in 1898), Aalto is not only one of our greatest doers, he is also a great humanistic thinker. In the last half-dozen years especially Aalto has emphasized the individual as the generator of our buildings and cities, not a pawn to operate them. He has become increasingly dissatisfied with the pristine cube as an architectural answer and with architecture concerned with its own importance, and which, far too often, is rigidly wrapped in one sterile curtain-wall after another. More than any other great architect of our time, Aalto designs his work as an end and sympathetic environment for human beings, not as an end for itself. As Giedion says: "He has brought human warmth and intimacy to the turmoil of the world" (*Arkkitehti,* No. 1-2, 1958). Aalto's genius has not gone unrewarded either at home or abroad, and he now enjoys substantial commissions in Sweden, Denmark, Germany, France, and Iraq. His most famous prewar buildings are the Turun Sanomat Plant, Turku (1930), his first widely known building; the marvelous tuberculosis sanatorium at Paimio, 16 miles east of Turku (1933); the heraldic Library in Vipurii (1935), lost to the Soviets, abandoned but now reportedly restored; the Sunila plant (q.v.), near Kotka, whose first phase prewar buildings (1936–39) many feel are the finest that Aalto has ever done; the Villa Mairea in 1939; and his Finnish Pavilion for the New York World's Fair (1939). His outstanding postwar work (in Finland) is shown later.

Aalto is, however, not alone. A clever, sensitive younger group has also risen. Among its members Viljo Revell is outstanding; in 1958 he became internationally known when he won the Toronto City Hall competition. His clothing factory at Hanko (q.v.) climaxes his Finnish achievements, followed by an unusual school in Tuusula (with Osmo Sipari) and work at Tapiola (q.v.). Aarne Ervi, who designed much of Tapiola, has also done several strong powerhouses and, somewhat formalistically, work for the universities of Turku and Helsinki. Kaija and Heikki Siren are a talented husband and wife team. Their wonderful chapel at the Technical University (q.v.) received world acclaim. They, too, have worked at Tapiola. Finally the splendid hospital at Jyväskyla by Jonas Cedercreutz and Helge Railo should be mentioned.

All of the above, Aalto particularly, have developed in a tradition more of Scandinavian humanism than of international rationalism. This concern for the occupant, this self-reliance and self-evolution, as it might be termed, away from supertechnology, slick glass, and the cube was little noticed in the first decade following the war, but is now being fully appreciated abroad. Natural materials (particularly wood, brick, and copper) are also stressed. The above does not mean that a folksy romanticism is arising around the shores of the Baltic. It does suggest that a more human and personal style of architecture will be found in Finland—and its northern neighbors—than elsewhere in Europe.

Comment on Finnish architecture would not be complete without reference to the complementary arts of furniture design, textiles, and handicrafts—in which the Finns are outstanding. In the last two Triennales in Milan they have won more than twice as many Grand Prix (12) as any other country except Italy (14). The architectural climate in Suomi—except for the weather—seems bright.

1 National Pensions Institute

Mannerheimvägen at Nordenskiöldsgatan, Helsinki
Alvar Aalto, architect

A strong, impressive statement in red brick and copper:
dignity without pompousness. Its sloping, symmetrically
triangular site (not far from the Olympic stadium) imposed
severe planning difficulties and gave rise to a solution that,
on the stepped-back flanks especially, is very expressionistic.
The complexity thus largely generated by the location produces a type of building far from the "rationalism" and
pellucid clarity of Aalto's prewar work. To some this seeming indeterminedness comes as a disappointment; to others
it carries a welcome affirmation of attack on what Aalto himself terms "Parallelepipeds of glass squares and synthetic
metals—the inhuman dandy-purism" (*Arkkitehti*, No. 1–2,
1958). The result in this case is a warm, glowing building of
friendly scale, stepped around a private garden and pool
that are raised slightly above street noises and disturbances
and that form the visual focus of much of the building. The
site, level changes, work flow, and design considerations
gave rise to a building of eight stories (including basements)
in some parts and two in others, with a lofty single story
(and basement) staff restaurant in the garden. The public
has access only to the large central hall at the entry on the
point of the triangular site. This is a room two stories high,

with steeply pitched inverted-V double-thick skylights in the ceiling, the outer "skin" of which is in Plexiglas. Counters as well as an extensive series of small cubicles for private consultation occupy the work space in this hall. A toplighted research library (recalling Vipurii) and the restaurant in the garden are the two other large rooms in this 350-office complex. All furniture and fixtures were designed by the architect.

2 Rautatalo Office Building
Keskuskatu 3 (Centralgatan 3), Helsinki
Alvar Aalto, architect

This discrete 8-story office-block for a steel corporation—its name means iron in Finnish—does not create architectural fireworks, but it merits a look. Adjacent to a romantically arcaded building done in 1925 by Eliel Saarinen, it carries out only the roof line of its neighbor, but its own quiet restraint keeps it gracious in its ambience. The most unusual feature of the façade is its projected "frame," which extends slightly in front of the window plane and is horizontally aligned with the window sills (i.e., waist level within). Thus the frame does not reflect the floor level. The tops of the window frames on each floor are actually on a level with the finished floor above, a splay upward in the outer concrete frame permitting this. The façade and roof are finished exclusively in copper in both flat and corrugated form. Within rises a 3-story "Marble Hall" with gay little café and shops, and two gallery floors of shops above. This is lit by a series of circular skylights, above which are placed artificial lights; the source of illumination thus remains the same day and dark. A certain heaviness characterizes the unbroken depth of the gallery balustrade, but the over-all "interior piazza" atmosphere is attractive. The famous Artek Shop occupies one corner of the building, adjacent both to the street and to the inner court.

3 House of Culture
Sturenkatu (Sturegatan), Helsinki
Alvar Aalto, architect

A sometimes fascinating, sometimes puzzling bifurcated structure in north Helsinki. The fascination lies in the wonderful, towering band of unbroken brick wrapped around—with ideas of its own—the 1,500-seat auditorium on the left. The puzzlement resides in the distracting marquee across the entire front, the unprepossessing entry, and the fact that the 5-story office-block on the right has too little family relation to the great mass opposite. The building was built for the Finnish Communist and other left-wing parties as a "house of culture," with propaganda never far away; it carefully provides more seats than any other assembly hall in Helsinki. The exterior of this hall carries an impressive statement, and plays with the sun dramatically. Selected angles suggest the fortified cathedral of Albi in the south of France. Its heavy concrete walls, soundproofed against traffic noises, are revetted externally with a special square-faced, wedge-shaped brick, which Aalto designed; the wedge permits it to be laid with a narrow radius. A precise and thin coping terminates this sinusoidal red wall, with a steeply pitched copper roof rising behind. Within, the congress-concert hall creates a pleasant intimacy, marred slightly by distracting acoustic panels on the side walls and an overelaborate lighting system near the stage. The first eleven ranks of seats about the stage are on a flat floor and can be removed for special events and dances. A large foyer with adjacent restaurant takes up the ground floor. A cinema for 300, garage, and storage are placed in the basement.

4 Alppila Church

Viborsgatan at Kotkagatan, Helsinki
Keijo Ström and Olavi Tuomisto, architects

A compact but manifold religious workshop, dominated by the church proper, in a poorer section of north Helsinki. The commission resulted from a competition. A gymnasium, 15 clubrooms for various youth and young adult organizations, and several apartments—plus a triangular lot—complicated circulation and imposed difficult problems. These, however, were well solved. The church itself has an appealing freshness, inside and out, largely due to its white painted-brick construction. The nave, although somewhat marred by heavy detailing about the altar, has a simple worshipful atmosphere. The church seats 500; 200 more can be added by lowering an unusual concrete wall-panel on the right side. Of necessity

chopped up in the over-all, the nave is well worth a look if one is in the vicinity.

5 Tapiola Garden City

Tapiola (5 miles W of downtown Helsinki)
Aarne Ervi, chief architect

Tapiola is a lovely, well-planned community to the west of Helsinki and separated from it by a picturesque series of islands and bays. Although unfortunately in little contact with water itself, it does enjoy a 640-acre site of unspoiled forest land. Established by Heikki von Hertzen in 1951 with a special housing foundation supported by six trade-union and social-welfare organizations, a competition for its design was held in 1953 and won by Aarne Ervi. The entire project will not be completed before 1962. Its avowed purpose is to create "a socially and above all biologically suitable environment for man to live in," a setting in direct contrast with the soul-crushing, unhealthy city. Tapiola is divided into three residential zones well separated by green belts; each zone has 4,000 to 6,000 inhabitants, 26 to 30 people per acre. Two of these have thus far been built. Each residential unit has its own shopping facilities and schools, but an over-all town center with a 14-story office building, extensive shops, theater, library, large restaurant, and church will soon be commenced. In addition to the 15,000 population of Tapiola itself this

centrum will serve an additional 15,000 people from the surrounding neighborhood, particularly the new Technical University at Otaniemi, just northeast of Tapiola. Busses on frequent schedules provide 15-minute service to downtown Helsinki. A considerable variety of housing abounds, from single-family detached houses to 11-story apartments, with 3- and 4-story walk-ups predominating. Each dwelling, even those in tall apartments, has its private allotment-garden. Ninety per cent of the accommodations are owned by their tenants. Intimate contact with nature, freedom from traffic, a human scale, were all prime considerations in planning the housing. A further effort was made to alternate housing types and sizes to provide greater visual variety and social intermingling. The close following of contours by the housing at times produces awkward angles, but in the main, building relations are satisfactory though not distinguished. Nowhere does a rigid, abstract formalism appear. The designs of the various housing types, being done in neighborhood groupings by a number of different architects, vary from the fairly good to the very good, the 11-story block (by Aarne Ervi) attached to the cinema in the local shopping center being among the best. Viljo Rewell has also done several good buildings, especially three identical 7-story blocks, and Kaija and Heikki Siren have done some nice row-houses and a pleasant school. A limited amount of light industry is being built; this will employ some 15% of the population. A central plant provides heat and hot water. One of the finer suburban developments in Europe.

6 Chapel of the Technical University

Otaniemi (6 miles W of Helsinki)

Kaija and Heikki Siren

A totally ingratiating chapel, nestled intimately among the trees and indeed almost growing from them. For many Finns nature itself is a pantheistic religious expression and experience and this sensitive chapel is scarce more than a shelter in its lovely setting. It might be said that the Sirens made the chapel as simple and pure as possible and left the rest to nature. One approaches by a path winding through the pines. The gracious entry forecourt of the chapel is formed by two low solid walls (extensions of the sides of the church) topped by a horizontal screen of slender wood rounds. The wall closing the end of this court consists completely of these wood rounds, stained dark and separated slightly so that light and space flow through them. An elevated belfry in the court—which stems from the churchyard tradition of old Finnish churches—is also of these slender rounds. On entering the church, passing two meeting and conference rooms that are separated from the nave only by folding doors, one feels in immediate contact with nature again, for clear glass overlooking the forest fills the whole chancel wall. To further this intimate identity with the setting, the cross is placed outside the church directly behind the altar. At night this is spotlighted. A day glare would normally result from such a window-wall facing the congregation, but the Sirens cleverly counterbalanced this by providing a window 50% larger behind and above the congregation. The side walls are of natural red brick. Four exposed deep wood trusses with horizontal bottom chords visually lower the pronounced slant of the wood ceiling. This is one of the finest new churches in Europe. (Be sure to take a look at the surrounding university —site plan by Aalto—especially interior of the student restaurant by the Sirens.)

7 Knitted Goods Factory

Hanko, Hopearanta (90 miles W of Helsinki)
Viljo Revell, architect

An extraordinary factory composed of two long blocks, parallel to each other. The smaller (85 feet distant from and 10 feet lower than the other) is bridged and connected to the larger by three wings elevated on stilts. Parks and a pool flow underneath. The upper block, some 725 feet long, houses all fabrication and machinery. Air-conditioned and artificially lighted, it is capable of almost unlimited straight-line future expansion. Power plant and 2-story dye-room are directly behind. The three "flying" office wings contain administration, locker rooms for over 200 employees, and special departments. The long wing at lower level (and at right angles to the elevated offices above) contains reception, guest room, general staff restaurant, kitchen, and recreation room. Glazed from floor to ceiling in clear glass, it permits the bosky setting to be an intimate part of the interior. The factory and office wings are also well glazed and are clad in white anodized-aluminum. With its airy elegance, reflecting pool, lively piece of sculpture by Arni Tynys, and parklike setting, the group has more the atmosphere of a country club than a clothing factory. A scintillating addition to industrial architecture.

8 Cemetery Chapel

City Cemetery, Turku (Åbo)

Erik Bryggman, architect

This famous church by the late Erik Bryggman was one of the first to draw international attention to Scandinavian religious architecture. It was finished in 1941. Though the exterior is ill-resolved in parts, the interior remains so ingratiating that it is included here so that the tourist taking the Stockholm-Turku boat can have it on his agenda. It is located off the main road to Helsinki, southeast of the city. The exterior shows boxiness and heavy detailing, but the wonderfully asymmetric nave radiates charm. The soft arch framing the chancel also screens the full window behind that gives a sweep of light across the sanctuary wall. The low aisle on the right is separated from the trees outside by full-height sheets of glass, so that the interior of the church is intimately tied to its cemetery setting.

9 Cemetery Chapel

Järvenpää (22 miles N of Helsinki)

Tarja and Esko Toiviainen, architects

A simple, ingratiating cemetery chapel, well stated in concept
and structure, well finished in detail, well worth a drive from
Helsinki. The over-all plan is a rectangle, one third of which
consists of an open but framed porch—an intermedium between nature and enclosure—punctuated by a freestanding
cross. This entry "court" opens into the vestibule, with
benches and hooks for coats, and this in turn leads directly
into the chapel proper. This square chamber has solid brick
walls below and continuous clerestory above. Unfortunately
the clerestory is not shielded by an overhanging roof, so a
certain amount of glare assaults the congregation during daylight services. The room itself is pleasant, however, with an
accent of a nice tapestry (by Laila Karttunen) directly behind the catafalque on which the coffin is placed, and by which

it is lowered into the basement before interment or crema-
tion. Behind the sanctuary wall on one side is the choir,
separated from the nave by deep mahogany louvers, and on
the other a small "relatives' room." Stairs to the basement
are placed between.

10 Sunila Sulphatecellulose Plant

above Kotka (86 miles E of Helsinki)
Alvar Aalto, architect

Architecturally this is the finest and probably the most famous
industrial complex in the world. Completed in its first phase
in 1939, it was expanded from 1951 to 1957. The plant is
located at the mouth of the Kymijoki River across from the
port of Kotka; thus it can receive directly the logs floated
down from the interior and can ship out the pulp by ocean-
going freighters. The factory rises on a small but rugged
island, the natural features of which Aalto preserved as much
as possible—instead of bulldozing. As a result a magnificent
massing of units builds up along various levels. One of the
most striking features of the buildings is the expressive
variety of shapes and forms that each takes. Here stands no
uniform, pat module, but a series of bold statements, a clear
functional expression in brick and concrete dramatically tied
together by airily supported conveyor belts. Each unit states
its own form and is visually tied to the others by consistent
use of materials: variations within unity. On the mainland
behind the industrial island, and well out of sight in an ex-

tensive pine forest, are the housing and various community facilities, in effect an entire village. The new units here lack the light clarity of the early ones, but together they form an extraordinarily benevolent group of employee housing. As an industrial complex Sunila reigns supreme.

11 Vuoksenniska Church
Imatra (166 miles ENE of Helsinki)
Alvar Aalto, architect

In eastern Finland, within sight of the Soviet border, a group of industrial communities has coalesced into the spread-out town of Imatra. The visitor is not certain that these settlements have found the town yet, but Aalto has drawn up a wonderful plan for future development and given it testament with this unusual church. The master's first firm interest in sinusoidal forms was expressed in the marvelous undulations of the Vipurii Library ceiling (1935), continued in vertical form in the startlingly fresh Finnish Pavilion for the New York World's Fair (1939), broadly stroked in the river façade of the M.I.T. Dormitory (1948), and has come home to roost in the House of Culture (q.v.) and this church (both 1958). The rounded ternary form of the plan here arose through function, not whimsey. It evolved so that the church could accommodate three separate weekday sessions at one time—such lay functions being the greatest stress of the church—or all sections could be thrown together on

Sunday, when they can seat almost 1,000. Thus a funeral, a church guild, and a youth meeting take place at once, no unhappy cross-traffic occurring, no adjacent noise penetrating those massive concrete sliding doors. From a captious viewpoint it might be said that the resulting church is a reasonable solution to a somewhat unreasonable premise. However, though a superfluity of overlapping means was used—no two windows being alike among other things—a surprising effect of winsome simplicity results. As one enters one is projected into a pure white environment of highly friendly scale. Decidedly there are three sections to the church, apparent in plan and emphasized volumetrically by the fact that each divisible section is vaulted separately, but this does not altogether negate a total atmosphere of religious repose. This is an exciting, if at times arbitrary, building, full of alive spaces that must be witnessed to be appreciated. Bizarrely enough for this part of the world, a freak tornado destroyed many of the trees among which Aalto had carefully placed his church, leaving the exterior more bereft than intended.

12 University and Teachers' College
Seminaarinkatu, Jyväskylä (182 miles N of Helsinki)
Alvar Aalto, architect

Aalto was born near this key center of south central Finland (1898), went to school here, and two years out of the Technical University, designed and built his first building here—a sturdily neo-Classic *folkets hus* (1923–25). It is appropriate that he has lately returned to do this important group of buildings on the outskirts of town—a group deployed easily on the sloping site about a central garden. The university's architecture has a studied informality of grouping that seems almost haphazard both from the open south end and from the north (main) approach, which is alongside the auditorium. Other features, both pro and con, reveal a complexity both in plan and form (especially in the auditorium and the classroom building to which it is attached), an interesting number of brick terraces on the "garden" side of the two restaurants and dormitory, a clean-cut statement of the various buildings (in contradistinction to much recent Aalto work no curves or soft shapes are used), a play (particularly in the auditorium-class building) of blank areas of brick alternating with glass, and a feeling of contact with setting. Some of the above is negative, some quite positive. In any case the university provides an interesting, if at times uneven, group of buildings certain to provoke a response.

13 Town Hall (Kunnantalo)
Säynätsalo (8 miles SE of Jyväskylä)
Alvar Aalto, architect

Aalto's "revolt" against what might be termed the Miesian cube is nowhere better illustrated than in this community hall for an island village of 3,000 in central Finland. The Finns' almost passionate love of and respect for nature cannot brook a cubic intrusion into the wilderness, and Aalto has sought in this unspoiled setting to be as architecturally gracious as possible. This sensitive group on an uneven site consists of a U-shaped block with municipal offices, council chamber, and two apartments, faced by a detached library. The whole is built around an open court raised by uneven grade a full story above ground level on three sides. Various shops, a bank, and post office are placed beneath, opening onto street and sidewalk. Apartment units and the offices for the local plywood company—the village's chief employer—are nearby. The commanding interest in the Town Hall lies in its undeniably picturesque architecture, particularly the southeast approach up grass-planted, irregularly shaped stairs (see photograph). San Gimignano and Italian hill towns have been mentioned as influences (*Casabella*, No.

200), and there is undoubtedly much primitive and unin-
hibited (but here calculated) joy of shapes in space, and a
verity of natural materials in Säynätsalo. Aalto feels that too
much contemporary architecture has been homogenized and
overpurified. This town hall stands forth as his most positive
contrecoup. The interior of the council hall has a pair of
marvelously imaginative wood trusses, which splay outward
into eight auxiliary supports on either side. This small building represents the apotheosis of The New Humanism.

DENMARK

The new architecture in Denmark, like the hospitality of
its people, is friendly, elegant, and imaginative. As does
most architecture in Scandinavia, it shows a keen sensitivity to scale—a "chummy" scale Frederick Gutheim
aptly calls it—to materials (here primarily yellow brick),
and to detailing and color, especially on the inside. With
a flat, unprotected landscape, and in winter a damp,
windy, and dour climate, the importance of a cheerful
interior is primary. Largely as a result of the above one
might say that the main contribution of contemporary
Danish work is to be found in interior design and small-
scale building. The Danes, even in housing, do not build

with anything like the vast scope that is common in Sweden and Finland. Although they have built one fairly extensive—and fairly good—project at Bellahöjvej, Copenhagen, a Swedish Vällingby or Finnish Tapiola is not in the Danish blood. This can perhaps be explained by the fact that although Denmark and Finland have roughly the same population (around four and a half million), Finland is eight times as large, or one eighth as dense. (Sweden has less than one sixth and Norway less than one ninth the density of Denmark.) Denmark furthermore has no natural resources for building except clay, so that a reinforced-concrete construction with brick panel-walls is typical for larger structures, with brick bearing-walls and tile roofs for smaller. The country must get most of its wood and all of its metal from abroad.

The architectural training at the Royal Academy in Copenhagen has evolved consistently and with enlightenment through the years so that the wretched academy-modernist struggle did not hamstring architecture in Denmark as it did in France, for instance—and still does in several countries brushed by the Atlantic. Beginning with their excellent instruction and continuing throughout practice, Danish architects more than any others concern themselves with all facets of building, down to the paper or paint on the walls and the furniture on the floor. Not as capable as the Swedes in planning and architecture-and-environment, they are cleverer and more imaginative at the other end—detailing and furnishing. Indeed, Danish architects are probably the most sensitive in the world toward this important—and in the U.S. neglected—aspect of building. The Royal Academy has, for instance, an excellent department of furniture design. Thus men like Finn Juhl and Hans Wegner, plus a half dozen younger ones, are turning out what is unquestionably the most elegant production furniture available. Ability to deal with all kinds of interior and furniture work can be seen afloat in Kay Kørbing's sophisticated M/S *Princess Margrethe*, which plies between Copenhagen and Oslo.

Denmark's outstanding architect—one who works from housing to landscaping to wallpaper—is Arne Jacobsen. Jacobsen since the early 30's has been turning out the country's leading work. His Bellavista Flats of 1934 are still wonderful. His housing has continually sought fresh

261

statements and a personal stamp. His Søholm Row Houses (q.v.) near Bellavista are the climax of this search, but other projects of interest can be seen in his apartments for young people on Hørsholmvejen, Gentofte, and on Jaegersborg Allé. All three of these have rediscovered, so to speak, the interest roof lines can give. Jacobsen has also built several town halls, of which the latest, at Rødovre, is illustrated. Two earlier ones—designed before the war—which have some points of merit are at Aarhus and Søllerød, the latter a suburb of Copenhagen. His Munkegård School (q.v.) has been called the finest school in Europe. Another, more modest but still interesting, school is at Hårby, a town in southwest Fyn, the major island between the capital and the mainland. Jacobsen of late has occasionally let U.S. prototypes overly influence him (e.g., Rødovre Town Hall and the new S.A.S. building), but even then he uses the curtain cliché with logic and finesse, while his interiors are superior. His major works will be illustrated later.

Two architects of mark who bracket Jacobsen in age are the distinguished and genial Kay Fisker—architect (Aarhus University; the new Nygaard Section of Bröndbyöster, west of Copenhagen; etc.), chronicler, and teacher—and young Jørn Utzon, the brilliantly imaginative winner of the competition for the Sydney, Australia, Opera House. Utzon may well develop into the most personal and challenging designer in Scandinavia. The future of architecture in Denmark is promising: there will not be a flood of outstanding new work but the best will be top notch.

1 Munkegård School

Vangedevej, Gentofte, Copenhagen
Arne Jacobsen, architect

This original and wonderful building represents a very fresh look at school design. Designed for 1,000 boys and girls between 7 and 16, it is laid out in an unusual checkerboard pattern, based on east-west class-blocks served by north-south corridors. Four rows of classrooms run east and west, giving south orientation to the classes. All rows are identical, with eight single-story classrooms, except the last, or back, row, which is two stories high and has special rooms, labs, kitchen,

and the library. The four rows are divided from each other by three rows of garden courts. Access to the various classrooms is via five north-south corridors, each corridor serving two classrooms per east-west row. Administration, assembly hall, and faculty room occupy a middle block, dividing the upper grades (left) from the lower (right). Bicycle sheds and three gymnasiums are detached and placed in front, the double gym (left) for the older children being adjacent to their large playground. The kernel of this plan can be seen in the unusual classroom-and-court that Jacobsen devised. The classroom is divided into two sections, a class proper, approximately 25 feet deep by 23 wide, with an anteroom 9 feet deep by 23 wide beside it but separated by wall and clerestory. This serves as coatroom and for group activities. Light for the class pours in from the large south-facing main window and a high, set-back "roof window." Each classroom opens onto a court, which it shares with the adjacent classroom. These open-yet-protected yards are one of the great features of the school. In addition to serving as teaching spaces in favorable weather, they double as recess areas through the year. Each is different in treatment though identical in form. Each has a different paving, different landscaping—all by Arne Jacobsen—and each is embellished with different works of art. Thus a distinctive, intimate individuality runs through the entire school, making it far more child-scaled than its capacity of 1,000 would normally indicate. Construction is primarily of yellow brick, which is double and

sand filled between the classrooms. The roof is aluminum. Munkegård has lessons for us all—it is the finest secondary school in Europe.

2 S.A.S. Building

Banegaardspladsen, Copenhagen
Arne Jacobsen, architect

A handsomely assured air terminal and 22-story hotel—the highest building in Scandinavia—directly opposite the Copenhagen Central Station and diagonally across from the delightful Tivoli. It comprises two distinct sections: a long, low block and a skyscraper surmounting it. Scandinavian Airlines System occupies the north half of the low slab, with the south half (on the square) taken by the Hotel Royal. The prismatic tower houses the hotel's 275 well-finished bedrooms. In exterior form, materials, and spirit the influence

of American skyscrapers, particularly Lever House, is evident, too evident. One would have liked more native imagiation here, especially when that native imagination is so outstanding. But within, the relaxed scale, agreeable simplicity, excellent colors, meticulous detailing—all superbly carried through in the furniture as well as in the architecture—are very commendable.

3 Langelinie Pavilion

foot of Amaliegade, Copenhagen
Eva and Nils Koppel, architects

Set at the mouth of the Inner Harbor, opposite the ancient
Vaubanesque citadel of the city, this pristine restaurant and
club occupies an enviable position. The commission for its
design was won in competition. The building forms three
square layers: a ground floor containing covered drive and
entry, bar, and services; a main floor, cantilevered on all
sides beyond the lower, containing restaurants and kitchens
and a smaller square atop for the premises of the Royal Danish
Yacht Club. A broad dropped dining-terrace with splendid
view of the harbor projects on the east. The entry floor—
with a large open fireplace cheerily greeting one in the center
of the hall—is almost totally enclosed. Thus when one leaves
this meeting hall or the bar and mounts to the almost all
glass restaurant, one experiences a stimulating spatial contrast. The kitchen and pantry are placed on the south side
of the restaurant level so that three dining rooms can enjoy
the superior views to west, north, and east. The lamps
(by Poul Henningsen), particularly those in the Yacht
Club's conference room, are very imaginative.

4 Church of the Advent

Sallingvej and Bellahöjvej, Copenhagen
Erik Møller, architect

A pleasant little brick church located on a sharp, triangular
site in west Copenhagen. Its basic plan is a square, and to
this can be added—by opening folding doors—the community

266

room at right, doubling the seating capacity for important services. The square plan brings the center of gravity of the congregation forward and in close relation with the simple sanctuary, itself within the fabric of the square, not projecting out from it. This clergy-congregation intimacy is emphasized visually by the built-up roof trusses parallel to the pews and chancel wall. The natural light, coming almost exclusively from one side, inclines to the glarish, even though tempered by a small garden without and vines within. The artificial light fixtures are good.

5 St. Knud Lavard Church

Lyngbygårdsvej, Kongens Lyngby (Copenhagen)
Carl R. Frederiksen, architect

A well-articulated and expressed structure markedly improves
a routine plan in this Roman Catholic church for 400 in a
northern suburb of Copenhagen. Its elements are clearly set
forth, inside and out. Note, for instance, the side walls and
the expression of their columns, and the free plane of the roof
above a continuous clerestory. The entrance, though nicely
landscaped and adapted to its grade, falters somewhat
amateurishly. Its art is not integrated and the doors are
puzzling. The interior, however, has a simple, pleasant air,
the narrow clerestory at ceiling giving an over-all light ac-
cented at the chancel by a large floor-to-ceiling window. A
narrow band of horizontal "relief" windows placed on either
side 8 feet above the floor (and under the masonry panel
of the side walls) obviates a closed-in feeling. The wood
circular stair to the organ gallery (inside front door to right)
is excellent.

Buddinge School and Community Center

Buddinge Hovedgade at Gladsakse Ringvej, Gladsakse
(Copenhagen)

Eva and Nils Koppel, architects

This school and center in an industrial suburb of northwest
Copenhagen cleverly demonstrates what an ingenious architectural team can do to squeeze an impossible program onto
an impossible site. The competition for its design called for
a community center with cinema and public library, plus a
primary school and a secondary school for some 1,200 boys
and girls from 7 to 17 years of age on a small triangular plot
bounded by two express streets. Bemusing. The Koppels (husband and wife) broke these requirements down into a series
of four 1-story buildings for the primary grades (southeast
corner), three 2-story buildings for the secondary (southwest
corner), the two groups loosely joined across the bottom of
the triangle by two gymnasiums and a swimming pool, with
the assembly hall at the top. The cinema and library are
placed at the apex of the site. The classrooms in the low
primary school are grouped in four staggered but connected
banks of four, each class opening southward onto a small
garden court. Special teaching rooms, toilets, and coatrooms
are placed on the north side of the corridor. The 2-story
secondary-school buildings are similarly deployed but are
more concentrated. The south-facing fenestration in all classrooms is identical—and interesting. The windows are divided
into an upper section (one third of the total) and a lower;
the upper part is screened with adjustable exterior Venetian
blinds of aluminum so that the daylight can be thrown deep

into the room, while the lower and larger section is protected by bright orange awnings, which can, of course, be rolled to suit conditions. Against black precast concrete wall-section and green planting, these awnings produce an energetic effect. The school is characterized by excellent scale throughout.

7 Town Hall
Rødovre Parkvej and Taarnvej, Rødovre (Copenhagen)
Arne Jacobsen, architect

A binuclear 3-story shoe-box and council chamber of elegant, mechanistic, and pure, very pure design. It is also cold as the Baltic on its lonely site, with little of the warmth—the community-belonging feeling—that its function suggests. In spirit it diametrically challenges Aalto's small Town Hall (q.v.) at Säynätsalo, Finland. However, it is a beautifully put together building, and in spite of the fact that it is reminiscent of the General Motors Technical Center outside Detroit, one that the visitor might want to see. In essence the building suggests simplicity compounded: one double-loaded corridor-block, with offices on either side and the council chamber as a separate unit behind. The main building was built with a central cantilevered frame supported on two columns, thus completely freeing the outside walls structurally. The ceilings of the offices were all finished before partitions were put up, providing complete flexibility in office layouts. Divisions can be erected on any meter module. The interiors of the Town Hall are its finest features. The main stairway is refined to the absolute, while the screws are loosened in the council room and a more relaxed elegance appears. Note the imaginative lighting fixture of scores of small suspended units and the furniture, particularly the cantilevered desks. The farther from America it gets the better it becomes.

8 Town Hall

Tårnbyvej at Amager Landvej, Tårnby (SE Copenhagen)
Halldor Gunnløgsson and Jørn Nielsen, architects

The municipalities surrounding Copenhagen are proving very alert to their independent status, and several have erected excellent town halls. This, the most recent (the commission for which was won by a competition), presents a friendly disposition on the exterior which blossoms into an inner atmosphere of some delight. The 2-story building is constructed about two courts, one open, the other lofty and enclosed. Most of the municipal offices encircle the large hall—whose roof clerestory can be seen in the photograph—a pleasant gregarious "forum" with excellent furniture by Poul Kjaerholm and Hans Wegner. This hall can also be used for concerts, exhibitions, and assemblies. The other court, though open to the sky, is completely glazed for its two floors and sports a spirited "fountain-sculpture" by Torsteen Johansson in the pool that fills its entire area. This was donated to the municipality by the National Foundation of Art. The building's double-court plan, direct simplicity, careful details, and furnishings are all commendable.

9 Søholm Row Houses

Strandevejen, Klampenborg (Copenhagen)
Arne Jacobsen, architect

The Bellevue seaside development (7 miles north of down-town Copenhagen) has fascinated Arne Jacobsen since he played on its beach as a boy. As an architect he made his first mark there as long ago as 1930, when, three years out of the Royal Academy, he built a barrel-vaulted riding hall. This was soon (1934) followed by the famous Bellavista Flats and a nearby theater with restaurant. The flats were—and are still —among the finest apartments in the earlier days of contempo-rary architecture. To those who saw them in the mid-30's when most of the world's apartments were decidedly dreary affairs, they were a revelation in bright, wonderful livability. Almost twenty years later, Jacobsen was able to build this new apartment group virtually next door to Bellavista, and in the design differences evident in these can be read much of the evolution of both man and movement. Gone is the white stucco "doctrinaire" of Bellavista, its somewhat abrupt angularity, its flat roofs—all of which were the international trade-marks of the early 30's. At Søholm we find a return to natural materials throughout (yellow brick, black tile, wood) an engagingly rhythmic play of roof planes, and a far greater statement of architectural individuality. The fourteen houses, particularly the five in the sharply staggered group nearest the road, are complicated in their 3-story corpus, but clever as can be and full of flowing space. The living room is placed on top for unobstructed view over the sea across the road, while each house has a completely private dining porch opening onto the garden. The exterior provides an ex-cellent demonstration of what can be done with a diverting play of roof lines. Highly imaginative.

10 Louisiana Museum

Ny Strandveg at Gammel Strandvej, Humlebaek (22 miles N of Copenhagen)
Jörgen Bo and Vilhelm Wohlert, architects

Attached to a nineteenth-century house on a beautiful estate north of Copenhagen, overlooking the Öre Sound of the Katte-gat and not far distant Sweden, this museum provides the most ingratiating setting imaginable for art. The new build-ing is no rigid foursquare block but a series of connected galleries laced through the trees and culminating in the main exhibition room, library, and reading rooms. In these reception areas a series of lectures and discussions, chamber music, cool jazz, and other arts hold forth, particularly during the winter evenings. In the long twilight of the Danish summer this end of the museum is filled with visitors, who after seeing the art,

linger for a cup of tea or a drink—and one of the loveliest views in Scandinavia. All the architecture was kept low so that it would not compete with the old trees of the setting. Using brick (whitewashed on the walls, natural on the floors), wood (natural throughout), glass with unbroken directness, and a simple (and Neutra-inspired) concrete structure, the minimum means was employed with the maximum effect and subtlety. The pulsation of spaces from enclosed to open, from low to high, with side lighting in some areas and top lighting in others, with sculpture inside, sculpture outside, with changes in volume, changes in direction: all is so artfully—and smoothly—developed that the very stroll through is pleasurable. As a result, more people have visited the museum and been exposed to its art than was ever dreamed possible. The Louisiana is enormously perceptive and sensitive, the most enjoyable museum in Europe.

11 Kingo Houses

Kingosvej, Helsingör
Jørn Utzon, architect

The young Utzon, who sprang full-blown to world prominence on winning the Sydney Opera House competition, has thus far built little. However, each of his projects, constructed or projected, has a personal—at times poetic—content that places him among the most genuinely creative architects of

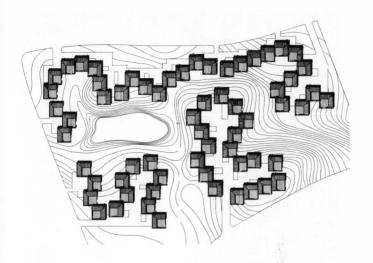

our era. This development of sixty-three "court" houses outside Hamlet's town belongs to Utzon's earlier works, and
though too many wavy tiles and stepped brick walls dominate
the architecture, the concept of the plan is absolutely superb.
Its nuclei consist of square walled-courts, each with a "window" in one side of the wall permitting a view out over the
small lake or the countryside. These courts, all the same size,
and each contiguous to at least one other, group in clusters
up and down the topography. The upper chain is serviced by
branches from a main road, the two lower groups by cul-de-
sacs. Within the walled enclosures, houses of a variety of
types have been tailored to fit individual needs. Many include
carports; a few even incorporate small shops. The houses
provide a fine feeling of privacy—although neighboring houses
are attached—splendid protection from blustery winds on a
flat coastal strip, a far greater density per acre than detached
houses, and flexibility in meeting topographical changes.

12 Aarhus University

Katrinebjerv, Aarhus
Kay Fisker, C. F. Møller, and Povl Stegmann, architects

Commenced well before the war, partly bombed during the
war, and rebuilt after it, this large complex has suffered its
vicissitudes. It has also seen a good deal of the evolution of
contemporary Danish architecture. Spread over an attractive

275

rolling site—a novel notion for a European university in the 30's—it has taken maximum advantage of changes in level and freedom of space, making the over-all campus-planning highly agreeable. The architecture, all in yellowish brick and tile, produces trim, eaveless buildings, simple and well scaled. None of it is particularly startling, except that of the interior of the great *aula* in the main building. This large assembly hall (by Møller) has been little noted by the architectural public, in spite of the fact that many critics number it among the noble rooms of modern architecture. With its exposed and lofty white concrete trusses, yellow brick infill, dark, dramatic acoustic-baffles and well-scaled lamps it well deserves a visit, in spite of a certain glare from its towering single window-wall.

13 Aarhus State High School

Fenrisvej, Aarhus

Arne Gravers and Johan Richter, architects

A large, low school of almost irreducible simplicity. A peripheral ring of classrooms is placed about a quadrangle (with auditorium at one end and special laboratories at the other). The center of the quadrangle remains open and is landscaped. Dining hall and kitchen occupy the basement level at entrance end, with a separate gymnasium formally related to the approach. The somewhat pompous flight of steps to the front door suggests a self-importance that will not be found within. The entrance hall, for instance, sports one of the most unusual murals in European schools. This trisectional fantasy by Asger Jorn, stretches a total of 88 feet and is 10 feet high. Made in deep-relief ceramic, with subject matter filled with whimsey, it exerts a powerful imprint on the entire school. The auditorium (on the opposite side of the mural's wall) is a colorful chamber with light-blue ceiling and naturally finished bent-plywood (Oregon pine) chairs. A good but not a brilliantly imaginative building, it still suggests attention, if only to the mural.

14 Carl Christenson Motor Works

Hobro Vej, Aalborg

Arne Jacobsen, architect

A small cylinder-boring plant south of a city near the north end of Jutland, providing a nicely wrought manifestation of solid geometry—a Mondrian in three dimensions. One closely shaved main block, an attached office and storeroom, a low

wall—all of brick—and a bright cylindrical metal stack comprise its elements. The end walls on the road are blank. Each element was seemingly cut out with a cheese knife, with no hint of projection at any eave edge. The structure of the building is in reinforced concrete, with steel and glass partitions and steel sash. The artificial lighting, being concentrated along the top of the 13-foot-high continuous window on the east side, provides a light source that will not vary. A good clean job in general perspective, it snaps into a Euclidian statement when seen in direct elevation, as in the photograph opposite.

Vitoria 7-8

Barcelona 5-6

Miraflores 4

Madrid 1-3

Lisbon 1-3

SPAIN AND PORTUGAL

50   100   150 M
50   100 150 200 250 KM

SPAIN AND PORTUGAL

Celestially (?) directed, the fascinating Iberian peninsula needs only greater official understanding and a
higher quality of instruction before producing at home
what its emigré sons have already produced in architecture, art, and music abroad. Even in spite of official-
dom, cultural and geographic isolation, shocking class
differences, and grinding poverty, Spain is making one
of the most surprising architectural contributions of any
country of Europe today. (This finds a parallel in art,
as recent prizes in the Venice and São Paulo Biennials
attest.) Architectural distinction can be seen in only a
few buildings to be sure—always, however, in the structures of the famous Eduardo Torroja—but an exciting
freshness and imagination sprout in the finest recent
work. It will be recalled that Spanish architects won the
first R. S. Reynolds Memorial Award, in 1957 (for the
dining pavilions—shown later—of the S.E.A.T. factory).
Many of Spain's new achievements were realized under
conditions of struggle for decent design which would
make most architects lose heart altogether. The state,
for instance, generally favors such outrageous monsters
as the new University of Gijon (on Bay of Biscay).

A cauldron of ideas has always seemed to simmer on
the stove of Spain. This boils over into frenetic output
at times. Its most tragic manifestations result in such
conflicts as the Spanish Civil War, and it is pertinent to
keep in mind, even in discussing architecture, that this
country with approximately 30,000,000 people lost
1,000,000 in this war—which figure is within a few per
cent of the fatalities suffered by *all* U.S. forces in World
War II. In happier times the Spanish temperament gives
us such men as Casals, Picasso, Miró, in the fine arts,
and Harvard's dean of the School of Design (José Luis
Sert) and Mexico's brilliant Felix Candela in architecture—to say nothing of the late, heteroclite Antonio
Gaudí.

Eduardo Torroja, mentioned above, the founder and
head of Madrid's outstanding Technical Institute of
Construction and Cement, is one of the greatest archi-

tectural engineers in the world. The late Frank Lloyd Wright said of him that he "expresses the principles of organic construction better than any engineer I know." For years, although he has built little, and most of this has been in industrial work, Torroja's designs have had top place. His most famous early work (done in 1935) is the Zarzuela Hippodrome outside Madrid. The roof of this has been described as "a veritable ballet of egg-shell concrete butterflies." The Las Corts Football Stadium, also in Madrid, provides an impressive statement in its steel roof, which cantilevers 83 feet over the spectators. High in the Pyrenees, 55 miles north of Lerida, at Pont de Suert, Torroja did a small church that though pretty grim in façade (not by Torroja) is intriguing in its structure of intersecting concrete shells. His project for the stepped-shell Club de Tachira in Caracas, Venezuela, will be sensational if carried through. Torroja's most recent completed structure is the elegantly scalloped Sidi Bernoussi Water Tower in Casablanca, Morocco, which was finished late in 1960. His buildings for the Instituto Tecnico are described later.

Two older, antipodal building types are to be seen in Spain in the fantastic Barcelona works of Gaudí, particularly his Sagrada Familia Church (begun in the 1890's but not finished in 1926 when Gaudí died), which looks as though it had been built of wet sand drops; and the prismatic white cubes of buildings on Ibiza and other islands in the Balearics. Here, indeed, are the poles of architectural expression. It might be said that their disparity represents one facet of the contrariant tensions endemic in Spain.

1 Instituto Tecnico de la Construccion y del Cemento

Costillares (Chamartin), Madrid

Eduardo Torroja, engineer; G. Echegaray and M. Barbero, architects

This large group of buildings is a postgraduate school and a research center. Its model-testing laboratories, under the directorship of Torroja, are among the finest in the world. Several of its buildings are distinguished, although the general architectural level is not. Torroja's perceptive brilliance is best illustrated by the coal bunker shown opposite. This utili-

tarian nuisance would be ignored by most architects and engineers; in Torroja's sensitive hands it becomes an alive piece of abstract sculpture, playing with sun and shadow by day and artfully floodlighted by night. Although connected to a row of workshops (with unusual triangulated roof) and the adjacent boiler-plant, the bunker nonetheless occupies a dominating visual position. It couldn't be better placed, or better designed for its position. Its dodecahedral shape 26 feet high approximates the theoretical optimum of the sphere yet is far easier to construct and far more interesting to observe. Coal is trucked in by an upper service road and dumped in storage hoppers to be transported to the dodecahedron and gravity fed to automatic stokers. Also worth seeing at the Instituto are the circular dining-hall, particularly its roof structure, and the imaginative pergola that swoops in a cantilevered parabola from the retaining wall over the walk with a shape that engineers describe as "Bernoullian lemniscates with zero end curvature." A somewhat similar but more angular pergola protects the parking lot opposite the main entrance.

2 The Spanish Pavilion from the Brussels World's Fair

Casa de Campo, Madrid

José Antonio Corrales and Ramón Vázquez Molezún, architects

The unexpectedly fresh Spanish Pavilion at the Brussels Fair of 1958 was one of the great surprises—and great delights—of that exhibition. Simple in concept and totally different from the usual "great hall" type of solution, it proved to be an oasis of understatement and spatial pleasure. This now has been dismantled and re-erected in the Feria del Campo outside Madrid. Its last use was for a shameful storehouse for the grounds, and its last condition was not precisely pristine. However, it may well have been fixed up in the interim. It is composed of combinations of one unit: a hexagonal steel "umbrella." A solid series of these clusters to form an amorphous shape of various heights and irregular outline, fitting the terrain and juggling among the trees. The interior effect throughout at Brussels was one of transparent informality—man-made "trees" with natural trees—with a minimum of bombast and "message" in the exhibitions. The columnar supports, or stems, of the umbrellas are hollow, permitting rain to drain effectively. Height differential is taken up by clerestories. Some walls are of glass, others are brick. Though somewhat disjointed from the exterior, this pavilion possesses great charm within. Let us hope that the Madrid city fathers have turned

it by now into a light, transparent, and totally delightful restaurant and exhibition area.

3 School Center in the University City

Ciudad Universitaria de Madrid

Miguel Fisac, architect

Though at times somewhat mannered with its wrap-around brick walls and the technical bravura of its covered walks, there are rewarding moments in this adjunct to the University City. The complex consists of a series of lecture halls, laboratories, and classrooms, administration building and quarters for concierge. The most unusual design can be seen in the combination lecture-halls-cum-laboratories. These fan-shaped rooms hold 50 students each; by facing forward the students receive theoretic instruction from the professor, then by swinging their seats 90° they can carry out practical experiments at laboratory benches. A somewhat disjointed relationship exists between many of the various buildings, but at times both buildings and landscaping reveal a sharp clarity. The sensuous covered walks are almost worth the trip themselves.

4 Summer Home for Children

Miraflores de la Sierra (45 miles N of Madrid)

José Antonio Corrales, Ramón Vázquez Molezún and Alejandro de la Sota, architects

High in the mountains north of Madrid, this children's colony was built to provide healthy summer vacations for 96 boys and girls. Stepped down the steep, south-facing slope of the mountain—with its roof accurately mirroring the grade—it might well be called a leading example of Spanish "organic" architecture. Because winters are severe in this region and little local construction industry exists, the building was erected by two groups: local stone-cutters laid the foundation and base; the upper section, of steel and wood, which rests almost delicately upon it, was largely prefabricated in Madrid. It comprises two main parallel units (under one roof). The lower contains playroom, chapel, assembly room, and dining room at one end, with all services and washrooms at the other. The upper section contains lecture room, instruction rooms, eight 12-bed dormitories, rooms for monitors, and related services. The entire building was constructed on a 3-by-6-meter module. Architecturally the dramatic sweep of the roof binds the building to the site, although on the exterior the roof's bright (sun-reflecting) color is somewhat disturbing. Within, the delightful airiness of the wood-and-steel construction on a firm masonry base—particularly the "transparency" and the spacious continuity of the ceiling down the grade—is highly effective, making this one of the most flowing interiors in contemporary Spain.

5 Dining Hall and Lounge, S.E.A.T. Automobile Factory

Barcelona (NE edge of city)

Rafael de la Joya, Manuel Barbero Rebolledo and César Ortiz-Echagüe, architects

This delightful group of five dining pavilions, each with a garden court, stands as the foremost recent building in Spain. In 1957 it won the first R. S. Reynolds Memorial Award as "a significant work of architecture, in the creation of which aluminum has been an important contributing factor." The excellence of this Barcelona project lies in its basic concept of separate dining pavilions, instead of one mammoth, anonymous hall. This encourages eating to be the relaxed pleasure it should be. This "spiritual" consideration of factory personnel, particularly those workers engaged in dulling, repetitive assembly, is very refreshing—and too rarely seen in any country. The pavilions accommodate 1,600 workers, 300 clerks, and 100 engineers. The southernmost pavilion (left in photograph) is reserved for engineers and guests, and also doubles as a lecture or exhibition hall and lounge. The other four are for general employees. The merit of the project continues in its architectural realization and in its technical ingenuity. Aluminum (for structural frame and roof), brick (for side walls), and glass (as "connector") are its primary elements; each is used with exposed directness. All framing and truss work is open—and well detailed. Electrically actuated *brise-soleils* of aluminum screen the southerly windows. Landscaping is well done, and very much a part of the ambience. An excellent building throughout.

6 School of Law

University of Barcelona, Avenida del Generalísimo, Barcelona
G. Giráldez Dávila, P. López Iñigo and J. Subías Fages, architects

One of the largest examples of modern architecture in Spain. With its crisp cubic massing and prominent frame-and-panel construction it also represents one of the most international. The school consists of three main sections: a low wing of small auditoriums and classrooms, at left; a 5-story wing, at right angles in the middle, for administration and study rooms; and a 404-set lecture-hall, at right. A library of 40,000-volume capacity and a museum of criminology, plus unusually considerate facilities for the students, complete the scene. The plan is both generous and fluid. The relation to the parklike site has also been worked out well. One definitely questions, however, the expanse of unshielded glass with no external sun-protection whatever.

7 Church of the Coronation of Our Lady (Iglesia de la Coronacion)

Vitoria (36 miles S of Bilbao)

Miguel Fisac, architect

An extraordinarily dynamic church in a manufacturing city in northeast Spain. Full of learned sophistication, it was realized with simple means. Its form comprises a solid white wall of "soft" shape wrapped around two thirds of the church, beginning to the left at the entrance and continuing behind the altar, and opposing this on the right, a "rigid" straight wall of raw stone pierced with an alternating pattern of slender rectangular windows. These are filled with stained glass by Francisco Farreras. A tall window pouring a flood of light on the sanctuary hides behind the junction of the right-hand wall with the curved wall. A simple block altar stands starkly revealed against this backdrop, with an expressive attenuated crucifix (by Pablo Serrano) suspended on a series of wires directly behind. Sacristy, a small chapel, and the baptistery are found on the right; confessionals in rear wall to left. Materials are raw and direct, and the entrance severe, but the result within asserts power. One of the better.

8 Church of Our Lady of the Angels

Calle Norte-Sur at Calle Bastiturri, Vitoria

Javier Carvajal Ferrer and José M. García de Paredes, architects

Although in the same city and of the same recent date as Miguel Fisac's Church of the Coronation of Our Lady—and though both are extraordinarily provocative—this follows a totally different approach from Fisac's sculptured shape. The Church of Our Lady of the Angels comprises a basically simple, but intricate appearing, relation of flat planes. There is not a curve in it. A sharply triangular site generated its arrow shape, and the proximity of apartments prompted the small garden separation at the entrance (at base of triangle) and the location here of a future belfry. One enters happily through the garden, not directly from the street. The church plan makes a triangle plus an additional side band of sacristy, chapel, confessionals, and baptistery (with flat roof). The lower part is encased in a solid wall of light-ocher brick. The

roof is divided into two sections the outer of which extends laterally beyond the low brick walls and is joined to them by a near-horizontal strip of glazing. This roof-section rises very high above the chancel and tapers down to a height of only a few feet at the entrance end, thus having near-triangular flanks. It is covered with dark-gray slate. The second, or inner, roof-section, which has a horizontal ridge, is also triangular but in the opposite direction, being deep at the entrance end and tapering to a point above the presbytery. The two roofs thus complement each other. They are joined by continuous glazing creating on the interior a "floating" ceiling and an impressive over-all rim of light. The structural framework is in light exposed steel, with wood ceiling naturally finished. An appropriate and well-done statue of the Virgin rising heavenward (by J. Garcia Donaire) is suspended from the open steel structure above the simple block altar. This extremely interesting church, together with Fisac's, makes Vitoria one of the most progressive smaller (population under 75,000) European cities in the field of church architecture.

PORTUGAL

The new architecture in Portugal is tamer than that in its only neighbor. "Official architecture" here (as, indeed, in Spain) bears a dubious stamp. And—also as in Spain—planning is very poor, the weakest element of both building programs. The Portuguese have, however, turned out several reasonable buildings, as those fortunate enough to have seen the "Contemporary Portuguese Architecture 1958" exhibition circulated by the Smithsonian Institution in Washington can attest. A few years ago such a show would have been impossible. The two housing examples shown in this book are particularly good: let us hope that they will be joined by many other fine buildings in the years to come.

1 The Infante Santo Housing

Avenida Infante Santo at Rua Sant'Ana á Lappa, Lisbon

Alberto José Pessoa, Hernani Gandra and João Abel Manta, architects

The four blocks (of five total) on *pilotis* shown here are among the finest examples of Mediterranean housing to be

290

seen: they adapt imposingly to their steep grade; their façades both front and rear are thoroughly competent; their duplex planning is extremely good. Furthermore, sculpture and polychrome *azulejos* (the famous Portuguese tiles) have been made part of the design. The five blocks are of eight floors and accommodate 24 families each. The apartments are of the balcony-access type; only kitchen and bath open onto the balcony. Closet banks miraculously divide the bedrooms—most European housing totally ignores the storage problem. Living rooms and dining rooms have loggias, as do all southwest-facing bedrooms. On the roof are placed storage and drying rooms for each apartment; on the ground floor terrace there is a garden and a space for protected play. Shops line the street at right angles to the axis of the apartments. It would be pleasant to stop this rosy picture at once, but the five buildings mentioned are only part of a development that contains 112 more apartments (vs. the 120 in five buildings described) stretched out in a solid line along the street, opposite and perpendicular to the five on *pilotis*. These last are perfectly competent buildings, but they are not of the caliber of the others, and the over-all urbanism that allows a main avenue to bisect the development is just plain poor. But look at the five blocks on stilts: they are good, very good.

2 S. João de Deus Housing

Alvalade, Lisbon

*Ruy Jervis d'Athouguia and Sebastiao Formosinho Sanchez,
architects*

The central and finest part of this development consists of
four parallel blocks of attractive and ingeniously planned
apartments. Each block consists of seven units, the two end
buildings being somewhat larger than those between. The
three central apartments are on *pilotis;* thus free circulation
knits all four groups together, and no street has to be crossed
to get from one to the other. The ingenuity of the individual
plans can be seen in the apartment arrangement: the two
lower floors (above the ground-floor services and storage) are
single-floor apartments with two bedrooms in the five central
units, three on the wings. These occupy the whole floor and
face both east and west. The upper two floors are duplexes,
thus the topmost floor can eliminate completely the public
hall needed for the others. The duplexes do, however, have
only a single exposure. Room-width loggias—which also act
as sunbreaks—line both sides of all floors. Although built by
more than a score of contractors, some with little experience
in this field, the over-all effect is agreeable even though at
times weak in detail.

3 Exhibition Hall

Industrial Fair Grounds, Lisbon

Francisco Keil Amaral, architect; Alberto Cruz, associate

Industrial fairs and other annual exhibitions are far more a part of the European economy than that of the United States. Several fine postwar buildings have been erected in various countries to house such activities, and though Nervi's building in Turin and the great C.N.I.T. in Paris are certainly the most outstanding yet built, a few more modest ones deserve a look. Among them is this recent two-section building in Lisbon, comprising a main exhibition-hall with mezzanine, 395 by 140 feet in size, and a wing in front (with separate doors and control) at right angles. A cinema-auditorium and various offices are placed on the second floor of this wing, which extends across the entire front of the auditorium. The fine interior of the exhibition hall is explicitly expressed and clean, with graceful reinforced-concrete arches bridging the floor span, and without break or joint, branching outward to carry the beams for the side aisle. Excellent construction technique. The lateral purlins between these well-formed arches are of prestressed concrete. On them rests the roof of corrugated asbestos sheets. *Brise-soleils* protect the main windows from the hot Lisbon sun.

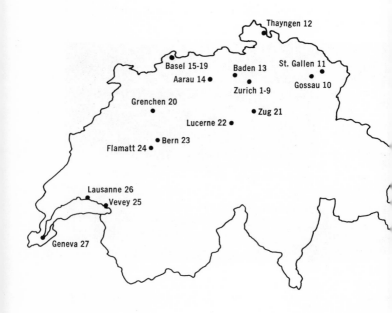

Thayngen 12

Basel 15-19   Baden 13   St. Gallen 11

Aarau 14 ●   Gossau 10

Zurich 1-9 ●

Grenchen 20 ●

● Zug 21

Lucerne 22 ●

● Bern 23

Flamatt 24 ●

Lausanne 26

Vevey 25

Geneva 27 ●

SWITZERLAND

10   20   30   40   50
20   40   60   80 M

SWITZERLAND

Switzerland, the microcosmic confederation of the Continent's three great cultures, its crossroads of communications and ideas, has produced an impressive amount of sound new architecture. The word "sound" was chosen purposely, for the new architecture in Switzerland generally does not scintillate the way much of Italy's does, it does not encompass the scale found in Sweden, nor is it often tinged with genius. However, much of the new Swiss building, particularly of the last few years, has demonstrated an unexpected virility of idiom and freshness of thinking. The future looms very bright.

The Swiss, like the Scandinavians, are fully sold on a contemporary architectural approach, and have been for years. Furthermore, their city fathers are determined to make their cities, even commercial ones like Zurich, as pleasant to stroll in as possible, and no urban stroll, they rightly reason, can be agreeable without expert planting, flowers, well-designed street-furniture and signs, and appropriate sculpture at strategic points. It is not insignificant that Maillol's bronze "Source," one copy of which graces the garden of the Museum of Modern Art in New York, decorates a parking lot in downtown Zurich (Talackerstrasse)!

Alert to what is happening about them, the Swiss study their neighbors' achievements in their excellent architectural magazines, *Werk* and *Bauen + Wohnen,* and in a series of distinguished trilingual books. The finest of their several jealously independent architectural schools, the E.T.H. in Zurich, carries an international reputation. It should be noted that both the U.I.A. (International Union of Architects) and the recently disbanded C.I.A.M. (International Congresses for Modern Architecture) were inaugurated on Swiss soil.

Obviously a certain conservatism marks contemporary Swiss architecture—and always has. Many of its genius sons emigrate. Le Corbusier, whom most consider the greatest architect since Michelangelo, lives and works in Paris. If the Swiss gave no one else to the world, they should be enshrined for this incredible man. However, the Helvetian Confederation should hang its head in shame for having totally ignored this restless giant: not one publicly commissioned building by Le Corbusier appears in his native country. Actually his only works there are the tiny villa for his mother on the Lake of Geneva (1925), and the Clarté Flats in Geneva (1930). Mortifying.

Other great Swiss in the arts who found freer and greater opportunities abroad include the late Arthur Honneger, the distinguished composer, who lived much of his life in France; Paul Klee, who spent most of his in Germany—but who did return to Switzerland seven years before he died; and O. H. Ammann, who came to the United States, where he designed (or was consultant for) the George Washington, Golden Gate, Bronx Whitestone, and the new Verrazzano-Narrows bridges. William Lescaze is another distinguished Swiss in this country. A brilliant exception to emigration was the late Robert Maillart (1872–1940), who not only gave the world its most ethereal arch bridges—slab mathematics in airy space—but who opened new visions of poured concrete as a building material. The most exciting Maillart bridges are Le Châtelard on the French border above Martigny, Wallis; the Salginatobel Bridge near Schiers (northwest of Davos); the Schwandbach Bridge and the nearby and earlier Rossgraben Bridge between Hinterfultigen and Schönentannen, east of Schwarzenburg (12 miles south of Bern); and the bridge over the Arve between Vessey and Geneva.

The architectural moderation mentioned remains always on a high general level and always within a contemporary mold: "traditional" architecture is not built. The strongest contributions this miniscule country (half the size of South Carolina) makes in architecture can be seen in churches, open-air baths, schools, and hospitals (compare Italy in these regards), exhibitions and graphics, and a humanization of the urban scene. Swiss industrial work is also of the highest order.

The contemporary Swiss churches are both numerous and of excellent quality. For many years they were the finest in Europe, and only recently have they been surpassed by those in Germany and France. The late Karl Moser, one of the founders of modern architecture in Switzerland, startled the country in 1927 with his powerful St. Antonius in Basel (Kannenfeldstrasse), still one of the country's strongest. Then, through the years, a succession of fine new churches has been erected. Among the better (sometimes in part only) are St. Johannes at Basel, by Burckhardt and Egender, right down the street from St. Antonius, which was the first important modern Protestant church (1936); the First Church of Christ Scientist in Zurich (Kreuzbühlstrasse), by Kellermüller and Hofmann; St. Francis, Riehen (Aussere Baselstrasse), near Basel, by Fritz Metzger; Neo-Apostolic Church, Geneva (rue Liotard), by Haefeli, Moser and Steiger; St. Marks, Zurich-Seebach (Höhenring), by A. H. Steiner; Felix-und-Regula, Zurich (Hardstrasse), by Fritz Metzger; Bullinger Church, Zurich (Bullinger-platz), by the Pfister Brothers; the Church of Our Lady, Solothurn-Weststadt (Wildbachstrasse), by Josef Schütz (good in structure only); St. Thomas, Basel (Luzerner-ring), by Benedikt Huber; and the tiny Reformed Church at Bottmingen, just southwest of Basel, by Walter Wurster. Others are illustrated later.

Swiss open-air baths have been famous since the sixteenth-century Swiss physician Paracelsus reinitiated the spa habit. The Allenmoos Bath in Zurich (Allenmoos-strasse), by Haefeli, Moser and Steiger, though one of the first large ones (finished in 1939) remains one of the very finest in its sympathetic scale and almost transparent architecture. Others of merit can be seen in the Bellerive Lido at Lausanne, by Marc Piccard; the small bath at Zurich-Schlieren (Schulstrasse), by Haefeli, Moser and Steiger; the bath at Dübendorf (just east of Zurich), by Oskar Stock; the very large Letzigraben in Zurich (Letzigraben), by Max Frisch; and the lido at Horgen, on the west shore of the Lake of Zurich, by Escher and Weilenmann.

The land of Johann Heinrich Pestalozzi (1746–1827) would be expected to carry out the forward precepts in architecture of this great Swiss educator. Switzerland is, indeed, rich in fine new schools, the most provocative of which are illustrated below. Also worth a look are two famous prewar examples: the Bruderholz School in Basel (Reservoir Strasse), by Hermann Baur, and the Industrial School in Bern (Lorraine Strasse), by Hans Brechbühler; both were finished in 1939. Others of more recent interest are the Untermoos School at Zurich-

Altstetten (Altstetter Strasse), by Eduard Del Fabro, the Wasgenring School in Basel (Welschmattstrasse), by Bruno and Fritz Haller, the Bannfield Primary School in Olten (Katzenhubelweg), by Hermann Frey, and the Geisendorf Primary School in Geneva (rue Liotard), by Brera and Waltenspuhl.

Swiss housing for years has been thoroughly competent in an uninspired, virtuous mold. Just as the wonderful Neubühl Housing of the early 30's in Zurich (Kalchbühlstrasse) has never been equaled by subsequent low-cost examples, the equally distinguished Doldertal Flats in Zurich (Doldertal) of 1936 by Alfred and Emil Roth and Marcel Breuer have never been surpassed as luxury dwellings. Housing since these has been proper, very well equipped, and beautifully built, but almost totally without architectural spark.

A final word should be said on art-and-architecture, industrial design, and graphics—facets of Swiss art related to architecture. Each is excellent. By law every Swiss school has some original art works, often a large mural. Those by the late Hans Fischer are the most delightful ever seen by boy or girl. (Among the best of these are those in the Primary School, Köniz, just south of Bern, in Saatlen Primary School, Zurich, and in the Im Erb Primary School, Küsnacht, just southeast of Zurich.) Hospitals, too, have a continuing art program, purchasing annually from exhibitions by local artists. Both the Waid Hospital (Tiechestrasse) and the University Hospital (Rämistrasse) in Zurich have first-rate paintings, mosaics, and outdoor sculpture. Industrial design is given every encouragement by the well-known Swiss *Werkbund,* with department stores as well as museums constantly pushing good design. Graphics are considered so important by architects that an entire issue of *Werk,* the Swiss architectural magazine, was recently devoted to them.

Competitions are held for almost all important Swiss public buildings, with the happy result that not only does the best solution emerge, but also younger men have a series of opportunities, while the public is thus urged to take a keen interest in what is being built.

Lastly, one should call attention to detail and the quality of construction in Swiss architecture: it is the highest in the world. Swiss buildings actually improve with age!

Note to the motorist: when driving through Switzerland keep an eye out for the extraordinary "native" architecture—the barns, farms, and vernacular buildings—that one will see in ever-changing fashion throughout the country, especially off the major roads. Switzerland's geographic and ethnic diversity, plus keenly marked regional construction resources—from solid wood to solid stone—have produced buildings of widely varied architectural expression. These are probably unequaled elsewhere in the world for such abrupt changes over such relatively short distances. Almost each canton has distinctly recognizable building patterns. Most important, architecture grew in each section from its particular needs and was realized with its particular means. Here is fundamental architecture: unadorned, unadulterated, magnificently conceived.

1 Freudenberg High School
Bederstrasse at Steinentisch Strasse, Zurich
Jacques Schader, architect

One of the greatest high schools of Europe, occupying a limited but unspoiled ancient estate just a few minutes from downtown Zurich. The chief problem with this school's beautiful tree-filled lot was how to deal with the hill in the center without ravaging the setting. Bulldozers were left at home and the site difficulty was resolved by putting a long double-deck wing for the natural sciences on one side of the rise and a rank of three gymnasiums in line on the other, and "bridging" the two with a "plateau"—man-made on two sides, natural ground in the middle. On this rest the 2-story high-school on one side and the 3-story trade or commercial school on the other—both for boys. A separate auditorium, focused on the open space between these two main elements, is placed just off the "plateau" and in the trees, where it is also convenient for public use from the street that bounds the lot on the northwest. Brilliant imagination was shown in this grouping of units so that the difficult topography was utilized, not vandalized. The architecture itself reveals a design superiority matching site utilization. Crisp elegance characterizes all buildings, inside and out. Note the relatively narrow strip of classroom windows, supplemented above by a relatively deep band with exterior blinds adjustable to reflect maximum light into the depth of the room. A touch of Le Corbusier appears in the over-all treatment, but a touch only. One of the finest new buildings to be seen.

2 Chriesiweg Primary School

Eugen Huber-Strasse at Loogartenstrasse, Zurich-Altstetten
Cramer, Jaray and Paillard, architects

This highly interesting school in a western suburb of Zurich won a competition held by the city to explore new possibilities in school design. So successful was the finished group that it was awarded the 1957 "Prize of the City" as the outstanding building of the year. The basic layout of the school comprises three separate pavilions of four classrooms each, to right up a slight grade, with a double kindergarten-unit on the left, an assembly hall and *Singsaal* for 135 behind, and a gymnasium at top left attached to the uppermost class pavilion. Beautifully landscaped and maintained grounds flow between all units. The exteriors are characterized by a playful homogeneity and excellent scale throughout. The three classroom blocks are the most original feature: each group, containing four classes and four hobby-rooms, is approached by a covered arcade, which leads not directly into the classrooms themselves but into hobby-room anterooms, each of which faces an inner courtyard. The hobby-rooms also serve as coat-rooms, for special small-group studies, and as "projects corners." Opening from each is the class proper, a square room with low window-wall facing southeast supplemented by a high set-back window-strip in the up-slanting ceiling. The whole school was imaginatively conceived and meticulously realized. It is marred only slightly by the somewhat heavy wood window-frames and mullions.

3 Reformed Church

Badener Strasse at Pfarrhausstrasse, Zurich-Altstetten
Werner Moser, architect

Moser's Protestant church in Altstetten remains one of the
finest modern churches in Switzerland. It stands on the edge
of a low hill beside an old church the congregation had
outgrown. Instead of destroying the old, it was carefully preserved and the new was related to it by angle and space
relation and by the repetition of a mutual eave-height. The
interior, one room of simplicity and dignity, binds the pulpit
and altar to the congregation in respectful unity. The windows
were designed to give a soft, general light, with an accent at
the altar end. They consist of a narrow strip high on the
sunny side, with taller windows to the north. An antidazzle
screen subdues glare from the larger windows, while the
sloping soffit of the ceiling helps spread the light uniformly.
Considerable sensation of space results from having a diagonal
entrance instead of the more prosaic axial doorway. This
feeling is augmented further by the slight change in level
of the pews on the north side, the plasticity of the pierced
"glare" screen, and the absence of right angles in ceiling and
end walls, all of which are slightly canted. In addition to increasing the sensation of space, each of these elements con-
tributes to better acoustics. The floor and pews are somewhat
fussy, the pulpit a bit heavy, and the gourd-shaped lamps not
altogether satisfactory. However, these are detail carpings at
a lovely church.

302

4 Letzi Kindergarten and Secondary School

Langgrütstrasse at Espenhofweg, Zurich-Albisrieden
Ernst Gisel, architect

The plan of this school—which has a good deal more to it than meets the casual eye—is developed somewhat rigidly around a central court, framed by three 2-story classroom-blocks in a U-shape, with a fourth block across the top of the U containing special rooms and two gymnasiums. A detached music-and-art-building occupies the center of the court. The three general class-units are identical and contain eight classrooms each, four to a floor. These are reached on both floors from two generous stairhalls per unit, each stairhall serving a classroom on each side. Thus the classrooms, having their access in an end (i.e., inside) wall, can have windows along the width of both sides, providing bilateral light and ventilation. The major windows face the lawn side, with a smaller, higher band on the court exposure. The corners resulting from the right-angle meetings of the three class-wings are given to semicovered play areas of considerable interest. Excellent art can be seen in both the music room (a mural on concrete by Max Truninger) and the art room (by the late and greatly talented Hans Fischer). The Letzi School represents an uncompromising statement, harsh in line and arbitrary in the placement of such elements as the music auditorium. Nonetheless it takes a perceptive look at the compacted-school concept, with several excellent points and a determined—at times too determined—quality quite unique. Construction is largely of red brick and copper. A hard but entertaining kindergarten with a childproof series of concrete playhouses has just been finished by the same architect near the southwest corner of the school.

5 Children's Center and Playground
Bucheggstrasse near Hofwiesenstrasse, Zurich
Hans Litz and Fritz Schwarz, architects

The cultural morphology of town planning has received far too little attention from architects as well as specialists. The enjoyable and healthy use of leisure, which is increasing constantly; play and hobby facilities for various—and all—age groups; multipurpose community-centers: these, and other factors, must be studied and incorporated in our cities if they are to create the full level of culture cities alone can produce. Zurich, being particularly alert to the problems of the use of leisure, is setting up sixteen strategically scattered centers, eleven are finished or under construction. Among the most delightful is this, for children, in a north-central, older section

of town. Divided into several groups along the periphery of a small park it provides the usual playgrounds and facilities, plus two highly imaginative and appealing constructions. The first of these contains hobby and work rooms and a yard with a small outdoor theater facing a wonderful concrete labyrinth that serves as backdrop and stage access; small community-hall with fireplace and library; and a children's village, in and on and over which the children can play. All is planned with a fey imagination and delight—and constructed in indestructible reinforced-concrete. A captivating "town" occupies the east end of the small park setting (see photograph). Made largely of concrete culvert sections, this "town," with its own private roads and traffic lights, serves as a "traffic school" in addition to play area. Would that more cities had more facilities with this imaginative spirit!

6 The University Hospital

Rämi Strasse at Gloria Strasse, Zurich

A.K.Z. Associated Architects (Steiger, Fietz, Haefeli, Weideli, Schütz and Moser)

A large $23,000,000 hospital complex—one of the more important in Europe. Occupying a 9-acre park on the hillside overlooking the city, directly across from the Technical Uni-

versity, it enjoys a fine, convenient site, which the architects were strict to preserve. One's first impression on seeing the Polyclinic, the only building on the main approach street (Rämi Strasse), results in a questioning disappointment. However, this building was designed and built during the war (it was finished in 1945), when severe restrictions on all materials limited even hospitals to a small-scale module with much masonry and wood. Rightly or wrongly, this scale has been the determinant *au fond* of all subsequent units for the following eight years. The result is that from the detached design point of view—a difficult viewpoint with the complexities of contemporary hospitals—the University Hospital's appearance is not prepossessing. Its contributions lie elsewhere: in its wonderful use of the site, with private rooms and wards opening onto the full extent of the park—and with low-silled windows so that most of the 1,200 patients can look southerly onto this park; in the sympathetic, inviting scale of all buildings—no monument complex, no awe-inspiring solid mass; in the deeply reasoned relation of the various units, which combines the best features of both block and pavilion systems; in basic flexibility; in its profusion of balconies and roof gardens; in its wonderful art program, which puts paintings or drawings in countless patients' rooms, murals at every landing of the Polyclinic, and sculpture throughout the garden; and finally, in its meticulous detailing. The general impression does not excite—neither does the interior design of the wards—and in some respects the hospital's architecture carries more conviction in detail than in the over-all. Nonetheless it represents some of the soundest hospital thinking on the Continent.

7 Tiefenbrunnen Lido

Bellerive Strasse, Zurich
Josef Schütz, architect; Otto Dürr and Willy Roost, associates

Built on the eastern shore of the Lake of Zurich only a few minutes from the center of the city, this beach resort stresses landscaping even more than architecture. Indeed, the architect's motivation was to make his own works as invisible as possible. This care of setting was particularly important since the site is used as a park for eight months of the year while the bathing facilities are open only during the summer. Beginning with the entry, gaily formed by six freestanding concrete mushrooms, and continuing through the various dressing-room buildings and the restaurant—in red, yellow, and white—there is a friendly, even festive, quality about the whole setting. Roofs of the dressing blocks "float" to minimize mass, and small units are preferred to large. The dressing facilities are primarily of the cubicle type, to which one takes a special hanger-basket, changes into bathing suit, checks the "loaded" hanger with attendant, and leaves the cubicle free for the next

person. The only building of questionable merit is the cone-topped tea pavilion, which looks like a Kentish oast. As the swimmers use the lake, no pools were necessary. However, the architect provided a merry touch for the nonswimmers by creating a round, shallow pool floating in the lake and attached to land by a gracefully arched little bridge. Although up to 3,000 can use Tiefenbrunnen at one time, none of that impersonal, dreary endlessness appears which characterizes most American public strands.

8 Aluminum Industries Headquarters
Seefeldquai, Zurich
Hans Hofmann, architect

It is significant to realize that the city of Zurich has followed through the years a careful policy of improving and even extending its lovely lakeside site so that the whole shore is a landscaped garden development for the enjoyment of people, not the speeding of automobiles. This enlightened—but unfortunately too rare—policy has benefited not only those who live in or visit this lively city, but the businesses that increasingly place their headquarters and offices about the lake. Unquestionably a parklike setting such as this building enjoys is far more valuable than a lake site without the park in front—to say nothing of a treeless mid-city location. The meticulous building the late Prof. Hofmann designed here naturally provides a showcase for aluminum, but always with logic and generally with beauty. Somewhat grandiloquently surrounded by its own private moat, its three floors and penthouse rise precisely from the waters with a well-framed fabric. It is an exoskeletal building, the first in Switzerland, its steel frame being clad with asbestos and revetted with natural aluminum. The spandrels, of dark brown color, are anodized aluminum, with a flat roof of aluminum sheets. The building is planned around a lofty central hall, with all offices opening from galleries that surround it. A spirited circular stair supplements the elevators.

9 Artists' Colony

Gockhauserstrasse, Gockhausen (Zurich)
Rudolf Brennenstuhl, architect; Gustav Kruck, engineer

This expressionistic building represents the first stage of a projected "colony" for artists outside Zurich. If the entire community is carried through with the architectural vigor evident here, it will indeed be an interesting and unusual group. The first unit, shown opposite, provides an atelier for an advertising executive, and consists solely of a series of offices and drawing rooms: no living quarters are incorporated. It is stepped down the hillside and divided into two connected sections, the upper houses office staff; the lower, the north-facing ateliers, conference room, and library. A kitchen and related services are placed in the basement. A conscious effort

throughout sought to establish an intimate contact with the surrounding nature. On the uphill sides, for instance, the ground level, almost up to the window sills, furthers this relation. Although an obvious personal and arbitrary quality marks much of the design, it is positive and unflinching. If this character can run through the remaining buildings and not be vitiated (as happened next door) this should be a powerful group.

10 Goldzack Elasticized Fabric Plant

Stadtbühlstrasse 12, Gossau (7 miles W of Saint Gallen)
Danzeisen and Voser, architects; Heinz Hossdorf, engineer

A dramatic, inexpensive, thoroughly workable factory housing elasticized-fabric looms. Situated in too-little-visited (but lovely) northeast Switzerland, it provides an unencumbered, flexible, north-lighted space, some 93 feet wide by 165 long. After studying several structural systems, the architects settled on an unusual design of seven cylindrical sections canted and abutted, their junctures providing lunettes of north-facing windows. This turned out to be 12% less expensive than ordinary saw-tooth factory-construction. The shells are made of reinforced concrete applied by spraying, and are tied below floor level by prestressed rods. On top of the shells, which vary in thickness from 2.75 inches to 4.75 inches, are placed two layers of cork, and corrugated-asbestos roofing. The windows, whose steel frames also act as trusses, are double glazed to facilitate strict temperature control. Fluorescent tubes are fastened to the lower chords of the shells. By day the plant is flooded with natural light, both direct and reflected from the canted ceilings, while at night artificial light comes from the same direction and not only fills the interior but makes a striking effect on the corrugations without. The entrance, unhappily, is weak.

11 Bruder Klaus Church

Hauptstrasse, Saint Gallen-Winkeln
Ernest Brantschen, architect

The exterior of this Catholic church in a western suburb of Saint Gallen is labored and self-conscious, the warped velum of its roof seeming contrived, and its corner windows "modernistic." However, the interior (excepting all windows) is both spatial and powerful. The twisted wave of the ceiling gives an accent that rises and emphasizes the chancel with a commanding flourish, while the extreme simplicity of the altar,

311

its fittings, and the choir pews play off against the exuberance of the ceiling. The sweep of natural light here is also effective. The stained-glass windows are not distinguished either in art or architectural frame, but the entrance door in cast aluminum (by Michael Grossert) is very good, as is the tabernacle on the altar (by J. Tannheimer). Heinz Hossdorf was the engineer.

12 Village Church

Thayngen (NE of Schaffhausen)
Josef Schütz, architect

This unpretentious church in a small village almost on the Swiss-German border possesses a boxlike exterior and a fumbling campanile, but its interior is full of a warm, religious atmosphere. In the late afternoon with the sun patterning the sanctuary wall it is especially agreeable. The simplicity of the structure and its direct expression are the interior's strong points. The finely finished white concrete frame, the red brick chancel wall, and the clear wood panels between concrete ribs are cleanly stated and juxtaposed. Only when the unnecessarily heavy mullions of the large chancel window are carried through the ceiling and falsely repeated on the other side does the integrity of the structural expression waver. A sculptured Last Supper by Josef Rickenbacher occupies a prominent spot on the sanctuary wall; although well located it does not warrant detailed inspection. The altar, unfortunately, is very poor indeed. The lightly suspended lamps of direct-indirect double-cone shape are excellent.

13 Chapel and Crematorium

Liebenfels Cemetery, Baden (just S of town, above main road
   to Zurich)

Edi and Ruth Lanners and Res Wahlen, architects

Baden, a bustling town 15 miles northwest of Zurich, has in this crematorium one of the most powerful recent Swiss buildings. Hard and cold—befitting the subject—it is nonetheless extremely competently realized. The approach takes one through a supernal "arch" composed of three thin flat planes of concrete, then along a row of trees and a 6-foot-high wall (on right) that shields the service drive. Directly on axis lies the rectangular parvis with the tilt-roof chapel at left and crematory at right. (The crematory, incidentally, belonged to an older building that was redesigned and incorporated into this new group.) A large bronze bowl-shaped fountain plays a single jet in the center. The side walls of the entrance court extend leftward to surround the chapel, which is thus placed within the walled area with access walks to the chapel on either side. The chapel roof overhangs these side approaches to provide shelter and to meet the total width of the enclosing perimeter walls. Within, one finds one room of great simplicity: low side walls of glass, usually curtained, with a large triangle of clear glass above on either side; natural-finish wood ceiling at pronounced slope, dropping at right angles to the cant behind the sanctuary; starkly sized cross, catafalque, and pulpit (this last rather too heavy); and open wood pews for 200. By drawing the curtains, 180 standees can be accommodated in the sideways. A "relatives' room" and room for the minister are placed along the back wall. Beyond the chapel and mortuary, the quiet old cemetery is ranged over the well-treed hills. A deeply impressive building.

14 Open Air Bath

Uferpromenade and Schützenhausweg, Aarau
Haefeli, Moser and Steiger, architects

The basic aim in the designing of most Swiss open-air baths—there are scores throughout the country—is to make them appear as invisible as possible. In this bath on the banks of the Aare River in an industrial town 31 miles west of Zurich, Haefeli, Moser and Steiger have repeated much of the success of their memorable prewar Allenmoos Bath in Zurich. Numerous "detached" planes sheltering the dressing pavilions float in the air to avoid the pressing insistence on one's head which would result if one straight-line, hard-edged roof were used; planting and trees are part of these dressing rooms even inside, while without, trees and shrubbery are employed to break up the masses of even these fragmented shelters. Several pools are used, each composed solely of straight lines but none with an assertive shape: there is a wading pool for small

314

children, a pool for nonswimmers and a 50-meter (165-foot)
pool for the energetic. Gardens and other plantings divide
quiet play and relaxing from active sports; a restaurant and
snack-bar enable one to spend the day here; and finally, a
delightful play sculpture by Erwin Rehmann completes the
scene.

15 Citizens' Hospital

Spitalstrasse at Petersgraben, Basel

E. and P. Vischer, Hermann Baur, Bräuning, Leu and Dürig,
  architects

One of the prime ideas generating the design of this 700-bed
hospital was based on giving the 7-story patients' block
southerly sunshine and orientation over the park and gardens
of a tight mid-city lot. The "bed house" accommodates 100
patients per floor, with all rooms facing south except a few
given to isolation cases. Men and women are grouped on
separate floors except for the uppermost, which has private
rooms and terraces. On the north side of the corridor are all
the necessary services, vertical circulation, nurses' stations,
etc. This arrangement gives the patients sun and quiet away

from the street, and the doctors and nurses undisturbed work places. All surgery cases are located in the east half of the block, while medical cases occupy the west. In a separate 3-story building to the north of the bed house are placed the treatment rooms, operating rooms, and polyclinic. The lecture halls and research laboratories for the university medical school are also here. This structure is connected with the patient block by four wings, which also contain treatment facilities for periodic patients. A wing projecting north from the treatment zone contains the kitchens and quarters for the staff. A low block (by Hans Schmidt) to the southwest of the main patient block contains tuberculosis and infectious cases. On the exterior this is an agreeable building, simple and well proportioned, its garden façade being particularly nice with its warm sand-color, boxes of flowers in almost every window, and balconied sunrooms at each end. Interiors, too, are bright and cheerful, with a maximum of sunshine. The design of this hospital with patient block to the south of staff block, though somewhat traditional, has been very influential in both Europe and the United States.

16 All Saints Church

Neubadstrasse at Laupen-Ring, Basel
Hermann Baur, architect

The over-all impression of this church, inside and out, is one of restrained dignity. Simple and lofty in its architecture, gray and white in its respectful colors, handsome in its details, it has a subdued patrician quality. The structure is both unusual and imaginative, consisting of seven bays of transverse barrel-vaulting, the lower chords of which bow slightly upward and are delicately supported by slender concrete columns set in from the side walls. The outside walls thus are masonry curtains. The inner effect of the structure is excellent, the rhythm of the vaulting and the lightness of its supports creating a refined if slightly dry atmosphere. The lunette windows formed by the ends of the vaulting provide a general light throughout the church; this is supplemented by two large grilled windows at the chancel. The large block altar of near-black granite (by Albert Schilling)—one of the finest one will see—was until recently shielded by a delicately suspended ciborium. A small chancel window by Albert Manessier should be noted, as should the beautifully simple baptismal font (left on entering) by Jean Arp. The exterior is of gray brick set in a white concrete frame. The structure that gives such interest to the interior is almost obliterated

317

without by a wide, flat cornice that masks the seven vaults except from a distance. If these had been emphasized instead of being timidly girdled and concealed, the church would be as fine outside as it is in.

17 Geigy Paint Warehouse

Sandgrubenstrasse at Bleichestrasse, Basel
Burckhardt Office, architects; J. Ochsner, engineer

Attached to a complex of older chemical factories, this new unit, though slightly grandiloquent from the design standpoint, adds a striking note to Swiss industrial architecture. The building, measuring 181 feet square and rising seven

318

stories above ground, with two basement floors, serves for mixing, packaging, storing, and shipping paint. Each of the upper floors is devoted to a single color—red, yellow, green, etc.—with mixing and packing on one side and storing on the other. Construction is reinforced concrete throughout with concrete vertical louvers shielding the work areas from direct sun yet admitting full natural light.

18 Electric Power Station

River Rhine, Birsfelden (Basel)
Hans Hofmann, architect

The main problem connected with this powerhouse was not just that of designing a hydroelectric station and its enclosure, nor even that of simply preserving the landscape about this handsome bend of the Rhine: it was the creation of a new man-made landscape, one that would be just as lovely to view as was nature before the dam and powerhouse were built. The late Prof. Hofmann, who had been retained for several years before construction to guard against possible "esthetic infringement" in connection with the over-all dam development, has achieved an excellent, sympathetic result in this building, one that fulfills all technical functions while at the same time embellishing the river site. His sinewy, expressive Y-framed powerhouse is not an intrusion: day or

night it has almost a pavilion elegance. Its folded-plane roof seems to dance across the river. Color, too, has been particularly well handled both inside and out. It is only unfortunate that the roofs of the five small weir-control buildings have self-consciously repeated the folded planes of the powerhouse, and that the service buildings behind are fussy in design. The power station itself remains an absolute model.

19 Bruder Klaus Church

Hardstrasse at Im Lerchengarten, Birsfelden (Basel)
Hermann Baur, architect

This Roman church (in a suburb adjacent to east Basel) reveals an interesting play of planes in floors and ceiling, punctuated by a dazzling splash of natural light over the chancel. The restrictions of its site pushed it almost into the hillside, which provides from the approach, a restful backdrop of trees. Baur, wanting to give importance to the entrance, created a slightly raised terrace in front, by which one enters the church. This intermedium between the setting and the fabric proper provides a fine transitional place and lets the priest chat with his parishioners in the open. One enters under a low ceiling that cants upward to the chancel. The church plan resembles a compact rectangle with two rounded ends—one at the chancel, the other at the baptismal font and confessionals. The apsidal chancel laps beyond the two side walls, and the spaces in these gaps are filled with glass, which lets the sun flood across the curved sanctuary. A too-elaborate spatial essay appears here, and the windows à la Ronchamp on the entrance wall are unfortunate, but the church warrants an inquiring look.

20 Park Theater and Hotel

Bahnhofplatz, Grenchen
Ernst Gisel, architect

One of the rewarding features of even the smaller Swiss communities rests in the high quality of accommodations. This small hotel, restaurant, and theater for a watch-making town of 17,000 some 20 miles north of Bern not only provides comfortable accommodations, but also is an excellent piece of architecture. Gisel, one of the very capable younger Zurich architects, plays here—as in most of his buildings—with sharply expressed juxtaposed masses. This segmented approach, plus the fact that he uses considerable red brick and copper, will of course suggest Aalto's work in Finland. The Park Theater is, however, no imitation: Aalto's Helsinki Pensions Building and Säynätsalo (q.v.) are its strict contemporaries. Gisel's interesting collection of pertinent forms is gathered into an over-all L-shape about an entrance court: 10-room hotel, and restaurant to the right; 600-seat theater in the background. A charming park lies beyond, with terrace restaurant between theater and hotel opening onto it. A handsome foil to the brick and copper of the building is provided by a superb Max Bill sculpture; its light-gray abstract shape, playing with the sun, brings life into the shadowed north-facing entrance-court. A clever, provocative building.

21 Terrace Apartments

Terrassenweg, Zug (18 miles S of Zurich)
Fritz Stucky and Rudolf Meuli, architects

A brilliant and fascinating use of an extremely difficult site. These dramatic apartments are staggered down a steep hillside, like a gigantic staircase, at an angle of 51°. Five overlapping floors of flats, with garage on lowest level, comprise each unit. The flats, the largest of which are elaborate villa types, vary in size, the smallest having three bedrooms, plus the usual living room, kitchen, bath, and utility room—and, interestingly enough, an air-raid shelter. Entrance to each is, of necessity, from the side, via a path that zig-zags up the grade. A Wrightian caste, recalling the never-built Crystal Heights project for Washington, is suggested, but these apartments go far beyond any influence from Wisconsin. In plan, each is well laid out and organized, with living room and bedrooms facing onto a broad southeast terrace, and with utilities against the hill. To prevent the upper terraces from overlooking those below, the baluster side (which in some houses stretches over 60 feet) is canted out at 60° and broadly planted along the leading edge, cleverly inhibiting tenants peering over. When totally completed, in 1962, the project will consist of five buildings with five apartments each. Highly imaginative. (And when in Zug—a charming lakeside town with several superb and unspoiled medieval streets—try the famous *Kirschtorten*, a heady local tart.)

22 Museum of Transport and Communications

Lidostrasse at Seeburgstrasse, Lucerne

Otto Dreyer, architect; Jean Huber, associate

A fascinating technical museum, consisting of six conjoined exhibition buildings and assorted services grouped around an open rectangular court—a vigorous and imaginative statement. Constructed by the Swiss Institute of Transport and Communications it shows all the major facets of surface (especially railroad) and air transport and communications. On the left as one enters are the railroad wing with an enormous, working scale-model (1:90) of the Gotthard Tunnel (appropriately enough, the railroad to the Gotthard is directly outside), then a room showing railroad controls and techniques, followed by a large hall with historic locomotives, all of which are maintained in running order. Another hall is devoted, delightfully enough, to that vanishing species of transport, the streetcar. Air and ship transport are placed in another hall, while the intriguing P.T.T. (Post, Telephone, and Telegraph) exhibits are in the final building. The oldest steamboat in Switzerland, laid down in 1847 in London and in constant use on Swiss lakes through 1952, fills most of the courtyard, where it serves as a diverting snack-bar and restaurant. A conference room holding 400 and a library complete the scene. Almost all of the exhibitions are very well done; some are wonderfully so. A certain tendency toward cramming too much into the available space crowds the right-hand buildings (air and ship transport, and P.T.T.), but the cleverness and imagination of the exhibits themselves soon make one forget this. The architecture, basically of simple shed-construction, is adequate to the requirements except at the rather stuffy entrance. Go, and by all means take the children!

23 The Halen Development (Siedlung Halen)

Halenbrücke, Länggasse, Bern (3 miles NW of city)

Atelier 5 (Fritz, Gerber, Hesterberg, Hostettler, Morgenthaler, Pini and Thormann) architects

A bold and imaginative look at suburban living. Based on a solution of terraced row-houses for maximum land utilization, Halen seeks to provide the economy of closely compacted city construction with the joy of the unspoiled countryside. Its 79 attached dwellings (33 large, 41 small, and 5 studios) step in two rows down a well-forested hillside overlooking the Aare River; each has a private garden facing south and the river, and each is three stories high, with entrance at mid-level. Communal facilities provide a small "piazza," with grocery store, delicatessen, and café (in center), swimming pool and sports ground (at edge), and central-heating plant. A large parking-lot and a garage are placed at the entrance side (west). The houses enjoy a pronounced feeling of privacy—due largely to their individual, fenced gardens—in spite of the fact that they are separated from neighbors only by party walls. The smaller (and more numerous) are minimal in planning, being less than 13 feet wide and 46 feet deep. The larger are 17 by 47.5 feet. Alternate room-arrangements could be made for each. This clever scheme provides each owner with peace, sun, quiet, and a lovely view—and does it at reasonable cost. Planning details (bathroom entered through kitchen, etc.) are certainly not common in the U.S., but then, the excellence of Halen's basic thinking is—unfortunately—not common in the U.S. either.

24 Small Apartment House

Flamatt (8 miles SW of Bern, on road to Freiburg)

Atelier 5 (Fritz, Gerber, Hesterberg, Hostettler, Morgenthaler and Pini), architects

ive apartments and a studio—in row-house form—outside
ern: rugged, hard, à la Corbusier, but clever and imagina-
ve. Like those in the Marseilles *unité,* the apartments are
oo deep for their 12-foot width, but the interior spaces are
ull of agreeableness. The ground floor of each apartment is
iven to storage; the living-dining room and kitchen are on
ae second floor, which has a loggia in front, facing south.
edrooms occupy the top floor, with roof garden above
accessible only to two apartments). Construction through-
ut is of concrete.

5 Nestlé International Headquarters

En Bergère," Lake of Geneva, Vevey
ean Tschumi, architect

With an assured sophistication in the over-all and refined
legance in detail, this 7-story lakeside building makes most
urtain-wall buildings oafish in comparison. The lucidity of
s thinking and the meticulous care for its realization were,
adeed, enough to give Prof. Tschumi the 1960 R. S. Reyn-
lds Award. Great care was exercised to fit the Y-shaped
uilding, which is situated in a lovely park directly at the
ast end of the Lake of Geneva, to its setting, and to make
he lake and the snow-capped mountains beyond an intimate
art of the concept. To further this rapport, the five floors of
he office block are raised on a podium of reinforced con-
rete supported by virile, polygonal columns enabling the
round floor to be transparent. Thus as one approaches under
striking marquee of aluminum, the sun-flecked lake and
nountains greet one through the door. Atop the office block
re the restaurants and kitchen—set back as a penthouse be-
ause of height restrictions—and a roof garden, all with
uperb views. The framework above the concrete of the base-
nent and ground floor is of steel on a 25-foot module. The
nost up-to-date mechanical facilities have been provided:
igh-velocity air-conditioning, tinted double-glazing (with
'enetian blinds *between* the panes), and completely flexible
artitioning. The exterior sun-control measures are note-
vorthy in that they are not only effective and refined, but
ary from orientation to orientation (as, of course, they
hould) and demonstrate what keenly detailed aluminum
an produce under trying technical demands. The glass of
he great south swoop of the façade is protected by project-
ng bands of horizontal louvers, each band being made of
n outer, large shield and a smaller, inner one to let the
ising warm air escape. In addition, slender vertical fins of

aluminum are affixed to each mullion. On the east and west end-walls, series of staggered and deeper vertical fins are used, producing an animated plastic effect without interfering with the view from within. A dramatic double staircase, largely of aluminum, winds up through the nodal point of the Y-shape. It is interesting to compare this Nestlé headquarters with a roughly similar building that Tschumi did five years earlier for the Mutuelle Vaudoise Accidents, at Lausanne (Place de Milan). Many of the same basic ideas are found in both, but the Nestlé building occupies a far loftier plane on every count: it is one of Europe's finest company headquarters. A postscript: Tschumi recently won first prize in the international competition for the design of the World Health Organization (WHO) at Geneva.

26 Grain Silo

Railroad Marshaling Yard, Lausanne-Renens (NW of city)
Jean Tschumi, architect

Appropriately topped by a meeting hall for the local farmers' co-operative, this 200-foot-high silo, though leaning toward the arbitrary, states with Swiss frankness that the utilitarian never need be an intrusion on the landscape. The floor level directly under the council chamber is filled with a complex of automatic pipe-machinery. Beneath are 42 divisions, or cells, for grain, with a total capacity of 3,300 tons. The elevator and stair to the top receive recognition in the angled planes at one end, planes with a highly sculpted bias express

sion that would warrant anyone's sticking his neck out a
coach window to see what imaginative railroad architecture
can be like.

27 The Chatelaine Church

avenue de Chatelaine at avenue de Balexert, Geneva
André Gaillard, architect

An accordion-roofed Protestant church in a northern suburb
of Geneva which carries several points of interest. The church
itself represents only the first stage of a projected parish
center, for which the architect won a competition. Its basic
concept provides a church surrounded by fieldstone walls
and topped by a folded-plane roof, with the side walls
extended to make a small enclosed, but unroofed, garden
beyond the sanctuary, in which the large cross is placed. The

329

only separation between "garden" and church is of plate glass. The narrow end of the garden is nearest the street and opens so that the passer-by will see that the cross is part of everyday life as well as religious life. The entrance, also topped by a folded-plane roof, projects to serve as a canopy. Building this part lower than the nave proper allowed a high clerestory to be fitted at the back of the church in an attempt to balance the light from the all-glass end at chancel. It doesn't. With so much light from the front and relatively little from behind, a glare results. (Cf. the Sirens' chapel in Finland.) The upper side-walls of the nave are also glass, this time in rather hectic colors and patterns, which, unfortunately, do nothing but establish a nervous scene. Beyond the entrance hall, which can be added to the nave by folding doors, are the parish hall, sacristy, and services. A competent straightforward detached campanile stands near the entry. If the light control and stained glass had been of a more understanding nature, this church would be excellent.

A NOTE ON EASTERN EUROPE

Although in recent years I have been unable to visit any of the countries of eastern Europe, conversation with nationals visiting the United States, and study of the Polish, Czech, Hungarian, Yugoslav, Romanian, and Soviet architectural magazines and books give cause for considerable architectural hope. There is no question but that a liberalization from dogma is taking place in these talented lands. Actually it would not be surprising if the Soviet Union itself took up modern architecture as successfully and as energetically as it has so many other facets of the twentieth century. (See *Architecture U.S.S.R.*, March 1959, dedicated to student work.) The atavism that produced the Stalin Allee in East Berlin and the Palace of Soviet Culture in Warsaw is definitely over.

Most of the countries under Russian domination did, in fact, make brave starts right after the war, but by 1949 it was obvious to the Soviet overlords that this forward-looking work represented "bourgeois formalism and decadence." The era of neocommunist classicism commenced. In the last few years this archaistic restraint has gradually eased: a few works of real merit are now appearing. It is not the province of this book to deal except in passing with eastern Europe, but a few words on the promising developments will not be amiss.

Poland has wisely instigated a substantial series of competitions. These range in subject matter from churches to cities. Although little of merit has yet materialized, the church competition for Nowa Huta, near Krakow, was as exciting as similar competitions elsewhere in Europe, while the Krakow-Bienczyce development for 29,000, won by Jadwiga Guzicka, appears (in model photographs) highly promising, as does the new Polish radio station awarded to Tadeusz Lobos. Perhaps the most fascinating of all is the design for a sports hall in Katowice, also won in competition, by the delightful Jerzy Hryniewiecki (who attended the A.I.A. Centennial in Washington). This "slipped bowl" with central dome promises to be one of Europe's outstanding arenas. Hryniewiecki's open-air stadium for 100,000, built several years ago, has proved its excellence. Other, already executed, works of interest: a small urban shopping group in downtown Warsaw, by Tomicki and Trzaska, which seems very fine; the low-cost housing of Helena and Szymon Syrkus (both familiar to the U.S.A.), especially that in the Kolo district of Warsaw; and several clever factories, particularly a thread-spinning plant in Kalisz by Glowczewski and Sikorski.

331

Czechoslovakia, which was little touched by war's destruction, has not lived up to its prewar promise, which was more brilliant than that of any other country in this group. Hospitals constitute the strongest single building type; that projected for Bratislava by B. Rozehnal looks impressive on paper, while the one he has already built at Brno (the city of Mies van der Rohe's famous Tugendhat House of 1930) appears very competent. A large "collective house" of some merit, for families with both parents working, has recently been built in Litvinov by Hilski and Linhart. The new cities are totally soulless.

Hungary, the land that for its population has in our time given more creativity to the world—in all fields—than any other, and which, in the field of design, sent to the U.S.A. Marcel Breuer, Roland Wank, Gyorgy Kepes, and the late Moholy-Nagy, among others, has recently finished at Pécsujhegy one of the most impressive power plants in all Europe. Designed by K. Pászti it stretches over 400 feet and is enclosed with prefabricated concrete V-shaped vertical wall-panels 108 feet high—in one piece! Other Hungarian industrial work has shown great ingenuity in the use of new concrete techniques, though over-all architectural design has not been distinguished. A building that should be almost sensationally handsome, however, is the new National Riding Hall by Emödi and Zentai.

Yugoslavia had not been noted before the war for any architecture except those delightful towns on the Dalmatian coast, some glorious Byzantine churches, and a few Bosnian mosques. However, even those who have not visited Yugoslavia were impressed in Brussels in 1958 by the quietly elegant and imaginative Yugoslav pavilion and its stream-girdling restaurant. "If there is an architecture which stands in need of shrewd and deep interpretative study at present, it is that of Yugoslavia" (*Architectural Review,* August 1960). On the home scene the most compelling architectural and urban development stretches along the Avenue of Proletarian Brigades in Zagreb. Several of the buildings there, notably those by Drago Galic and by Niksic and Kucan, are very fine. Le Corbusier obviously inspired them, but the results are local, and except for rigid planning, good. Other buildings of distinction: the new mining-town at Velenje (almost on Austrian border northwest of Zagreb), much of which seems surprisingly superior; the beach development at Zadar by Zvonimir Pozgay, which though not really important, is nicely grouped; and the community hall at Kranj (just above Ljubljana) by Edo Ravnikar.

Romania, which has not exactly been on everyone's lips

as a contemporary architectural oasis, is nonetheless building at Mamaia, just above Constanta on the Black Sea, and at Mangalia, a bit south of Constanta on this same sea, a series of developments several of which are in part (and only in part) noteworthy. Whereas one of the restaurants at Mangalia amusingly enough recalls Brasilia's Presidential Palace in clumsy fashion, the other and larger, by Lazarescu and Popovici, appears as sleek and competent as anything that the rest of Europe, or the United States, affords. It is an enormous and excellent building, raised on stilts, with a totally assured manner. A drive-in movie is placed directly behind! Eforie, too, has a very smart-looking restaurant-club, by N. Stopler. Bucharest has its encrusted Casa Scinteii (neo-Stalinism in architecture) and somewhat similar Congress House, and most of the country has monotonously dreary housing developments. But when Romanian architects with all their difficulties can turn out buildings such as the ones praised above, it is time to stand up and cheer.

BIBLIOGRAPHY

Numerous volumes both in hard and soft covers describe the modern architecture, the men, and the building types of most of the countries of western Europe. The books listed below are those thought to be most useful to the general reader who would like to explore postwar work in Europe. With few exceptions, each has English text, summaries, or captions. In addition, the leading architectural magazines—the most up-to-date sources of information—are listed under appropriate country. Almost all of the offices of these periodicals have stocks of back issues for on-the-spot additional research.

GENERAL BOOKS ON MODERN EUROPEAN ARCHITECTURE (alphabetically by author)

Banham, Reyner, *Theory and Design in the First Machine Age*—Praeger, 1960 (penetrating background). Behrendt, W. C., *Modern Building*—Harcourt, Brace, 1937 (dated but good). Blake, Peter, *Master Builders*—Knopf, 1960 (Le Corbusier, Mies, and F. L. Wright—excellent). Giedion, Siegfried, *Space, Time and Architecture*—Harvard, 1954 (inspiring and invaluable); *A Decade of Contemporary Architecture*—Girsberger, Zurich, 1951 (a catalog of achievement). Hitchcock, H.-R., *Architecture: Nineteenth and Twentieth Centuries*—Pelican History of Art, Baltimore, 1958 (primarily useful for research). Hitchcock, H.-R. and Johnson, P. C., *The International Style*—Museum of Modern Art, 1932 (good early treatise). Joedicke, Jürgen, *A History of Modern Architecture*—Praeger, 1959 (excellent survey). Jones, Cranston, *Architecture Today and Tomorrow*—McGraw-Hill, 1961 (lavish, perceptive). Kultermann, Udo, *Architecture of Today*—Universe Books, 1959 (uneven but useful in parts). Michaels, Leonard, *Contemporary Structure in Architecture*—Reinhold, 1950 (technical but interesting). Mumford, Lewis, *Technics and Civilization*—Harcourt, Brace, 1934 (early philosophical background); *The Culture of Cities*—Harcourt, Brace, 1938 (highly significant historically). Peter, John, *Masters of Modern Architecture*—Braziller, 1958 (brief text but handsome illustrations). Pevsner, Nikolaus, *An Outline of European Architecture*—Penguin, 1960 (wonderful coverage from sixth century to date, available in small Penguin or enormous hard-cover); *Pioneers of Modern Design*—Museum of Modern Art, 1950 (fine background on growth of modern movement). Richards, J. M., *An Introduction to*

Modern Architecture—Penguin, 1959 (inexpensive, irreplaceable—the one book all should have). Roth, Alfred, *The New Architecture*—Girsberger, Zurich, 1940 (useful for the professional). Whittick, Arnold, *European Architecture in the Twentieth Century*—Crosby, Lockwood, London, 1953 (primarily for the scholar). Zevi, Bruno, *Towards An Organic Architecture*—Faber & Faber, London, 1950 (largely on Frank Lloyd Wright but of merit on European developments). Several fine annuals, basically on recent European developments: *Architecture—Formes + Functions* (Swiss, mostly in French); *Architects' Year Book* (English, with very broad coverage); and *Zodiac* (Italian—and admirable—with full English translation).

BOOKS ON THE URBAN ASPECT (alphabetically by title)

Town Design, Frederick Gibberd—Reinhold, 1953 (somewhat technical but very good). *The Urban Scene*, Gordon Logie—Faber & Faber, London, 1954 (excellent for layman and architect alike).

BOOKS ON SPECIFIC BUILDING TYPES

Contemporary Church Art, Anton Henze—Sheed & Ward, 1956 (good but limited review of Continental work). *Liturgy and Architecture*, Peter Hammond—Barrie and Rockliff, London, 1960 (a sharp dissection of mainly English developments). *The Modern Church*, Edward D. Mills—Architectural Press, London, 1956 (mainly for the architect). *Modern Flats*, F. R. S. Yorke—Architectural Press, London, 1958 (well illustrated, primarily for the architect). *The New School*, Alfred Roth—Praeger, 1957 (technical analysis of European and U.S. developments).

AUSTRIA

Periodical: *Der Aufbau*, Neues Rathaus, Stiege 8, Vienna 1 ($12.20 per year).

BELGIUM

Periodical: *Habiter*, 86, rue Saint-Lazare, Brussels 3 (200 francs per year).

L'Architecture Vivante: Belgique—Albert Morancé, Paris, 1958 (poor but inclusive). *Modern Belgian Architecture*, Hugo van Kuyck—Belgian Government Information Service, 1946 (small booklet, useful for background).

DENMARK

Periodical: *Arkitektur*, Bredgade 66, Copenhagen (68 kroner per year).

The Architecture of Denmark—Architectural Press, London, 1949 (good earlier survey). *Arne Jacobsen,* Johan Pedersen—Arkitektens Forlag, Copenhagen, 1954 (good survey until 1954 of Denmark's leading architect). *Contemporary Danish Architecture,* Esbjørn Hior—Gjellerups Forlag, Copenhagen, 1949 (thoughtful coverage to 1949). *Contemporary Danish Architecture*—Arkitektens Forlag, Copenhagen, 1958 (good survey). *Housing in Denmark since 1930,* Esbjørn Hiort—Architectural Press, London, 1952 (mostly for the specialist). *100 New Buildings in Copenhagen*—Federation of Danish Architects, 1956 (a good but not sufficiently selective folder-guide).

ENGLAND

Periodicals: *Architectural Design,* 26 Bloomsbury Way, London WC 1 ($6.25 per year); *Architectural Review,* 9 Queen Anne's Gate, London SW 1 ($10.50 per year).

Guide to Modern Architecture in London—The Architectural Association, London, 1957 (handy folder, excellent map). *Modern Architecture in Britain,* Trevor Dannatt—Batsford, London, 1959 (excellent recent book). *The New Architecture in Great Britain, 1946–1953,* Edward D. Mills—Reinhold, 1954 (thorough study).

FINLAND

Periodical: *Arkkitehti,* Ainogatan 3, Helsinki (2,000 marks per year).

Alvar Aalto, Frederick Gutheim—Braziller, 1960 (brief but fine monograph on one of the world's great architects). *Contemporary Finnish Houses,* Becker and Schlote—Krämer Verlag, Stuttgart, 1958 (housing survey). *Finnish Buildings and Alvar Aalto,* E. and C. Neuenschwander—Verlag für Architektur, Zurich, 1954 (excellent coverage until 1951). *Industrial Architecture in Finland,* Finlands Arkitektförbund, Helsinki, 1952 (industrial towns until 1952).

FRANCE

Periodicals: *L'Architecture d'Aujourd'hui,* 5, rue Bartholdi, Boulogne, Seine ($16.00 per year); *L'Architecture Française,* 14, rue de l'Universe, Paris VII ($13.00 per year); *Techniques & Architecture,* 19, rue de Prony, Paris XVII ($14.50 per year).

Creation Is a Patient Search, Le Corbusier—Praeger, 1960 (a definitive work by the master himself). *Le Corbusier,* Françoise Choay—Braziller, 1960 (brief but inexpensive and useful). *Le Corbusier, His Works 1910–1960,* edited by W. Boesiger and H. Girsberger—Wittenborn, 1960 (comprehensive and detailed).

Periodicals: *Bauen + Wohnen,* Rosenheimer Strasse 145, Munich (Dm. 51 per year); *Baukunst und Werkform,* Marienplatz 5, Nürnberg (Dm. 37.20 per year); *Der Baumeister,* Finkenstrasse 2, Munich (Dm. 36 per year); *Die Deutsche Bauzeitung,* Neckarstrasse 121, Stuttgart; *Kunst und Kirche,* Bau-Muster-Haus, Darmstadt (Dm. 16 per year).

Bauten in Deutschland seit 1948, Bund Deutscher Architekten—Verlag "Das Beispiel," Darmstadt, 1959 (an over-all recent nonselective survey—German text). *Ludwig Mies van der Rohe,* Arthur Drexler—Braziller, 1960 (good on Mies's German background). *Mies van der Rohe,* Philip C. Johnson—Museum of Modern Art, 1947 (fine earlier biography). *Modern Architecture in Germany,* Bruno E. Werner—Bruckmann, Munich, 1956 (good small review). *The New Architecture and the Bauhaus,* Walter Gropius—Faber & Faber, London, 1935 (excellent early book on the approach of the famous Bauhaus). *New German Architecture,* Hatje, Hoffmann, and Kasper—Architectural Press, London, 1956 (good substantial survey). *Planen und Bauen im Neuen Deutschland,* Bund Deutscher Architekten—Westdeutscher Verlag, Cologne, 1960 (monumental 648 page review with English captions). *Walter Gropius,* Siegfried Giedion—Reinhold, 1954 (fine early work on Germany's master). *Walter Gropius,* James M. Fitch—Braziller, 1960 (good recent work). *Wassili und Hans Luckhardt,* Udo Kultermann—Wasmuth Verlag, Tübingen, 1958 (brief German text but good illustrations on two important German brothers).

Periodical: *Architectoniki,* 9a, Valaoritou Street, Athens ($15.00 per year).

Periodical: *The Irish Builder & Engineer,* 11 Findlater Place, Dublin.

Architectural Survey—Parkside Press, 43 Parkgate Street, Dublin (a well-illustrated annual survey).

Periodicals: *L'Architettura,* Via Nomentana 150, Rome ($21.00 per year); *Casabella-Continuitá,* Via Monte de Pietà 15, Milan ($20.00 per year); *Domus,* Via Monte de Pietà, Milan ($20.00 per year).

Gio Ponti—Aria d'Italia, Milan, 1954 (handsome monograph on a multitalented man). *Ignazio Gardella,* Giulio Carlo Argan—Edizioni di Comunità, Milan, 1959 (full biography on a sensitive architect). *Italy Builds*, G. E. Kidder Smith—Reinhold, 1955 (the most complete survey to date). *Italy's Architecture Today,* Carlo Pagani—Hoepli, Milan, 1955 (comprehensive but somewhat disordered). *Milan Today*—Milano Moderna, 1959 (a spritely scrapbook). *Nuove Architetture a Milano,* Roberto Aloi—Hoepli, Milan, 1959 (a large handsome, if at times uncritical, book). *Pier Luigi Nervi,* Ada Louise Huxtable—Braziller, 1960 (a fine, inexpensive biography). *Recent Italian Architecture,* Agnoldomencio Pica—Edizioni del Milione, Milan, 1959 (at times useful). *Structures,* Pier Luigi Nervi—Dodge, 1956 (primarily for the professional). *The Works of Pier Luigi Nervi,* Ernesto N. Rogers—Praeger, 1957 (excellent technical study).

NETHERLANDS

Periodical: *Forum,* Keizersgracht 546, Amsterdam C (35 florins per year).

Architecture in the Netherlands, Paul Bromberg—Netherlands Information Office, New York, 1944 (out of print but useful). *Na-oorlogse bouwkunst in Nederland,* J. P. Mieras—Kosmos, Amsterdam, 1954 (second-rate). *Netherlands Architecture since 1900,* R. Blijstra—Uitgeverij De Bezige Bij, Amsterdam, 1960 (small, recent, useful). *Rietveld,* T. M. Brown—Bruna & Zoon, Utrecht, 1958 (definitive biography on Dutch architectural pioneer of the 20's); *Willem M. Dudok,* Garmt Stuiveling—G. van Saane, Amsterdam, 1954 (biography of an older master).

NORWAY

Periodicals: *Bonytt,* Bygdoy Alle 9, Oslo (38 kroner per year); *Byggekunst,* Drammensveien 20, Oslo (33 kroner per year).

Norwegian Architecture, Past and Present, Guthorm Kavli—Dreyers Forlag, Oslo, 1958 (not much on the present, but interesting).

PORTUGAL

Periodical: *Arquitectura,* Rua Alexavre Braga 17, Lisbon (150 escudos per year).

"Contemporary Portuguese Architecture, 1958" (a thin catalog for exhibition circulated by Smithsonian Museum, Washington).

SCANDINAVIA

Nordisk Arkitektur (useful surveys published every three to four years by the Danish, Finnish, Icelandic, Norwegian and

Swedish architectural societies in concert). *Scandinavian Architecture,* Thomas Paulsson—Branford, 1959 (relatively little on contemporary work but good historically). *Wohnen in Skandinavien,* Andresen and Jordan—Hoffmann Verlag, Stuttgart, 1958 (housing and furniture).

SPAIN

Periodical: *Arquitectura,* Barquillo 12, Madrid (450 pesetas per year).

Antoni Gaudí, J. J. Sweeney and J. L. Sert—Praeger, 1960 (the definitive work on an extraordinary architect). *Antonio Gaudí,* G. R. Collins—Braziller, 1960 (good, inexpensive biography). *Philosophy of Structures,* Eduardo Torroja—University of California, 1958 (a technical work by Spain's brilliant engineer). *The Structures of Eduardo Torroja,* Eduardo Torroja—Dodge, 1958 (good survey for the professional).

SWEDEN

Periodical: *Arkitektur, The Swedish Architectural Review,* Kungsgatan 32, Stockholm C (40 kronor per year).

Guide for Visiting Builders and Architects to Malmö—Byggnadsnämnden, Malmö, 1958 (23 pages, no illustrations). *Guide to Architecture in Göteborg* (Gothenburg)—Orstadius Boktryckeri AB, Göteborg, 1960 (a handy, well-illustrated booklet). *Guide to Modern Architecture in Stockholm*—Svenska Arkitekters Riksförbund, Stockholm, 1959 (with excellent map and small photos and descriptions of 230 buildings this is very useful though not selective). *Sweden Builds,* G. E. Kidder Smith—Reinhold, 1957 (the only complete survey).

SWITZERLAND

Periodicals: *Bauen + Wohnen,* Winkelwiese 4, Zurich ($14.00 per year); *Werk,* Technikumstrasse 83, Winterthur (45 Swiss francs per year).

Moderne Schweizer Architektur—Verlag Karl Werner, Basel, 1945 (two loose-leaf, boxed volumes primarily useful to the professional). *Switzerland Builds,* G. E. Kidder Smith—Bonniers, 1950 (somewhat dated except for section on native architecture).

NOTE: 35 mm. color slides (from 9 x 12 cm. Ektacolor negatives) of most of the churches mentioned in *The New Architecture of Europe* can be ordered from Sandak, Inc., 39 West 53rd Street, New York 19, New York.

INDEX OF ARCHITECTS

Note: Dates given are those for the completed buildings.

341

AUBERT, ANDRE; BONIN, PIERRE; AND MARICAN, MAR-
CEL   3, rue Cité Universitaire, Paris (XIV), France (Tel.: KEL.
27-11)
Saint-Gobain Building, Neuilly (1959)   87

BACKSTROM AND REINIUS   Blasieholmstorg 11 C, Stockholm,
Sweden (Tel.: 23 58 50)
Gröndal Apartments, Stockholm (1947)   217
BAUR, HERMANN   Barfüsserhof, Basel, Switzerland (Tel.: 24
98 82)
All Saints Church, Basel (1953)   317
Bruder Klaus Church, Birsfelden (1958)   320
(see also Vischer, Baur and Bräuning)
B.B.P.R.: BELGIOJOSO, PERESSUTTI AND ROGERS   Via dei
Chiostri 2, Milan, Italy (Tel.: 80 42 20)
Torre Velasca, Milan (1958)   187
Monument to Those Fallen in Germany, Milan (1948)   188
Castel Sforzesco Museum, Milan (1956)   190
BERGH, ROLF   Rörstrandsgatan 32, Stockholm, Sweden (Tel.:
34 11 19)
St. Botvid's Church, Oxelösund (1957)   231
BERNASCONI, FIOCCHI AND NIZZOLI   c/o Olivetti, Via
Clerici, Milan, Italy (Tel.: 87 57 44)
Olivetti Headquarters, Milan (1954)   189
BILL, MAX   Jenatschstrasse 10, Zurich, Switzerland (Tel.: 23 72
37)
School of Design, Ulm (1955)   147
BLOM, HOLGER   Stockholms Parkavdelningen, Tulegatan 7,
Stockholm, Sweden (Tel.: 24 00 20)
Stockholm's Parks (various dates)   224
BLOME, BORJE   Lingvägen 103, Enskede, Sweden (Tel.: 94 76
46)
St. Michael's Chapel, Mora (1954)   241
BO, JORGEN   Frederiksberg Allé 32, Copenhagen V, Denmark
(Tel.: Vester 6267), and WOHLERT, VILHELM, Åbrinken 20,
Virum, Denmark (Tel.: 85 15 35)
Louisiana Museum, Humlebaek (1958)   273
BOHM, DOMINIKUS (†)
St. Maria Königin, Cologne-Marienburg (1954)   134
BOHM, GOTTFRIED   Aüf dem Römerberg 25, Cologne-Marien-
burg, Germany (Tel.: 32800)
St. Albert, Saarbrücken (1957)   140
BRANTSCHEN, ERNEST   Vadianstrasse 54, St. Gallen, Switzer-
land (Tel.: 22 50 41)
Bruder Klaus Church, Saint Gallen-Winkeln (1959)   311
BRENNENSTUHL, RUDOLF   Klosbachstrasse 15, Zurich, Swit-
zerland (Tel.: 47 09 40)
Artists' Colony, Gockhausen (1958–)   309

BREUER, MARCEL   201 East 57th Street, New York 22, N.Y., ZEHRFUSS, BERNARD, 9, rue Arsène-Houssaye, Paris (VIII), France (Tel.: WAG. 33-89), and NERVI, PIER LUIGI, Lungotevere Arnaldo da Brescia 9, Rome, Italy (Tel.: 35 55 76)

UNESCO Building, Paris (1958)   82

BRIZZI, GORI, GORI, RICCI AND SAVIOLI   Via Manin 3, Florence, Italy

Covered Market, Pescia (1951)   174

BRYGGMAN, ERIK (†)

Cemetery Chapel, Turku (1941)   254

BURCKHARDT OFFICE   Gellertstrasse 33, Basel, Switzerland (Tel.: 24 19 80)

Geigy Paint Warehouse, Basel (1959)   318

CACCIA DOMINIONI, LUIGI   Piazza San Ambrogio 16, Milan, Italy (Tel.: 89 30 53)

Office Building, Milan (1959)   186

CAMELOT, R.   10, rue des Nonnains-d'Hyères, Paris (IV), France (Tel.: ARC. 31-06), DE MAILLY, J., 7, rue Michel-Ange, Paris (XVI) (Tel.: BAG. 88-93), and ZEHRFUSS, B., 9, rue Arsène-Houssaye, Paris (VIII) (Tel.: WAG. 33-89)

Exhibition Hall of C.N.I.T., Paris (1958)   84

CARLIER, C.; LHOEST, H.; AND MOZIN, J.   Groupe Egau, rue Dartois 44, Liége, Belgium (Tel.: 52 40 53)

Champ des Manoeuvres Housing, Liége (1957)   23

CHAMBERLIN, POWELL AND BON   15 Avenue Studios, Sydney Mews, London SW 3, England (Tel.: KNI. 7243)

Golden Lane Housing, London (1961)   46
Bousfield Primary School, London (1956)   53

CLARKE HALL AND SCORER   6 Mason's Yard, Duke Street, St. James, London W 1, England (Tel.: WHI. 2951)

Secondary Modern School, Richmond (1959)   20

CORRALES, JOSE ANTONIO   Guadalquivir, 7, Madrid 16, Spain (Tel.: 34 85 70), MOLEZUN, RAMON VAZQUEZ, Bretón de los Herreros, 65, Madrid 3 (Tel.: 34 55 35), and DE LA SOTA, ALEJANDRO, Edificio Espana, Madrid (Tel.: 47 96 35)

The Spanish Pavilion from the Brussels World's Fair,
Madrid (Corrales and Molezún) (1958)   283
Summer Home for Children, Miraflores de la Sierra (1959)   285

COSENZA, LUIGI   Via Mergellina 226, Naples, Italy (Tel.: 85 5 98)

Olivetti Factory and Services, Pozzuoli (1954)   168

COULON, R. A.; MANEVAL, J.; AND DOUILLET, PH.   c/o S.N.P.A., 16, cours Albert Ier, Paris (VIII), France (Tel.: BAL. 93-09)

Housing of the S.N.P.A., Lacq (1961)   110

CRAMER, JARAY AND PAILLARD   Eierbrechtstrasse 16, Zurich 7, Switzerland (Tel.: 27 43 32)

Chriesiweg Primary School, Zurich-Altstetten (1957)   301

DANZEISEN AND VOSER Vadianstrasse 30, St. Gallen, Switzerland (Tel.: 22 23 52)

Goldzack Elasticized Fabric Plant, Gossau (1955)   310

D'ATHOUGUIA, RUY JERVIS   31, Rua de S. Pedro de Alcântara, Lisbon, Portugal, and SANCHEZ, SEBASTIAO FORMO-SINHO, 112, Rua Rodriques Sampaio, Lisbon (Tel.: 73 13 18)

S. João de Deus Housing, Lisbon (1953)   292

DAVILA, G. GIRALDEZ; INIGO, P. LOPEZ; AND FAGES, J. SUBIAS   Muntaner, 524, Barcelona, Spain

School of Law, Barcelona (1956)   287

DE BRAUER, J.   c/o S.N.P.A., 16, cours Albert Ier, Paris (VIII), France (Tel.: BAL. 93-09)

Industrial Complex, Lacq (1961)   110

DEILMANN, HARALD Jessingstrasse 11, Münster, Germany (Tel.: 23 121)

Sanatorium, Bad Salzuflen (1957)   123

DEILMANN, HARALD Jessingstrasse 11, Münster, Germany (Tel.: 23 121), VON HAUSEN, MAX, Wefeler Strasse 106, Münster (Tel.: 41 898), RAVE, ORTWIN, Warendorfer Strasse 34, Münster (Tel.: 36 114), and RUHNAU, WERNER, Husemannstrasse 43, Gelsenkirchen (Tel.: 219 28)

City Theater, Münster (1956)   123

DE LA JOYA, RAFAEL Paseo del Pintor Rosales, 10, Madrid, Spain (Tel.: 48 01 59), REBOLLEDO MANUEL BARBERO, General Mola, 47, Madrid, and ORTIZ-ECHAGUE, CESAR, Princesa, 81, Madrid (Tel.: 47 87 58)

Dining Hall and Lounge, Barcelona (1957)   286

DIETZ, ALBERT Scheidterstrasse 71, Saarbrücken, Germany (Tel.: 29013)

St. Mauritius, Saarbrücken (1956)   139

D'OLIVO, MARCELLO Via Manin 23, Udine, Italy (Tel.: 55 135)

Boys' Town, Trieste-Opicina (1957)   196

DOXIADIS, C. A.   24, Strat. Syndesmou, Athens (Tel.: 22 091)

Doxiadis Associates Building, Athens (1958)   153

DREYER, OTTO Moosmattstrasse 10, Lucerne, Switzerland (Tel.: 2 17 71)

Museum of Transport and Communications, Lucerne (1959)   324

DUINTJER, M. F.   Prisengracht 770, Amsterdam C, Netherlands (Tel.: 6 64 66)

Opstanding Church, Amsterdam-West (1956)   28

EGGER, RENE   73, La Canebière, Marseilles, France (Tel.: 20 43 83)

School of Medicine and Pharmacy, Marseilles (1959)   103

EKHOLM AND WHITE Drottninggatan 5, Gothenburg, Sweden (Tel.: 17 34 60)

Baronbäckarna Housing, Örebro (1957)   228

346

RUHNAU, WERNER Husemannstrasse 43, Gelsenkirchen, Germany (Tel.: 219 28), RAVE, ORTWIN, Warendorfer Strasse 34, Münster (Tel.: 36 114), and VON HAUSEN, MAX, Wefeler Strasse 106, Münster (Tel.: 41 898)

SAARINEN, EERO 1300 North Woodward, Birmingham, Michigan

SCHADEL, HANS Bischöfliches Baumt, Herrnstrasse 6, Würzburg, Germany (Tel.: 5 09 22)

SCHADER, JACQUES Parkring 37, Zurich 2, Switzerland (Tel.: 27 11 23)

SCHAROUN, HANS Hardenbergstrasse 35, Berlin-Charlottenburg, Germany (Tel.: 32 51 81)

SCHNEIDER-ESLEBEN, PAUL Leo-Statz-Strasse 27, Düsseldorf, Germany (Tel.: 4 72 35)

SCHREIER, F. Witzfeldstrasse 72, Düsseldorf-Büderich, Germany (Tel.: Büderich 2215)

SCHUTZ, JOSEF Nüschelerstrasse 22, Zurich 1, Switzerland (Tel.: 27 07 49)

SCHWARZ, RUDOLF (Died April 2, 1961)

SCOTT, MICHAEL 19 Merrion Square, Dublin, Ireland (Tel.: 66 464)

SHEPPARD, RICHARD, AND PARTNERS 5 Southampton Place, London WC 1, England (Tel.: CHA. 4261)

SIJMONS, KAREL, L. Rokin 62, Amsterdam, Netherlands (Tel.: 3 50 80)

SIMON AND MORISSEAU 33, rue Copernic, Paris (XVI), France

SIREN, KAIJA AND HEIKKI   Lounaisväylä 8, Lauttasaari, Helsinki, Finland (Tel.: 67 30 33)
  Chapel of the Technical University, Otaiemi (1957)   252
  (see also *Tapiola Garden City*, p. 250)

SKINNER, BAILEY AND LUBETKIN   74 Queensway, London W 2, England (Tel.: BAY. 6466)
  Holford Square Estate, London (1954)   48

SMITHSON, ALISON AND PETER   46 Limerston Street, Chelsea, London SW 10, England (Tel.: FLA. 7329)
  Secondary School, Hunstanton (1954)   60

SPENCE, BASIL, AND PARTNERS   1 Canonbury Place, London N 1, England (Tel.: CAN. 7175)
  St. Michael's Cathedral, Coventry (1962)   66

STAPELS, RENE   rue Berkendael 128, Brussels, Belgium (Tel.: 42 42 12)
  Apartment Hotel, Brussels (1957 ?)   22

STOCKHOLM TOWN PLANNING OFFICE   Stadshuset, Stockholm, Sweden (Tel.: 54 03 60)
  Vällingby, Stockholm (Sven Markelius, chief planner)
  (1953–59)   211
  Farsta, Stockholm (1960–   )   216

STRIFFLER, HELMUT   G 4 Block, Mannheim, Germany (Tel.: 24 516)
  Trinity Church, Mannheim (1959)   142

STROM, KEIJO, AND TUOMISTO, OLAVI   Hietalahdenkatu 8, Helsinki, Finland (Tel.: 61 654)
  Alppila Church, Helsinki (1957)   249

STUBBINS, HUGH, JR.   806 Massachusetts Avenue, Cambridge 39, Mass.
  Congress Hall, Berlin (1957)   120

STUCKY, FRITZ, AND MEULI, RUDOLF   Reiffergässchen 1, Zug, Switzerland (Tel.: 4 36 16)
  Terrace Apartments, Zug (1960–62)   323

TENGBOM, ANDERS   Kungsträdgårdsgatan 10, Stockholm, Sweden (Tel.: 10 82 81)
  Skogshem (*Employees' Training School*), Lidingö (1958)   218

TOIVIAINEN, TARJA AND ESKO   Rantapolku 7a, Munkkiniemi, Finland (Tel.: 48 45 42)
  Cemetery Chapel, Järvenpää (1957)   255

TORROJA, EDUARDO   Instituto de la Construccion, Costillares (Charmartin), Madrid, Spain (Tel.: 34 26 00)
  Instituto Tecnico, Madrid (1951)   281

TSCHUMI, JEAN   16, avenue Tissot, Lausanne, Switzerland (Tel.: 22 22 19)
  Nestlé International Headquarters, Vevey (1960)   327
  Grain Silo, Lausanne-Renens (1959)   328

UTZON, JORN   Hellebaek, Denmark (Tel.: 158)
  Kingo Houses, Helsingör (1953)   274

VAGO, PIERRE   17 quai Voltaire, Paris (VII), France (Tel.: LIT. 73-90)

St. Pius X Basilica, Lourdes (1958)   113

VAN DEN BROEK AND BAKEMA   Posthoornstraat 12B, Rotterdam 1, Netherlands (Tel.: 13 47 80)

World Broadcasting Center, Hilversum (1961)   29
Lijnbaan Shopping Center, Rotterdam (1951)   31

VAN EYCK, ALDO   Prinsengracht 1001, Amsterdam C, Netherlands (Tel.: 3 01 40)

Children's Home, Amsterdam (1960)   26

VAN KASTEEL, BART   Reguliersdwarsstraat 9, Amsterdam C, Netherlands (Tel.: 6 25 04)

Reformed Church, Geleen (1956)   32

VIGANO, VITTORIANO   Corso Vigentina 1, Milan, Italy (Tel.: 54 26 35)

Marchiondi Institute, Milan-Baggio (1959)   193

VIKSJO, ERLING   Torggatan 17, Oslo, Norway (Tel.: 41 20 86)
Government Office Building, Oslo (1959)   203

VISCHER, E. AND P.   Hardstrasse 10, Basel, Switzerland (Tel.: 41 66 99), BAUR, HERMANN, Barfüsserhof, Basel (Tel.: 24 98 82), and BRAUNING, LEU AND DURIG, St.-Alban-Anlage 15, Basel (Tel.: 24 19 80)

Citizens' Hospital, Basel (1945)   315

VOUREKAS, E., SAKELLARIOS, P., AND VASSILIADIS, P. 25 Queen Sophia Avenue, Athens, Greece (Tel.: 73 653)

Astir Beach Resort, Glyphada (1957?)   155

WEBER, GERHARD   Weserstrasse 18, Frankfurt, Germany (Tel.: 33 32 55)

National Theater, Mannheim (1957)   141

WEJKE AND ODEEN   Surbrunnsgatan 38, Stockholm, Sweden (Tel.: 34 34 21)

Royal Gymnastic Institute, Stockholm (1946)   221

WINDBRECHTINGER, WOLFGANG AND TRAUDE   Badhausgasse 22, Vienna VII, Austria (Tel.: 44 04 56)

Community Center, Kapfenberg (1959)   16

WORLE, EUGEN AND FELLERER, MAX (†)   Tuchlauben 7 a, Vienna I, Austria (Tel.: 63 54 22)

Gänsehäufel Lido, Vienna (1950)   15

YORKE, ROSENBERG AND MARDALL   2 Hyde Park Place, London W 2, England (Tel.: AMB. 4521)

Gatwick Airport, Sussex (1958)   56

INDEX OF BUILDING TYPES

Note: The following seventeen categories have been used: *Churches and Crematoriums, Exhibition Buildings, Hospitals and Sanatoriums, Hotels and Restaurants, Housing and Apartments, Industrial Architecture, Memorials, Museums, Office Buildings, Playgrounds and Parks, Public Buildings, Schools and Universities, Shopping Centers and Markets, Social Welfare Buildings, Sports Buildings, Theaters and Auditoriums, Transport Buildings.*

CHURCHES AND CREMATORIUMS

INDUSTRIAL ARCHITECTURE

MEMORIALS

MUSEUMS

OFFICE BUILDINGS

PLAYGROUNDS AND PARKS

PUBLIC BUILDINGS

SCHOOLS AND UNIVERSITIES

SHOPPING CENTERS AND MARKETS

SOCIAL WELFARE BUILDINGS

SPORTS BUILDINGS

THEATERS AND AUDITORIUMS

TRANSPORT BUILDINGS

PHOTOGRAPHIC CREDITS

Note: Most of the photographs not credited below are by the author. The numbers refer to pages.

AUSTRIA: 14, Landesbildstelle Vienna; 16, August Makart, Vienna.

BELGIUM: 22, Les Frères Haine, Brussels; 23, Francis-Niffle, Liége.

NETHERANDS: 27, K. L. M., Amsterdam; 30 (top), J. A. Vrijhof, Rotterdam; 33, W. K. Steffen.

ENGLAND: 42, W. J. Toomey (from *Architects' Journal*); 49, from Denys Lasdun, London; 51, Robert P. Hymers, Ltd. (from Denys Lasdun, London); 54, Sam Lambert (from *Architectural Design*, London); 57, Colin Westwood (from *The Architect and Building News*, London); 58, de Burgh Galwey (from *Architectural Review*, London); 59, Photoflight Limited, Elstree Aerodrome, Hertfordshire; 60, de Burgh Galwey (from *Architectural Review*, London); 62, General Electricity Authority, London; 63, Alfred Cracknell, London; 64, 65, de Burgh Galwey (from *Architectural Review*, London); 67, Alfred Cracknell, London; 68, Colin Westwood, Weybridge, Surrey; 69, John R. Pantlin, Radlett, Hertfordshire; 70, 71, de Burgh Galwey (from *Architectural Review*, London).

IRELAND: 73, de Burgh Galwey (from *Architectural Review*, London).

FRANCE: 87, Jean Biaugeaud, Arcueil; 88, 89, Etienne Weill, Paris; 91 (top), Georges Palot, Paris; 91 (bottom), Durand-Peyrebesse; 103, Henri Delleuse, Marseille; 104, Helene Adant, Paris; 105, Galf, Paris; 106, Duprat; 111, Reportage Yan, Toulouse; 112, Claude Roux, Arudy; 113, H. Baranger.

GERMANY: 123, Schmidt & Lueg, Iserlohn; 125, (bottom), Knorr; 126, Heidersberger; 133 (bottom), Hugo Schmölz; 144, Photoarchiv, Zeiss Ikon, Berlin; 146, Leonard Wett; 147, O. Aicher, Ulm.

GREECE: 155, D. A. Harissiadis.

ITALY: 168, Oscar Savio, Rome; 175, 190, 194, Fotogramma, Milan; 197, Italo Zannier; 199, Aldo Ballo, Milan.

NORWAY: 207 (top), Teigens, Oslo.

SWEDEN: 216, *Dagens Nyheter*, Stockholm; 218 (top), Oscar Bladh, Stockholm; 223, 235, Lennart Olson, Stockholm; 239, Ralph Erskine, Drottningholm; 240, Carl Larsson, Stockholm; 242, 243, Ralph Erskine, Drottningholm.

FINLAND: 247, Havas, Helsinki; 248, Jane Davis Doggett, New Canaan, Conn.; 253, 255, 258, Havas, Helsinki; 260, Valokuva Oy.

DENMARK: 263, 264, 266, 269, Strüwing, Copenhagen; 271, K. Helmer-Petersen, Copenhagen; 274, from *Zodiac*, Milan; 277, 278, Strüwing, Copenhagen.

SPAIN: 286, Trabajos Aereos y Fotogram; 288, 289, A. S. Koch, Detroit, Mich.

PORTUGAL: 291, Mario Novais.

SWITZERLAND: 299, Fachklasse für Fotografie; 301, Peter Grünert, Zurich; 307, Walter Binder, Zurich; 309, F. Maurer; 310, Gross; 311, Pius Rast; 315, Michael Wolgensinger, Zurich; 319, Peter Heman, Basel; 324, A. Waldis, Lucerne; 325, Albert Winkler, Bern; 326, Reihenhäuser, Flamatt; 328, Eric E. Guignard, Vevey; 329, Maurice Vulliemin, Lausanne.

NOTES